RESTORATION
AND
CONSERVATION ECOLOGY

By

Dr. Govind Prasad

M.A., Ph.D., D.litt., F.A.MSE (France)
Senior Reader
Deptt. of Geography
Rana Pratap Postgraduate College
Sultanpur (U.P.)
(India)

DISCOVERY PUBLISHING HOUSE PVT. LTD.
NEW DELHI-110 002

Published by:
Tilak Wasan

DISCOVERY PUBLISHING HOUSE PVT. LTD.
4383/4A, Ansari Road, Darya Ganj
New Delhi-110 002 (India)
Phone : +91-11-23279245, 43596064-65
Fax : +91-11-23253475
E-mail : parul.wasan@gmail.com
discoverypublishinghouse@gmail.com
web : www.discoverypublishinggroup.com

***First Edition:* 2012**

ISBN: 978-93-5056-117-1

Restoration and Conservation Ecology

Printed at:
Shree Balaji Art Press
Delhi

Preface

Restoration ecology is the scientific study and practice of renewing and restoring degraded, damaged, or destroyed ecosystems and habitats in the environment by active human intervention and action. Restoration ecology emerged as a separate field in ecology in the 1980s.

Land managers, laypeople, and stewards have been practicing restoration for many hundreds, if not thousands of years, yet the scientific field of 'restoration ecology' was first identified and coined in the late 1980s by John Aber and William Jordan. The study of restoration ecology has only become a robust and independent scientific discipline over the last two decades.

The Society for Ecological Restoration defines ecological restoration as an "intentional activity that initiates or accelerates the recovery of an ecosystem with respect to its health, integrity and sustainability". The practice of ecological restoration includes wide scope of projects including: erosion control, reforestation, removal of non-native species and weeds, revegetation of disturbed areas, daylighting streams, reintroduction of native species, as well as habitat and range improvement for targeted species. The term 'ecological restoration' refers to the practice of the discipline of 'restoration ecology'.

In the view of biologist E.O. Wilson, "Here is the means to end the great extinction spasm. The next century will, I believe, be the era of restoration in ecology".

There is consensus in the scientific community that the current environmental degradation and destruction of many of the Earth's biota is considerable, and is taking place on a 'catastrophically short timescale'. In fact, estimates of the current extinction rate are 1000 to 10,000 times the normal rate. For many people biological diversity (biodiversity) has an intrinsic value; humans have a responsibility toward other living things, and obligations to future generations.

On a more anthropocentric level, natural ecosystems provide human society with food, fuel and timber. More fundamentally, ecosystem services involve the purification of air and water, detoxification and decomposition of wastes, regulation of climate, regeneration of soil fertility, and pollination of crops. Such processes have been estimated to be worth trillions of dollars annually.

Habitat loss is the leading cause of both species extinctions and ecosystem service decline. There are two ways to reverse this trend of habitat loss: conservation of currently viable habitat and restoration of degraded habitats.

With regard to biodiversity preservation, it should be noted that restoration activities are complementary to, not a substitute for, conservation efforts. Many conservation programmes, however, are predicated on historical bio-physical conditions — i.e. they are incapable of responding to global climate change, and the assemblages 'locked in' that become increasingly fragile and liable to catastrophic collapse. In this sense, restoration is essential to provide new spaces for migration of habitats and their associated flora and fauna. Also, conservation biology often has organisms, and not entire ecosystems and their functions, as its focus, and therefore has limited goals and aims.

Author

Contents

1

Introduction

Restoration ecology is the scientific study and practice of renewing and restoring degraded, damaged, or destroyed ecosystems and habitats in the environment by active human intervention and action. Restoration ecology emerged as a separate field in ecology in the 1980s.

Land managers, laypeople, and stewards have been practicing restoration for many hundreds, if not thousands of years, yet the scientific field of 'restoration ecology' was first identified and coined in the late 1980s by John Aber and William Jordan. The study of restoration ecology has only become a robust and independent scientific discipline over the last two decades.

Definition

The Society for Ecological Restoration defines ecological restoration as an "intentional activity that initiates or accelerates the recovery of an ecosystem with respect to its health, integrity and sustainability". The practice of ecological restoration includes wide scope of projects including: erosion control, reforestation, removal of non-native species and weeds, revegetation of disturbed areas, daylighting streams, reintroduction of native species, as well as habitat and range improvement for targeted species. The term 'ecological restoration' refers to the practice of the discipline of 'restoration ecology'.

In the view of biologist E.O. Wilson, "Here is the means to end the great extinction spasm. The next century will, I believe, be the era of restoration in ecology".

Restoration Needs

There is consensus in the scientific community that the current environmental degradation and destruction of many of the Earth's biota is considerable, and is taking place on a 'catastrophically short timescale'. In fact, estimates of the current extinction rate are 1000 to 10,000 times the normal rate. For many people biological diversity (biodiversity) has an intrinsic value; humans have a responsibility toward other living things, and obligations to future generations.

On a more anthropocentric level, natural ecosystems provide human society with food, fuel and timber. More fundamentally, ecosystem services involve the purification of air and water, detoxification and decomposition of wastes, regulation of climate, regeneration of soil fertility, and pollination of crops. Such processes have been estimated to be worth trillions of dollars annually.

Habitat loss is the leading cause of both species extinctions and ecosystem service decline. There are two ways to reverse this trend of habitat loss: conservation of currently viable habitat and restoration of degraded habitats.

Conservation Biology and Restoration Ecology

With regard to biodiversity preservation, it should be noted that restoration activities are complementary to, not a substitute for, conservation efforts. Many conservation programmes, however, are predicated on historical bio-physical conditions — i.e. they are incapable of responding to global climate change, and the assemblages 'locked in' that become increasingly fragile and liable to catastrophic collapse. In this sense, restoration is essential to provide new spaces for migration of habitats and their associated flora and fauna. Also, conservation biology often has organisms, and not entire ecosystems and their functions, as its focus, and therefore has limited goals and aims.

Restoration ecology, as a scientific discipline, is theoretically rooted in conservation biology. While restoration ecology may be viewed as a sub-discipline of conservation biology, foundational differences exist between the disciplines' approaches, focuses and modes of inquiry.

Approaches

The fundamental difference between conservation biology and restoration ecology lies in their philosophical approaches to the same problem. Conservation biology attempts to preserve and maintain existing habitat and biodiversity. In contrast, restoration ecology assumes that environmental degradation and population declines are somewhat reversible processes.

Therefore, targeted human intervention can lead to habitat and biodiversity recovery and eventual gains. This does not provide, however, an excuse for converting extremely valuable 'pristine' habitat into other uses.

Focuses

First, both conservation biology and restoration ecology have an unfortunate temperate terrestrial bioregion bias. This issue is probably the result of these fields developing in the geopolitical north, and both fields should attempt to reconcile this bias.

Second, perhaps because plants tend to dominate most (terrestrial) ecosystems, restoration ecology has developed a strong botanical bias, while conservation biology is more strongly zoological.

Similarly, the principal systemic levels of interest differ between the disciplines. Conservation biology has historically focused on target individuals (i.e. endangered species), and has thus concentrated on genetic and population level dynamics. Since restoration ecology is aimed at rebuilding a functioning ecosystem, a broader (i.e. community or ecosystem) perspective is necessary.

Finally, since soils define the foundation of any functional terrestrial system, restoration ecology's ecosystem-level bias has placed more emphasis on the role of soil physical and microbial processes.

Modes of Inquiry

Conservation biology's focus on rare or endangered species limits the number of manipulative studies that can be performed. As a consequence, conservation studies tend to be descriptive, comparative and unreplicated. However, the highly manipulative nature of restoration ecology allows the researcher to more rigorously test hypotheses. In fact, every restorative activity is, in essence, an experimental test of what limits populations.

Disturbance

Disturbance is a change of environmental conditions, which interferes with the functioning of a biological system. Disturbance at a variety of spatial and temporal scales is a natural, and even essential, component of many communities.

Humans have had limited 'natural' impacts on ecosystems for as long as humans have existed, however the severity and scope of our modern influences has accelerated in the last few centuries. Understanding and minimizing the differences between modern anthropogenic and 'natural' disturbances is crucial to restoration ecology. For example, new forestry techniques that better imitate historical disturbances are now being implemented.

In addition, restoring a fully sustainable ecosystem often involves studying and attempting to restore a natural disturbance regime.

Succession

Ecological succession is the process by which the component species of a community changes over time. Following a disturbance, an ecosystem generally progresses from a simple level of organization (i.e. few dominant species) to a more complex community (i.e. many interdependent species) over a few generations. Depending on the severity of the disturbance, restoration often consists of initiating, assisting or accelerating ecological successional processes.

In many ecosystems, communities tend to recover following mild to moderate natural and anthropogenic disturbances. Restoration in these systems involves hastening natural successional trajectories. However, a system that has experienced a more severe disturbance (i.e. physical or chemical alteration of the environment) may require intensive restorative efforts to recreate environmental conditions that favour natural successional processes.

Fragmentation

Habitat fragmentation is the emergence of spatial discontinuities in a biological system. Through land use changes (e.g. agriculture) and 'natural' disturbance, ecosystems are broken up into smaller parts. Small fragments of habitat can support only small populations and small populations are more vulnerable to extinction. Further, fragmenting ecosystems decreases interior habitat. Habitat along the edge of a fragment has a different range of environmental conditions and therefore supports different species than the interior. Fragmentation effectively reduces interior habitat and may lead to the extinction of those species which require interior habitat. Restorative projects can increase the effective size of a habitat by simply adding area or by planting habitat corridors that link and fill in the gap between two isolated fragments. Reversing the effects of fragmentation and increasing habitat connectivity are central goals of restoration ecology.

Ecosystem Function

Ecosystem function describes the foundational processes of natural systems, including nutrient cycles and energy fluxes. These processes are the most basic and essential components of ecosystems. An understanding of the full complexity and intricacies of these cycles is necessary to address any ecological processes that may be degraded. A functional ecosystem, that is completely self-perpetuating (i.e. no management required), is the ultimate goal of restorative efforts. Because these ecosystem functions are emergent properties of the system as a whole, monitoring and management are crucial for the long-term stability of an ecosystem.

Evolving Concepts

Restoration ecology, because of its highly physical nature, is an ideal testing ground for emerging community ecological principles. There are also the emerging concepts of inventing new and successful restoration technologies, performance standards, time frames, local genetics, and society's relationship to restoration ecology, and new ethical and religious possibilities, as future topics of discussion and debate.

Assembly

Community assembly "is a framework that can unify virtually all of (community) ecology under a single conceptual umbrella". Community assembly theory attempts to explain the existence of environmentally similar sites with differing assemblages of species. It assumes that species have similar niche requirements, so that community formation is a product of random fluctuations from a common species pool. Essentially, if all species are fairly ecologically equivalent then random variation in colonization, migration and extinction rates, between species, drive differences in species composition between sites with comparable environmental conditions.

Stable States

Alternative stable states are discrete species compositional possibilities that may exist within a community. According to assembly theory, differences in species colonization, interspecific interactions and community establishment may result in distinct community species equilibria. A community has numerous possible compositional equilibria that are dependent on the initial assembly. That is, random fluctuations lead to a particular initial community assembly, which affects successional trajectories and the eventual species composition equilibrium.

Multiple stable states is a specific theoretical concept, where all species have equal access to a community (i.e., equal dispersal potential) and differences between communities arise simply because of the timing of each species' colonization.

These concepts are central to restoration ecology; restoring a community involves not only manipulating the timing and structure of the initial species composition, but also working toward a single desired stable state. In fact, a degraded ecosystem may be viewed as an alternative stable state under the altered environmental conditions.

Ontogeny

The ecology of ontogeny is the study of how ecological relationships change over the lifetime of an individual. Organisms require different environmental conditions during different stages of their life-cycle. For immobile organisms (e.g. plants) the conditions necessary for germination and establishment may be different from those of the adult stage. As an ecosystem is altered by anthropogenic processes the range of environmental variables may also be altered. A degraded ecosystem may not include the environmental conditions necessary for a particular stage of an organism's development. If a self-sustaining, functional ecosystem must contain environmental conditions for the perpetual reproduction of its species, restorative efforts must address the needs of organisms throughout their development.

Application of Theory

Restoration is defined as the application of ecological theory to ecological restoration. However, for many reasons, this can be a challenging prospect. Here are a few examples of theory informing practice.

Soil Heterogeneity Effects on Community Heterogeneity

Spatial heterogeneity of resources can influence plant community composition, diversity and assembly trajectory. Baer et al. (2005) manipulated soil resource heterogeneity in a tallgrass prairie restoration project. They found increasing resource heterogeneity alone was insufficient to insure species diversity in situations where one species may dominate across the range of resource levels. Their findings were consistent with theory regarding the role of ecological filters on community assembly. The establishment of a single species best adapted to the physical and biological conditions can play an inordinately important role in determining community structure.

Invasion, Competitive Dominance and Resource Use

"The dynamics of invasive species may depend on their abilities to compete for resources and exploit disturbances relative to the abilities of native species". Seabloom et al. (2003) tested this concept and its implications in a California grassland restoration context. They found native grass species were able to successfully compete with invasive exotics for a range of resources. This suggests native California grasses are dispersal limited and exotics may currently dominate because of historical land use patterns.

Successional Trajectories

Progress along a desired successional pathway may be difficult if multiple stable states exist. Looking at over 40 years of wetland restoration data Klotzi and Gootjans (2001) argue that unexpected and undesired vegetation assemblies "may indicate environmental conditions are not suitable for target communities". Succession may move in unpredicted directions, but constricting environmental conditions within a narrow range may rein in the possible successional trajectories and increase the likelihood of a desired outcome.

2

Conservation of Natural Resources

To address the problems of environment and development holistically, people have enunciated several policy instruments which takes into consideration various cross-sectoral issues having a direct bearing on conservation and sustainable uses of natural resources including forestry and wildlife.

Biosphere Reserves

Biosphere Reserves are areas of terrestrial and coastal ecosystems which are internationally recognized within the framework of UNESCO's Man and Biosphere (MAB) Programme. These reserves are required to meet a minimal set of criteria and adhere to a minimal set of conditions before being admitted to the World Network of Biosphere Reserve designated by UNESCO for inclusion in the World Network of Biosphere Reserves. The world's major ecosystem types and landscapes are represented in this network, which is devoted to conserving biological diversity, promoting research and monitoring as well as seeking to provide models of sustainable development in the service of humankind.

These reserves are rich in biological and cultural bdiversity and encompass unique features of exceptionally pristine nature. The goal is to facilitate conservation of representative landscapes and their immense biological diversity and cultural heritage, foster economic and human development which is culturally and ecologically sustainable and to provide support for research, monitoring, education and information exchange. The scheme is apioneering effort at pursuing the increasingly difficult yet urgent task of conserving ecological diversity under mounting pressures.

The thirteen Biosphere Reserves set up in the country so far not only aim to protect representative ecosystem, but also serve as laboratories for evolving alternative models of development. The Ministry provided financial assistance to the respective State Governments for conservation and management of these Biosphere Reserves. Research and development projects were also supported. On the basis of the proposal submitted by this Ministry to the International Coordinating Council (ICC) of Man and Biosphere Reserve (MAB) Programme of UNESCO, three Biosphere Reserves; Sunderban (West Bengal), Mannar (Tamil Nadu) and Nilgiri (Tamil Nadu) have been included in the International Network of Biosphere Reserves. Efforts are on for getting other Biosphere Reserves included in the World Network of Biosphere Reserves. This facilitates international recognition and attracts additional funding in these sites.

The Ministry provided financial support to the respective State Governments for management interventions in the buffer zones of these biosphere reserves based on the recommendations of the Indian National MAB Committee. A number of research projects have been completed during the year which provided baseline data helpful in the scientific management of these reserves. A number of new research projects were also initiated during the year.

Wetlands

Wetlands are lands transitional between terrestrial and aquatic system where the water table is usually or near the water surface and land is covered by shallow water. They are life support systems for people living around and are effective in flood control, waste water treatment, reducing sediment, recharging of aquifers and also winter resort for variety of birds for shelter and breeding and provide a suitable habitat for fish and other flora and fauna. They also act as buffer against the devastating effect of hurricanes and cyclones, stabilize the shore-line and act as bulwark against the encroachment by the sea and check soil erosion. Apart from that, they are valuable for their educational and scientific interest and provide durable timber, fuelwood, protein rich fodder for cattle, edible fruits, vegetables and traditional medicines.

Identification of wetlands can be attributed to the following three main factors, viz.

- When an area is permanently or periodically inundated
- When an area supports hydrophytic vegetation
- When an area has hydric soils that are saturated or flooded for a sufficiently long period to become anaerobic in the upper layers.

On these criteria, Ramsar Convention defines wetlands as areas of marsh or fen, peat-land or water, whether artificial or natural, permanent or temporary, with the water that is stastic or flowing, fresh, brackish or salt including areas of marine water, the depth of which at low tide does not exceed six meter. Mangroves, corals, estuaries, bays, creeks, flood plains, sea grasses, lakes etc are covered under this definition. Taking into consideration deterioration of water bodies, a programme on conservation of wetlands was initiated in 1987 with the basic objective of assessment of wetland resources, identification of wetlands of national importance, promotion of R&D activities and formulation and implementation of management action plans of theidentified wetlands, which are at present 27 covering 15 States. Under the management action plans for identified wetlands, activities also includes survey and demarcation, catchment area treatment, desiltation, weed control, fisheries development, community participation, water management, public awareness, pollution abatement, etc.

States Steering Committees have been constituted in all the concerned States under the chairmanship of Chief Secretary having members from various subject matter departments relating to wetland conservation in the State.

Significant achievements during the year

- Financial assistance increased from Rs. 5 crores to 6 crores.
- The main focus for wetland conservation is now on biological methods of conservation rather than of dopting engineering options under the catchment area treatment component. The main thrust is on waterhshed management and activities under this component is aimed at involving close participation of stakeholders in order to cover more conservation activities and also to see its sustainability.
- Four new wetlands have been added to the national list on recommendations of the Committee. New wetlands are: East Calcutta and Sunder bans wetland from West Bengal , Pt. Calimer from Tamil Nad and Kottuli wetland from Kerala.
- Management action plans have been prepared for twenty two wetlands out of twenty seven.
- Assistance released for conservation of Wetlands to following States during the current financial year J&K (Wullar), Himachal Pradesh (Renuka, Chandertal and Pong), Orissa (Chilka), Manipur (Loktak), W.Bengal (East Calcutta & Sunderbans), amil Nadu (Pt. Calimer) and Rajasthan (Sambhar), Kottuli and Sashthamkotta (Kerala).

- Two more proposals received from Mizoram andSikkim for their inclusion in the national list which is being processed.
- Four more research proposals approved for assistance during this year.
- On the basis of results obtained in UNDP project on inland wetlands of India, PDF-B project is proposed for taking up of intensive conservation of some wetlands in totality.
- Two Regional workshops on wetlands have already been organized in Gujarat, Cochin, Orissa and Imphal during the year. Two more workshops are scheduled to be held in Bhopal and Lucknow.
- Nineteen sites have already been designated as Ramsar sites in India till date. Information on six more sites, viz., Renuka and Chandertal (H.P.), Hokera & Surinsar/-Mansar (J&K), Pulicat (A.P) and Rudrasagar (Tripura) has been sent to Ramsar Bureau for being designated as Ramsar sites and data on six more sites, viz., Nalsarovar and Rann of Kutch (Gujarat), Upper Ganga (U.P.), Pangong Tso (J&K), Thane Creek (Maharashtra) and Sunderbans (W.Bengal) has been collected and their maps have been sent to Survey of India before sending to Ramsar Bureau. This will fulfill our commitment made in CoP7 meeting held in Coasta Rica in May, 1999 where India committed to declare twenty five more sites as Ramsar sites of international importance during the present triennium. India has achieved this feat within the stipulated time.

Mangroves

Mangroves plants are that survive high salinity, tidal extremes, strong wind velocity, high temperature and muddy anaerobic soil — a combination of conditions hostile for other plants. Mangroves are successfully adapted in colonizing saline intertidal zone at the interface between the land and sea along the deltas, shallow lagoons, mud flats, bays and backwaters in tropical and subtropical sheltered coast lines. Mangroves not only protect the coastal communities from the fury of cyclones and coastal storms, but also promote sustainable fisheries and prevent sea erosion. In addition, they provide medicine and fuelwood. They also serve as the home of a wide range of flora and fauna including crocodiles and tigers. The Orissa Super-cyclone of 1999 and the life saving role of mangrove forests became very apparent because areas adjoining mangrove forests either withstood the fury of the cyclones or suffered far less damage than other areas. This generated awareness among local communities of the importance of mangrove forests, and encouraged them to raise mangrove nurseries and plant saplings in degraded areas.

In spite of all such gifts they confer, many mangrove ecosystems have been cleared for aquaculture ponds and other alternative uses. Still others have been unsustainably exploited, leading to their degradation. Of late, the fragile mangrove ecosystems have been subjected to various anthropogenic and biotic pressures resulting in habitat destruction, loss of bio-diversity, affecting avifauna and their migration paths. Unsustainable aquaculture, siltation, weed infestation, uncontrolled discharge of waste-water, industrial effluents, surface un-off, encroachment around these water bodies, etc. is resulting in shrinkage of their area. Obviously, effective measures are needed to save the mangrove ecosystems.

With these aspects in mind, Ministry launched Mangrove Conservation programme in 1987 and, has so far, identified 35 mangrove areas for intensive conservation and management in the country These mangrove areas are identified on the recommendation of National Committee on Mangroves and Coral Reefs on the basis of their unique ecosystems, biodiversity etc. 100 per cent central assistance is give under Management Action Plans (MAPs) for undertaking activities like raising mangrove plantations, protection, catchment area treatment, siltation, control, pollution abatement, biodiversity conservation, sustainable resource utilization, survey and demarcation, education and awareness etc. This is further supplemented by research and developmental activities which can give scientific inputs for smooth execution of Management Action Plans. It may be recalled that some four years back there were only 15 Mangrove areas identified by the Ministry for intensive conservation and management. Recognizing the importance of mangrove ecosystem, the number ofmangrove areas has since grown from 15 to 35 and at present efforts have been on to persuade the State Governments to identify new and additional mangrove conservation areas.

The mangroves in India comprise 69 species under genera and 28 families. India is home to some of the best mangroves in the world. The Ministry has established a National Mangrove Genetic Resources Centre in Orissa. Two mangrove species are endemic to India. One species is *Rhizophora annamalayana*, occurring in Pichavaram, Tamil Nadu. Another species is *Heritiera kanikensis* that exists only in Bhitarkanika of Orissa. Sunderbans (West Bengal have been included in the World List of Biosphere Reserves by UNESCO. They represent the largest stretch of mangroves in the country. There were two separate schemes, one each on wetlands and mangroves earlier which have now been merged and permission from the competent authority for its continuation during the 10 Five Year Plan has been taken. All the concerned States/UTs have constituted Steering Committees to monitor implementation of Management Action Plans for mangroves and coral reefs.

During the year financial assistance was extended During the year, the National committee on Mangroves and Coral Reefs and the Research Subcommittee on Mangroves and Coral Reefs were reconstituted. A meeting of the Research Sub-committee on Mangroves & Coral reefs was held on 23 February, 2004 in the Ministry. The committee considered 17 fresh proposals and recommended six research proposals for financial support by the Ministry. A national workshop on "Conservation, Restoration and Sustainable Management of Mangrove Forests in India", was organized through Institute of Wood Science and Technology at Visakhapatnam, Andhra Pradesh from 18 to 22 February, 2004.

Coral Reefs

The National Committee on Mangroves and Coral Reefs had earlier recommended intensive conservation and management of corals in four areas, namely, Andaman & Nicobar Islands, Lakshadweep Islands, Gulf of Kachchh and Gulf of Mannar. The programme is continuing since 1987. Management Action Plans are under implementation in all the four areas through financial assistance extended by the Ministry to the respective States/UTs. Under Management Action Plan for Conservation and Management of Coral Reefs in Gulf of Mannar, Rs. 30.4 lakhs was released to the State Government in December, 2003 for High Speed Boat (one), Scientific Baseline Data Collection (14 islands), Museum-cum-Interpretation Centre.

Under Management Action Plan for conservation and management of coral reefs in Gulf of Kachchh, Gujarat, Rs. 73.8 lakhs was released to the State Government in December, 2003 for Awareness Programme, Protection and Vigilance, Maintenance of equipments, Purchase of Glass Bottom Boat, Snorkelling Sets, Purchase of OBM Boat, Twin Boat Engine with Hydraulic System, Binoculars, Underwater Camera and Photography, Interpretation Centre.

Under Management Action Plan for Conservation and management of coral reefs in Andaman and Nicobar Islands, Rs. 19.25 lakhs was released to the UT Administration in March, 2004 for Survey and Monitoring Health of Coral Reefs in A&N Islands, Establishment of Database Centre for Management and Monitoring of Coral Reefs, Procurement of Mobile set, Purchase of Speed Boat with two 40 HP OBM engine, Procurement of compressor, Safety equipments, Publicity/Education and Awareness activities, Procurement of equipment for interpretation centre (Microscope underwater camera) etc.

The National Coral Reef Research Centre at Port Blair was provided financial assistance for strengthening infrastructure of the Centre. The

Centre is continuing its activities of biophysical monitoring related to health of coral reefs. They were provided Rs. 17.46 lakhs in November, 2003 for salary to project staff, permanent equipment, books and periodicals, expendables, other project costs, travel, contingencies, etc. Research Sub-Committee on Mangroves and Coral Reefs during its meeting reviewed the progress on ongoing research projects on coral reefs.

Biodiversity Conservation

Biodiversity is the variability among living organisms and the ecological complexes of which they are part, including diversity within and between species and ecosystems. Biodiversity has direct consumptive value in food, agriculture, medicine, and in industry. India is one of the 17 mega diverse countries which together possess 60 to 70 per cent of the world's Biodiversity. It is encouraging to mention that India has taken over Presidency of the like-minded megadiverse group of countries on 19 February, 2004 during the Ministerial meeting of the group in Kuala Lumpur in the margins of CoP 7 meeting of Convention on Biological Diversity.

It may be worth mentioning that India ratified the International Convention on Biodiversity (CBD) on 18th February, 1994 and became party to the convention in May, 94. The CBD is an international legal instrument for promoting conservation and sustainable use of Biological Diversity taking into account "the need to share cost and benefit between developed and developing countries and the ways and means to support innovation by local people". Till date, seven ordinary meetings of the CoP have been held of the seventh meeting was held in Kuala Lampur from February 9-10, 2004. India chaired one of the two working groups of the CoP 7. One important decisions taken by the parties was related to Access and Benefit sharing as related to genetic resources. It was resolved to evolve an International regime on access to genetic resources and benefit sharing with the aim of adopting an instrument/instruments to effectively implement the provisions of CBD. A scheme on biodiversity conservation was initiated during 1991-92 to ensure coordination among various agencies dealing with the issues related to conservation of Biodiversity and to review, monitor and evolve adequate policy instrument for the same. Important steps taken during the year are as follows:

National Bio-diversity Strategy and Action Plan (NBSAP)

A comprehensive project with the financial support of UNDP-GEF was launched for producing a series of planning documents relating to ecological security and livelihood of people most dependent on natural resources. The ultimate aim is to develop a national plan for conservation of biodiversity and its sustainable use. A consultative and participatory approach was adopted by all the executing agencies. A draft National Action Plan (NAP) has been prepared and circulated to more than 500 experts and organisations for comments. The comments received were suitably incorporated and the report revised. A meeting of the Steering Committee under the Chairmanship of Secretary (E & F) was held on January 29, 2004 in which the submission of the draft NAP reportto the Ministry was recommended. The Ministry, based on this draft NAP, shall seek competent approval for a possible National Biodiversity Strategy and Action Plan in line with the National Environment Policy which isunder formulation.

Biological Diversity Act, 2002

A National Biodiversity Authority has been set up at Chennai vide Gazette Notification dated October 1, 2003 under the Act. The Act also provides for establishment of State level Boards and Local level Biodiversity Management Committees to deal with any matter concerning conservation of biological diversity, its sustainable use and fair and equitable sharing of benefits arising out of the use of biological resources and associated knowledge. Detailed rules under the Act have been notified in Gazette on April 15, 2004.

The Cartagena Protocol on Biosafety

The Cartagena Protocol on Biosafety, the firstinternational regulatory framework for safe transfer, handling and use of living Modified Organisms (LMOs) was negotiated under the aegis of the convention on the Convention on Biological Diversity. The Protocol seeks to protect biological diversity from the potential risks posed by living modified organisms resulting from modern biotechnology. It establishes an Advance Informed Agreement (AIA) procedure for ensuring that countries are provided with the information necessary to make informed decisions before agreeing to the import of such organisms into their territory. It further incorporates procedure for import of LMOs with respect to Food Feed and Product (FFP), Risk Assessment and Risk Management Framework and Capacity Building. The protocol contains reference to a precautionary approach. The protocol also establishes a Biosafety Clearing House to facilitate the exchange of information on living modified organisms and to assist countries in the implementation of the protocol.

The protocol was adopted on 29th January, 2000. The protocol has been signed by 103 countries (except USA). India signed the Biosafety Protocol on 23 January, 2001 and acceded to the Protocol on 17th January, 2003. The protocol has come into force on 11th September, 2003, so far 84 countries have ratified the protocol. *Anaphyllum wightii* Schott — endemic to S.W. Ghats Following the entry into force of the protocol the decision making body of the protocol, called the Conference of Parties serving as the Meeting of the Parties to the Protocol (CoP-MoP) will manage and keep under review its development and implementation.

The first meeting of the CoP serving as the first Meeting of the Parties (MoP I) was held at Kuala Lumpur, Malaysia from 23rd - 27th February, 2004. The meeting adopted important decisions on substantive issues related to AIA procedure, handling transport, packaging and identification of LMOs, compliance and liability and redress. Subsequent to the MoP I Meeting, a meeting of Core Expert Group on Biodiversity was held for initiating necessary follow-up.

The Genetic Engineering Approval Committee (Biosafety Regulatory Framework in India)

The Ministry has also initiated measures for streamlining the regulatory procedures for Genetically Modified Organisms (GMOs) in India under 1989 Rules. In this context the Ministry has constituted a task force on Recombinant Pharma Sector under the chairmanship of R.A. Mashelkar, DG, CSIR for streamlining the procedures for Pharma industry. It has also been decided to hold the GEAC Meeting every month. The GEAC has recently approved commercial release of RCH 2 Bt. Cotton hybrid developed by M/s Rasi Seeds Pvt. Ltd. for the Central and South zones. The GEAC has also recommended large scale trials of a number of Bt. Cotton hybrids developed by various companies.

All India Coordinated Project on Capacity Building in Taxonomy (AICOPTAX)

India is one of the mega biodiversity nations of the world and it has a variety of ecological habitats with arge variations in species of plants, animals and microorganisms. On account of such diverse ecosystems present in the country, we have a rich bio-diversity to be identifies, classified and nurtured for present as well as future generations. So far about 90,000 species of animals and 47,000 species of plants have been identified and described. But, this is not the complete picture. Large number of animals and plants are yet to be explored, identified and described.

Taxonomy is the science which helps in exploration, identification and description of living organisms. However, the scope of taxonomy does not end with this. A sound taxonomic base is a pre-requisite for environmental assessment, ecological research, effective conservation, management and sustainable use of biological resources. The All India coordinated Project on Taxonomy (AICOPTAX) was started during the Ninth Plan. The aim of the project was to encourage excellence in the field of taxonomy and motivate the experts to undertake work in hitherto neglected groups of organisms such as microbes, lower groups of plants, animals etc. The scheme envisaged establishment of centres for research in identified priority gap areas such as viruses, bacteria, microlepidopetra, lichens, gymnosperms etc. The centres for research and two centres for training and coordination were identified during the first phase. Simultaneously, steps have been taken to strengthen Botanical Survey of India and Zoological Survey of India so that these organizations could actively participate in the taxonomic work.

A complete list of coordinating and collaborating units operational during the year under the AICOPTAX project is given at Annexure-X. Approval of competent authority has been obtained to continue the entire AICOPTAX project during the remaining part of the enth Five Year Plan.

Assistance to Botanical Gardens

The scheme on assistance to botanical gardens and centres for *ex-situ* conservation was initiated in 1992 to augment *ex-situ* conservation of rare endemic plants.

One time financial assistance is provided to the existing botanical gardens for improvement of their infrastructural facilities to augment *ex-situ* conservation of rare endemic plants. The achievements made in these botanic gardens are periodically monitored with the help of Botanical Survey of India and regional offices of the Ministry. The Ministry has constituted an expert group to identify and recommend proposals received under the scheme. The Botanical Survey of India helps in identification of rare endemic plants requiring ex-situ conservation. During the year, following institutions were provided financial support for improvement of infrastructure facility in their botanical garden:

- Shri Anand College (Arts and Science), Pathardi Distt., Ahmednagar, Maharashtra
- University of Hyderabad, Dept. of Plant Sciences, Hyderabad
- Navarasam Arts & Science College for Women, Nagamalai, Arachalur, Erode
- Dr. Balasaheb Sawant Konkan Krishi Vidyapeeth, Dapoli, Ratnagiri, Maharashtra
- Forest Research Institute (Botany Division), ICFRE, Dehradun
- Shri Kaliswari College, Meenakashipuram Anaikuttam Branch, Thiruthangal Post, Sivakasi, T.N.
- Madurai Kamaraj University, Madurai

- Deptt. Of Botany, Government of Institute of Science, Nipat Niranjan Nagar, Caves Road, Aurangabad
- Late Karmveer Dr. P.R. Ghorey Science College, Dhule – Development of Eco-park and Botanical garden at Bagafa Shantirbazar, South Tripura, Department of Forests and Wildlife, Government of Tripura
- Padamashri Vikhe Patil College of Arts, Science & Commerce, Pravaranagar, Distt. Ahmednagar, Maharashtra Kisan Veer Mahavidyalaya Wai, Dist- Satara
- Majalgaon Arts, Science & Commerce college, Mjalgaon, Dist Beed.
- Uttarkashi Forest Division, conservator of Forests, Bhagirathi Circle, Munikireti
- Lions Deaf, Dumb and physically Handicapped School, Koparagaon
- Nagaland University, Kohima
- University of Kashmir, Srinagar
- The Ranipet Herbarium, St. Joseph's College, Tiruchirapalli
- New Horizon Society, Imphal
- Department of Botany, T.M. Bhagalpur University, Bhagalpur
- Department of Environmental Science, University of Kalyani, West Bengal
- Creation and maintenance of Botanical Garden Complex at Sepahijala, Department of Forests and Wildlife, Government of Tripura.

Botanic Garden of Indian Republic (BGIR), NOIDA

The Botanic Garden of Indian Republic (BGIR) was established at NOIDA in April 2002 as part of the Botanical Survey of India(BSI) to address the long felt need for a conservation-oriented botanic garden specifically for the threatened plants of the country. The project proposal had received full support from the Planning Commission and other relevant Ministries and Departments including the Department of Biotechnology, Ministry of Science and Technology, Finance Ministry, etc. It was also identified as one the projects under the Prime Minister's Jai Vigyan Science and Technology Mission Scheme for expeditious implementation. The BGIR was set up primarily with the following objectives:

- *Ex-situ* conservation and propagation of important threatened points of the country.
- Serve as a Centre of Excellence for conservation research and training.
- Build public awareness through education on plant diversity and need for conservation.

As part of the project implementation the preliminary step has been the initiation of the selection process of a landscape architect for BGIR since all developmental works in the garden hinge on the selected master plan/ landscape design. The process of selection decided upon is through a two-stage open design competition with call for 'expression of interest' letters through wide publicity and detailed landscape/layout designs conceptualized and submitted by the qualifying competitors. A fourteen member Board of Assessors constituted by the ministry is evaluating the entries.

Civil works completed at the BGIR site include completion/raising of boundary wall, laying of bituminous approach roads in parking area and construction of a portacabin to house the site office, herbarium and seed bank. The BGIR has taken up specific field activities in accordance with its mandate. Woodland development work along the peripheral areas has been initiated with indigenous trees being planted to recreate a deciduous forest ecosystem. A plant procurement programme has been initiated on a priority basis with seedlings being collected from different parts of the country. About nine thousand saplings have already been procured for introduction in the garden. These saplings are being stocked and acclimatized in net houses developed for the purpose. A nursery has also been developed for raising seedlings of indigenous tree species of the country. Seeds for the purpose are being procured from various State forest nurseries. A medicinal plants section is under development; about 70 medicinal plants have been procured so far towards development of the medicinal plants section. Apart from the basic plantation work, conservation biology studies of RET species particularly some critically endangered species, have been taken up. Floristic survey of the National Capital Region has also been initiated by way of a research programme; the plant specimens collected in the process are being housed in the herbarium. As part of its conservation research and education programme database development work has also been initiated.

Forest Conservation

Till March 2004, the Ministry received 14,621 proposals from the State/ Union Territories for getting approval under the Forest (Conservation) Act 1980 for diversion of forest land for non-forestry purpose.General Guidelines issued under Forest (Conservation) Act, 1980 have been revised.

- ➢ To promote investment in power sector 'Wind Energy Policy' under Forest (Conservation) Act, 1980 has been put into place.
- ➢ In conformity with the National Forest Policy, 1988 and to provide boost to the development of tribal areas, new guidelines for 'Development projects in tribal areas' have also been formulated and

one time clearance has been granted for public utility development projects like drinking water, electricity etc.

- The period of general approval under Section–2 of Forest (Conservation) Act, 1980 for public utility development projects has been extended upto 15/10/2005.
- A road map has been provided to the State/UT Government to expedite action for conversion of forest villages into revenue villages.
- Guidelines have been issued for regularization/recognition of tribal rights on forest lands.The implementation of these Guidelines have been stayed by the Hon'ble Supreme Court vide their order dated 23.2.2004 in IA No. 1126 of 2004 in Writ Petition (C) No. 202 of 1995.
- A Monitoring Cell has been created for data base management, updating the website for Forestry Clearance, monitoring the movement of proposals inthe State and at the Central Government level and also to monitor the compliance of the stipulated conditions of the approved cases.

Regional Offices of the Ministry

The primary functions of the Regional Offices of the Ministry are to monitor and evaluate the ongoing forestry projects and schemes with specific emphasis on conservation of forests and follow-up action on the implementation of conditions and safeguards laid down by the Ministry while granting clearance to development projects under FCA/E(P)A. The Regional Chief Conservator of Forests are empowered to decide cases for diversion of forest land for non-forestry purposes upto the extent of 40 ha. except mining and regularization of encroachment.

The Ministry has six Regional Offices located the Bangalore, Bhopal, Bhubaneswar, Lucknow, Shillong and Chandigarh with its headquarter in the Ministry at New Delhi. The seventh Regional Office at Ranchi could not be made functional due to financial constraint.

Forest Policy

The Forest Policy Division provides policy support in respect of forestry matters, and reviews the forest policy and its relation to policies of other relevant sectors. Various legal issues viz., the State / Central Bills related with the forestry matters that re required to receive the assent of the President of India are examined by the division.

North East Forest Policy

In pursuance of the recommendation of Shukla Commission which was set up by the Planning Commission to examine the backlog in basic minimum services and gaps infrastructure sectors for the development in the North East, the North East Forest Policy Committee was constituted in November, 1998 under the chairmanship of Shri S.C. Dey to suggest a suitable Forest Policy for the North East within the framework of National Forest Policy, 1988. Some of the modifications/changes that have been recommended to the North East region are as follows:

- Increased focuses on weaning away the people from Jhum cultivation area.
- Conservation of natural heritage, genepool and biodiversity and maintenance of environmental stability through preservation and soil and moisture conservation specifically on steep slopes, river catchment and eco-fragile areas.
- Encourage efficient utilization of forest produce and maximum value addition.
- Survey and demarcation and preparation of working plans/working schemes for all forests for sustainable and scientific management.

Amendment of Indian Forest Act, 1927

As forestry has undergone many conceptual changes since the adoption of Indian Forest Act, 1927, it was decided to bring suitable amendments to this Act. After receiving the comments and suggestions on the proposed amendments from various Ministries, organizations and NGOs the final draft has been prepared for placing it before the Cabinet of approval.

National Forest Commission

The Ministry of Environment and Forests has constituted the National Forest Commission on 7.02.03 to review the working of Forests and Wildlife Sector with the following terms of reference:

- Review and assess the existing policy and legal framework and their impact in a holistic manner rom the ecological, scientific, economic, social and cultural viewpoint.
- Examine the current status of forest administration and the forestry institutions both on all India and State level to meet the emerging needs of the civil society.
- Make recommendations indicating policy options for achieving sustainable forest and wildlife management and development, bio-diversity conservation and ecological security.
- Suggest ways and means to make forest administration more effective with a view to help to achieve the above policy options.

- Establish meaningful partnership and interface between forestry management and local communities including tribals. The composition of the Commission includes a chairperson, member secretary and five members. The tenure of the commission is of 2 years. The commission functions under the administrative control of the Central Government in the Ministry of Environment and Forests with headquarters at New Delhi.

Integrated Forest Protection Scheme

Integrated Forest Protection Scheme has been formulated by the merger of the schemes of the 9th Five Year Plan 'Forest Fire Control and Management' and 'Bridging of Infrastructure Gaps in the Forestry Sector in the North Eastern Region and Sikkim. It is operational from 2002-03. The scheme covers all the States and UTs for the 10th Five Year Plan period.The main components of the scheme are:

- Infrastructure development
- Working plan preparation/survey and demarcation strengthening of infrastructure for forest protection.
- Forest fire control and management the central sector component of forest fire control and management will be implemented by the forest protection division of the ministry and by the forest survey of India, Dehradun and other central institutions like Indian council of forestry research and education, Dehradun, Indian Institute of Forest Management, Bhopal, National Centre for Medium Range Weather Forecasting. The state sector component of the scheme will be implemented by the forest departments/of the concern State Governments and UTs. The central assistance is provided for various activities which will help to protect and improve the existing forest. The major items of expenditure include communication, mobility, fire fighting measures, construction of offices and residences particularly of the front line staff, technology upgradation and skill development, survey & demarcation and writing of working plans, assistance to JFMS's etc. The 10th Plan outlay for the Scheme is Rs. 445 crore. The total expenditure in current during the year 2003-04 is Rs. 25.40 Crores.

Joint Forest Management

The Joint Forest Management (JFM) Programme was pursued vigorously with the result that JFM resolution has now been adopted in all the 28 States. 84632 JFM Committees have been formed and 17.33 million ha forest area have been brought under JFM Programme. About 85.28

lakhs families are involved in JFM Programme invarious states all over the country. The state-wise progress of JFM Programme in the country is given A meeting of JFM Network and Slake holder forum was also organized in September, 2003 where various issues related to Joint Forest Management was discussed in detail.

A scheme for providing Seed Money has also been prepared for providing financial assistance for creation of new Joint Forest Management Committees and to meet their various expenses so that all the villages in the country are covered under JFM Programme and universalization of JFM takes place. The scheme has been sent to the Planning Commission for approval.

Wildlife Conservation

Various activities relating to wild life conservation and implementation of the Wild Life (Protection) Act, 1972 were carried out by the Ministry during the year. The details are as follows:

Enforcement of Wildlife (Protection) Act, 1972 and Export- Import Policy

The Wildlife (Protection) Act, 1972, the provisions of the Convention on International Trade in Endangered Species (CITES) and Export and Import Policy of India were continued to be enforced through the offices of the Regional Deputy Directors of Wildlife Preservation located at Delhi, Mumbai, Calcutta and Chennai with the help of State Wildlife Department, the State Police Departments, the Customs Departments, Border Security Force (BSF) and Coast-Guards. The Regional Deputy Directors detected several cases of poaching and illegal trade in wildlife products during the year. During the year ban on export of 29 species of plant, plant portions and their derivatives obtained from wild were continued. Export of six species of exotic birds was continued subject to pre shipment inspection and CITES permit wherever required.

Wildlife (Protection) Act, 1972

The various amendments made to the Wildlife (Protection) Act, 1972 came into force from 1st April 2003 except for the provision relating to constitution of National Board for Wildlife.

National Board for Wildlife (NBWL)

As per the provisions of the Wild Life (Protection) Act, 1972 as amended in 2002, the National Board for Wild Life was constituted vide notification dated 21 September, 2003. The first meeting of the NBWL was held on 15 October, 2003 under the chairmanship of Hon'ble Prime Minister. The

Standing Committee of the NBWL was also constituted and has met twice on 24th December 2003 and 18th March 2004 to discuss important aspects related to wildlife.

Development of National Parks and Sanctuaries

There are 92 National Parks and 500 Wildlife Sanctuaries in the country covering an area of 15.67 million hectares. During the year, financial assistance for Development of National Parks and Sanctuaries has been provided to 269 National Parks and Sanctuaries in 28 states including north-eastern states. During the year 2003-2004 Rs. 43.19 crores have been released. Under this scheme 100 per cent Central assistance is provided for non-recurring item of expenditure for both national parks and sanctuaries. 50 per cent assistance is also provided for recurring items of expenditure in case of national parks where the State Government provides 50 per cent of matching share. Further, protected areas in mountains, deserts and coastal regions supporting large population of endangered species like Snow leopard, Red Panda, Rhino, Sangai deer, Pharys' af monkey, Musk Deer, Hangul, Great Indian Bustard,Chinkara and Black buck, are eligible for 100 per cent Central ssistance for both, recurring and non-recurring item of expenditure.

Animal Welfare

The Animal Welfare Division became a part of Ministry of Environment and Forests in the month of July 2002. Earlier the Division was under Ministry of Statistics and Programme Implementation. The Mandata of Animal Welfare Division is to prevent the infliction of unnecessary pain or suffering on animals. To accomplish this mission three-pronged approach is being adopted by the division:

Regulatory

The main task of the division is to implement effectively the various provision of Prevention of Cruelty to Animals Act, 1960. Under this Act, a number of Rules have been framed for various purposes. Some of the important Rules framed are:

- Performing Animals Rules, 1973 and Performing Animals (Registration) Rules, 1972.
- Transport of Animals Rules, 1978 and 2001.
- Prevention of Cruelty (Slaughter Houses) Rules, 2000.
- Prevention of Cruelty to Animals (Establishment and Regulation of Society for Prevention of Cruelty to Animals) Rules 2001.

- ➢ Animal Birth Control (Dogs) Rules, 2001; and
- ➢ Breeding of and Experiments on Animals (Control and Supervision) Rules, 1998 as amended in February, 2001.

The following action has been taken for ensuring more effective regulation of these Rules:

- ➢ Rules under the Prevention of Cruelty to Animals Avt, 1960 were notified by Animal Welfare Division as under:
  - — Performing Animals (Registration) Rules, 2001. (Notified on 26th March 2001)
  - — Prevention of Cruelty to Animals (Transport of Animals on Foot) Rules, 2001. (Notified on 26th March 2001)
  - — Transport of Animals (Amendment) Rules, 2001.(Notified on 26th March 2001)
  - — Prevention of Cruelty to Animals (Slaughter House) Rules, 2001. (Notified on 26th March 2001)
  - — Prevention of Cruelty to Animals (Establishment and Regulation of Societies for the Prevention of Cruelty to Animals) Rules, 2001. (Notified on 26th March 2001)
  - — Animal Birth Control (Dogs) Rules, 2001. (Notified on 24th December, 2001)
  - — Performing Animals (Registration) Amendment Rules, 2001. (Notified on 8th January, 2002).
  - — Experiments on Animals (Control and Supervision) (Amendment) Rules, 1998. (Notified on 26th August, 1998).
  - — Breeding of and Experiments on Animals (Control and Supervision) Rules, 1998. (Notified on 15th December 1998).
  - — Breeding of and Experiments on Animals (Control and Supervision) Amendment Rules, 2001. (Notified on 15th February 2001).
  - — Two hundred and twenty five number of animals from circuses viz. Ajanta Circus, Asian Circus, Komal Circus etc. have been seized and transported to rescue centres at Chennai, Visakhapatnam, Bangalore and Tirupati.
  - — Made timely intervention in likely cases of animal sacrifices in various states including Andhra Pradesh, Tamil Nadu, Orissa and Kerala and prevented the same.

— A total of 307 Societies for Prevention of Cruelty to Animals (SPCAs) stand constituted. The number rose to this level from around 250.

— Five proformae for monitoring compliance of Transport Rules, Slaughter House Rules, Performing Animals and Registration Rules, Registration of Cattle Premises Rules and Draught and Pack Rules have been sent to all State Department of Animal Husbandry, Home, Urban Development and Transport for furnishing quarterly performance report.

Developmental

The Division provides assistance for construction of shelter houses, dispensaries etc. for stray, infirm & abandoned animals. It also gives grants for ambulances and vehicles in connection with treatment and transportation of sick, injured and rescued animals. Another major developmental programme is immunization and sterillization of stray dogs.

Various Schemes Implemented by the Animal Welfare Division

Scheme for Shelter Houses for Looking After the Animals: The objective of this scheme is to establish and maintain shelter houses for distressed animals in the country. Primarily NGOs, SPCAs are given grant up to Rs.22.50 lakhs. During the year, Rs.2.96 crore has been released to 38 organizations in the states of Rajasthan, New Delhi, Gujarat, Orissa, Punjab, Haryana, West Bengal, Maharashtra, U.P., Madhya Pradesh, Andhra Pradesh and Goa. Some of the beneficiary organizations are Adinath Pashu Raksha Sanstha Gaushala; Udaipur, Rajasthan; Wild life S.O.S, New Delhi; People For Animals, Solapur, Maharashtra; NICCD, Khoda, Orissa; Bishwa Bharti Shiksha Sansthan, Gurukul Gaushala, Rohtak, Haryana; Shri Gopal Gaushala, Patiala, Punjab; SPCA Udgir, Maharashtra; Dayodaya Pashu Sansthan, Lalitpur, U.P.; Shri Gopal Goshala Nyas, Ratlam, Madhya Pradesh; Friendicoes SECA, New Delhi; Sri Raghvendra Pashu Samraksha Sangha, Cuddapah, Andhra Pradesh; People For Animals, Panaji, Goa.

Scheme for Animal Birth Control and Immunization of Stray Dogs: The scheme is meant for controlling the population of stray dogs by sterilization and reducing incidences of rabies by immunization. The NGOs and SPCAs working in collaboration with local bodies are eligible for this grant. The scheme has had the desired impact specially in large cities like, New Delhi, Mumbai, Ahmedabad, Panaji, Vishakhapatnam, Pune, Kolkata, Chennai, Bangalore and Hyderabad and there has been a perceptible improvement in controlling the dog population. During the year, an amount of Rs. 1.697 crore has been released to 65 organizations in the states of punjab, Karnataka, Goa, New Delhi, Rajasthan, Gujarat, Andhra Pradesh, West Bengal, U.P., Maharashtra, Tamil Nadu, Orissa, Assam and Arunachal Pradesh. Some organizations given grant under this schemes are Circle of Animal Lovers, New Delhi; Sanjay Gandhi Animal Care Centre, New Delhi; Friendicoes SECA, New Delhi; Visakha SPCA, Vishakhapatnam; Blue Cross Society of Pune, Blue Cross of India, Chennai; SPCA, Chennai; SPCA & PFA Kolkata. During the year around 63,000 dogs have been covered under this programme.

Scheme for Provision of Ambulance Services to Animals in Distress: Under this scheme the animal welfare organizations are given grant for purchase of suitable vehicle for transportation, rescue and also for providing emergency services to animals in distressed. An amount of Rs. 47.50 lakh has been released during the year to 12 organizations like Early Birds, Assam; PFA, Imphal; Gram Vikas Kalyan Samiti, Mathura; Shri Krishna Gau Seva Sansthan, Rajasthan; International Wildlife and Tiger Conservation, Jabalpur; PFA Sadhrana, Gurgaon), Haryana.

Scheme for Relief to Animals During Natural Calamities and Unforeseen Circumstances: The animal welfare organization, State Government, Local Bodies etc. are given grant to make available emergency services to animals in distress on account of natural calamities like earthquakes, cyclone, flood, drought etc. During this financial year the target set by the division was for giving grant of Rs. 35 lakhs. Two States, through organizations namely Rajasthan Livestok Development Board, Jaipur and UP Go Seva Ayog, Lucknow, have been given grant totaling to Rs. 30.00 lakhs under Natural Calamity Scheme. Educational Seminars and workshops at national, zonal and state levels on various issues is another activity in which the division is engaged. A workshop on 'Laboratory Animal Science & Welfare' at Mumbai was organized by CPCSEA in April 2003.

The regular publication of Newsletters of CPCSEA & AWBI have also been carried for dissemination of information.

National Institute of Animal Welfare (NIAW)

An Institute is being constructed at Ballabhgarh, District, Faridabad, Haryana for providing various Graduate and Post Graduate courses on animal welfare. The institute would also offer intensive specialized diplomas in specific streams. Besides it would also provide guidance to research scholars.

The National Institute of Animal Welfare, will work as a Teaching, Research and Extension Centre. It will impart teaching in disciplines like History of Animal Welfare Movement, Psychology of Animal Behaviour,

Animal diversity, Animal Laws, Animals Nursing, Animal Breeding, Zoo Management, Park Management, Aquatic Management, Animal Stress and Pain etc. It is proposed to start the academic session w.e.f. 1.10.2004. Before the institute in a full fledged manner, a number of issues are being to be firmed up. These are:

(a) assessment of market demand to ensure employability of candidates;

(b) decision regarding degree or diploma and its due recognition;

(c) evolving the course content and finalization of the curriculum;

(d) deemed University status for the NIAW;

(e) finalization of the Recruitment Rules for the faculty members, and

(f) appointment of Director and other core faculty members.

As all this would take some more time, in the first year it is proposed to start with in-service training. Simultaneously a road map is being developed for turning the institute into one for degree courses. In-service training course in the first year is proposed to assign to ED.Cil on turnkey basis.

STATUTORY BODIES

Animal Welfare Board of India (AWBI)

This is a statutory body under Section 4 of the Prevention of Cruelty to Animals Act, 1960 with head quarters at Chennai. Its basic mandate is to advise the Government on animal welfare issues, and create awareness in animal welfare. Animal Welfare Board of India (AWBI) gives financial assistance to eligible Animal Welfare Organizations for Shelter Houses, Model Gaushalas for setting up Bio-Gas Plants, Famine/Drought Relief Earthquake Relief etc. in various states. The number of Animal Welfare Organization (AWOs) registered with AWBI went up to 2100 during the year.

An amount of Rs. 4.95 crore under Plan scheme and Rs. 65 lakhs under non-plan scheme have been released under the scheme during the year. A provision of Rs. 4.50 crores under plan scheme and Rs. 68 lakhs under non plan scheme has been made in the budget estimate for Animal Welfare Board of India. So far State Animal Welfare Boards (SAWBs) have been constituted in 24 States/UTs.

Committee for Purpose of Control and Supervision of Experiments on Animals (CPCSEA)

This is also a statutory body under Section 15 of Prevention of Cruelty to Animals Act, 1960 with head quarters at Chennai. The mandate of this committee is to register and monitor the animal breeders and institutions conducting experiments on animals. So far 820 units have been registered with this committee.

During current financial year 91 new Institutions have been registered with this committee. A provision of Rs. 45 Lakh was made in the year 2003-200 Budget and the entire amount was released.

Project Tiger

'Project Tiger' was launched in 1973 with an objective "to ensure maintenance of a viable population of tigers in India for scientific, economic, aesthetic, cultural and ecological values, and to preserve for all times, areas of biological importance as a national heritage for the benefit, education and enjoyment of the people". The Project has been successfully implemented, and at present there are 281 Tiger Reserves in 17 states, covering an area of 37761 sq. km. The selection of reserves was guided by the need to conserve unique ecosystem/habitat types across the geographic distribution of tigers in the country. The network of tiger reserves include high mountainous terrains of Arunachal Pradesh, the heavy rainfall areas of Assam and West Bengal, the estuarinemangroves of Sunderbans, the dry forests of Rajasthan, the foothills of the Himalayas in Uttaranchal, Uttar Pradesh and Bihar, the Central Indian Highlands of Madhya Pradesh, Chattisgarh, and Maharashtra, and the plateau of Chota Nagpur (Jharkhand), the hilly tropical and evergreen forests of Orissa, the evergreen forests of Western Ghats in Kerala and Karnataka, the dry deciduous forests of Andhra Pradesh and the Southern moist deciduous forests of Tamil Nadu. 'Project Tiger' is undisputedly the custodian of major gene pool of the country and a repository of some of the most valuable ecosystem and habitats for wildlife.

For the purpose of management, the tiger reserves are constituted on a 'core'-'buffer' strategy. In the core area, forestry operations, collection of non-timber forest produce, grazing, human settlement and other biotic disturbances are not allowed, and is singularly oriented towards conservation. The buffer zone is managed as a 'multiple use area', with conservation oriented land use, having the twin objectives of ensuring habitat supplement to the spillover population of wild animals from the core, apart from providing site specific eco-developmental inputs to fringe dwelling, stake holder communities. The main thrust of the project is protection and mitigation of deleterious human impacts with a view to comprehensively revive the natural ecosystem in the reserves. During the X Plan, the major thrust would beto further enlarge and diversify the activities and consolidate the progress made under the scheme hitherto.

Upto 1979-80, the scheme operated as a 100 per cent centrally financed (plan) scheme. However, during the VI Five Year Plan (1980-85), the central funding was reduced to 50 per cent for recurring items of expenditure with State Governments allocating the matching grant), while providing 100 per cent central funding support to non-recurring items.

Highlights of Achievements

- Launched in 1973 with nine reserves covering an area of 16339 sq. km, Project Tiger has been extended to 281 reserves in 17 States, encompassing 37761 sq. km, of tiger habitat, with the addition of four new tiger reserves viz. Pakui
- Nameri (Arunachal/Assam: 1206 km^2), Bori
- Satpura (MP: 1486 km^2), Bhadra (Karnataka: 492 km^2) and Pench (Maharashtra: 257 km^2). Project Tiger has been rated as a role model and has been noted as one of the 56 events that changed India since independence.
- Eight potential areas in the country have also been identified for subsequent inclusion under 'Project Tiger'.
- For the first time, 'Project Allowance' has been provided to all categories of field staff working in tiger reserves.
- The tiger population in the country has registered an increase from 1827 in 1972 to 3642 in 2001-02.
- Complementary inputs for eco-development and voluntary village relocation provided earlier in separate projects, have now been merged with 'Project Tiger as an Umbrella Scheme. Under the on-going, externally aided India Eco-development Project', as many as 572 eco-development committees have been formed in seven Protected Areas covering 75,600 families, to reduce the dependency of local people on Protected Area resources, with reciprocal commitments.
- 100 per cent central assistance is now being provided for deploying anti-poaching strike squads in tiger reserves, apart from inputs relating to research, veterinary, monitoring and evaluation, compensation to the legal heir of staff/person killed while performing duty, and for monitoring of tiger population. transboundary cooperation protocol with Bangladesh and Myanmar.
- For the first time, information and communication technology is being used for: linking important tiger reserves in the GIS Domain for evolving management support system including crime detection, dissemination of information through web and evolving a 'National Tiger Monitoring and Habitat Evaluation System' with regional protocols. A new Resolution on conservation of 'Asian Cats' was floored

by India in November 2002, during the 12th meeting of the Conference of Parties to CITES.

- The allocation under 'Project Tiger' has been enhanced from Rs. 7500 lakhs in the IX Plan to Rs. 15000 lakhs in the X Plan. During the year 2003-04, an amount of Rs 3067.21 lakhs was released to states under the project.

INDIAN ECO-DEVELOPMENT PROJECT – A WORLD BANK ASSISTED PROJECT

Objectives

Improved PA Management: To improve the capacity of Protected Area Management to conserve bio-diversity and gain support of the local people for conservation by increasing opportunities for local participation in Protected Area Management.

Village Eco-development: to reduce negative impact of the local people on bio-diversity.

Education and Awareness: Promoting, education and awareness, monitoring and research for further the cause of conservation in identified tiger reserves and national parks.

Project Management: To ensure effective management of the project at both PA and national level.

Achievements

Seven PAs covered in seven States, 572 microplans prepared which cover 75,600 households (26% tribals, 27% landless), 4500000 mandays generated in IX Plan, 1939000 man-days generated in X Plan, apart from improved PA management due to infrastructure, ecodevelopment and capacity building. A number of consultancies have been conducted both at State level as well as Centre level and their reports have been received. Total cost of the project is Rs. 200.97 crores, so far an amount of Rs. 198.99 crores has been released to the project states. This include Rs 3.94 crores released for current financial year (2004-05).

Project Elephant

Project Elephant was launched in February, 1992 to assist states having free ranging populations of wild elephants to ensure long term survival of identified viable populations of elephants in their natural habitats. The project is being implemented in 12 states, viz. Andhra Pradesh, Arunachal Pradesh, Assam, Jharkhand, Karnataka, Kerala, Meghalaya, Nagaland, Orissa, Tamilnadu, Uttaranchal and West Bengal. States are being given financial as well as technical assistance in achieving the objectives of the project. Help is also provided to other states with small populations of elephants for the purpose of census, training of field staff and mitigation of human-elephant conflict.

Main Activities of Project Elephant

- Strengthening of measure for protection of wild elephants from poachers.
- Development of scientific and planned management for conservation of elephant habitats and viable population of wild Asiatic elephants in India.
- Ecological restoration of existing natural habitats and migratory routes of elephants.
- Promotion of measures for mitigation of manelephant conflict in problem areas and moderating pressures of human and live stock on crucial elephant habitats.
- Eco-development.
- Veterinary care.
- Research on elephant issues relating to elephant onservation.
- Public education and awareness programme; and
- Capacity building of field staff, mahouts and veterinarians.

Achievement

- An amount of Rs. 12.85 crores (including Rs. 3.17 crores for North-Eastern States) was released during the year 2003-04 under the scheme Project Elephant to the elephant range states against the arget of Rs. 12.85 crores for the purpose of habitat management, mitigation of man-elephant conflict, payment of ex-gratia relief for loss of life human and crop caused by wild elephants, strengthening of anti-poaching measures, capacity building of the field staff, registration of domesticated elephants using microchips etc.
- Eight elephant reserves have been set up during the year which include Dihing – Patkai, Dhansiri – Lungding and Kaziranga – Karbi Anglong in Assam, Nilgiri, Coimbatore, Anaimalai and Srivilliputhur in Tamil Nadu and Royala in Andhra Pradesh. Total number of elephant reserves in the country stood at 24 as on 31.3.2004.
- Arrangements for refresher courses for elephant veterinarians were made with the help of the Assam Agricultural University (Guwahati) and Kerala Agricultural University (Trichur).

- A programmed for registration of domesticated elephants with the help of microchips has been initiated in the country during 2003-04.
- A national workshop on the management and welfare of domesticated elephants was organizsed at Thiruvananthapuram in August 2003.
- A programmed has been initiated during 2003-04 for the regular and systematic monitoring of wild elephants under the MIKE (Monitoring of Illegal Killing of Elephants) programmed of CITES (Convention on International Trade in Endangered Species of Wild Fauna and Flora). Ten sensitive sites have been identified for this purpose in different parts of the country. MIKE also provides a forum for collaboration with other South Asian countries (viz. Nepal, Bhutan, Bangladesh and Sri Lanka) for protection of elephants.
- A technical handbook on post-mortem techniques for elephants has been brought out during 2003-04.

Wildlife Institute of India

The Wildlife Institute of India (WII) was established in 1982 under the Ministry of Agriculture and subsequently brought under the Ministry of Environment and Forests. The mandate of the Institute is to impart training, carry out research and advise on matter of conservation and management of wildlife. Wildlife Institute of India is an autonomous institute of the Ministry, with a 48 member WII Society headed by the Union Minister for Environment and Forests as the apex body.

Central Zoo Authority

Central Zoo Authority (CZA) was established in 1992 under the provisions of Wild Life (Protection) Act, 1972. The Authority consists of 10 members and one whole time member secretary and is chaired by the Minister, Environment and Forests, Government of India. Two committees namely 'Administrative Committee' under the Chairmanship of Director General of Forests and Technical Committee under the Chairmanship of Additional Director General of Forests (Wildlife) have been constituted for carrying out the functions of the Central Zoo Authority.

Main functions of the Central Zoo Authority are:

- Specify minimum standards for housing, upkeep and veterinary care of the animals in the zoos.
- Recognition of zoos on the basis of evaluation of their functioning.

Biotechnological Intervention for Conservation of Endangered Species

In view of the fragmentation of habitats due to biotic pressures of various kinds, the survival of endangered species of wild fauna is not possible only through in-situ conservation efforts. These efforts need to be supplemented through ex-situ conservation of species which are under threat of extinction or likely to become extinct in future.The Central Zoo Authority had initiated a programme for biotechnological intervention for conservation of endangered species in 1994-95 at Centre for Cellular and Molecular Biology (CCMB). This programme was very successful and, therefore, supported in the 9th Five Year Plan period as a joint venture of CCMB, Department of Bio-Technology (DBT) and Central Zoo Authority. During its implementation, it has been felt that the programme needs to be enlarged in its scope and a separate laboratory should be established for this purpose. Accordingly, the foundation stone for the proposed Laboratory was laid by MEF on 16.9.2001.

The Government of India has approved establishment of National Facility for Conservation of Endangered Species of Animals, vide its letter No. BT/ PR/3210/BCE/08/241/2002 dated 14.8.2003, at a total cost of Rs. 746.787 lakhs (CZA share of Rs. 360.00 lakhs, DBT share of Rs. 290.760 lakhs and Council for Scientific & Industrial Research (CSIR) share of Rs. 167.027 lakhs). Central Zoo Authority share of Rs. 360.00 lakhs is proposed to be released in two installments of Rs. 180.00 lakhs each. An MoU was signed to the effect between all participates department/organizations. The first installment of Rs. 180.00 lakhs has been released to CCMB during the year.

Strengthening of Infrastructure in Veterinary Universities/ Colleges

In order to provide the Indian Zoos access to modern techniques for faster diagnosis of various diseases infecting the wild animals the Central Zoo Authority had taken an initiative to provide financial assistance to select Veterinary Universities/Colleges for strengthening their existing infrastructure, so that they can help the Zoos in their region. Accordingly, 6 such Universities/Institutes have been identified, namely:

1. Indian Veterinary Research Institute (IVRI), Bareilly;
2. Sher-E-Kashmir University of Agriculture and Technology, Jammu;
3. Orissa University of Agriculture & Technology, Bhubaneshwar;
4. Tamil Nadu University of Veterinary & Animal Sciences, Chennai;

5. Assam Agriculture University, Jorhat; and
6. Gujarat Agriculture University, Ahmedabad.

During the year, Rs.70.30 lakhs has been released to Gujarat Agricultural University and Assam Agriculture University to strengthen their existing disease diagnostic facilities.

As per the direction of the technical committee, appraisal of the above identified centres are being carried out to assess the extent of help that has been rendered by these centres to the Indian Zoos and also formulate an effective networking among the Zoos and the centres.

Rescue and Rehabilitation of Star Tortoises

The Central Zoo Authority took initiative and coordinated with the CITES authorities in Singapore and their Indian counterparts in the Ministry of Environment & Forests, the Wildlife Institute of India and Andhra Pradesh, Forest Department, to bring back 1830 star tortoises into the country, which were seized by the Singapore authorities. At present these tortoises have been rehabilitated at Nehru Zoological Park, Hyderabad. A strategy for their final rehabilitation in the wild has also been drawn up as per the IUCN protocol. A soft release programme of the star tortoises has already been carried out at Srisailam on 15.11.2003. 500 star tortoises which were rescued by the Malaysian CITES authorities have also been brought back to India and have been rehabilitated at Arignar Anna Zoological Park, Chennai.

Rehabilitation of Circus Animals

The Government of India has put a ban on performance of lion, tiger, panther, bear and monkeys by circuses. Consequent to the ban, these animals were to be rehabilitated by creating appropriate facilities. As Indian Zoos did not have adequate facilities to rehabilitate all these animals, the Central Government decided that rescue centres should be created by the Central Zoo Authority for the display areas of the various zoos. Accordingly, the Central Zoo Authority has established five rescue centres at the following Zoos:

- Arignar Anna Zoological Park, Chennai, Tamil Nadu
- Indira Gandhi Zoological Park, Visakapatnam, Andhra Pradesh
- Sri Venkateshwara Zoological Park, Tirupati, Andhra Pradesh
- Bannerghatta National Park, Bangalore, Karnataka
- Nahargarh Biological Park, Jaipur, Rajasthan

During the year 48 lions, 3 tigers, 6 bears and 6 monkeys have been rescued from the circuses and have been rehabilitated at Nahargarh Biological Park, Bannerghatta Biological Park and Arignar Anna Zoo logical Park, Chennai. Till date the Central Zoo Authority has rehabilitated 239 lions, 51 tigers, 8 bears, 2 panthers and 17 monkeys from various Indian circuses.

Publications

During the year Central Zoo Authority brought out following publications:

- Annual Inventory Report for the 2002-2003.
- Techniques and Procedure for Postmortem of Elephants.

Website

The website of Central Zoo Authority (www.cza.nic.in) was launched in March, 2003. This is an interactive website. The website has two main sections : a general section and administrative section. The general section has information about the Central Zoo Authority and Zoos, animal collections in major zoos, a bulletin board for exchange of views and information between the general public and zoos, events and news section and a section on frequently asked questions (FAQ) about Central Zoo Authority and Zoos in India. This section is open to all. The status of compliance of standards prescribed by Central Zoo Authority has been put up on its website so that people can know about it. Till date status of 20 Zoos out of 54 major Zoos have been uploaded to the website. Other zoos shall be covered after the ongoing evaluation work is completed. The website is quite popular as is evident from the number of hits registered by it. A total of 1,31,449 hits have been registered out of which 76.22 per cent has been from international visitors. The website is kept updated with a view to keep interest of its users alive.

National Zoological Park

Inaugurated on 1st November 1959, National Zoological Park (NZP) could boast of being the first Indian Zoo built on modern concept of open moated enclosures, simulating natural habitat of the animals housed. However, with the changing times, priorities and objectives of the zoo changed. These factors also had an effect on the number of species and heads of animals of a particular species. To respond to this changed scenario, a Master Layout Plan for National Zoological Park is in place and the Park is presently undergoing several changes in confirmity with it. The major changes that occurred during the year are:

- A pair of Chimpanzee viz. Ruby and Rustam who earlier occupied a small enclosure around 445m^2 in area were released in a improved enclosure of 5500 m^2 area that was newly constructed. The release took place on 12th June 2003. Shri M.K. Sharma, Director General of Forests released the animals.
- Enclosures of Royal Bengal Tiger and White Tiger have been extended by adding new arenas. This has facilitated simultaneous release of more animals. Hence, by rotating between animals and arenas, boredom and stress on animals can be reduced to some extent. Since some sites cannot be viewed by public animals can get some solace.
- The African Elephant enclosure, construction for which had begun last year, is likely to be completed soon. To enable denizens of National Zoological park overcome extremes of temperature in winter and summer months, appropriate summer gear and winter gears were launched well in time.
- During the year, National Zoological park received one palm civet cat, twelve tortoise from wildlife department (Haryana Div.) two rat snakes, one cobra and one sand boa from Wildlife Protection Society of India, five kalij pheasant from Srahan Phesantry (Himachal Pradesh) and one scavanger vulture.
- Two black buck were air lifted to Colombo Zoo, Sri Lanka, in exchange of jaguar.
- Eight pythons were released in Chambal Sanctuary. One male Hippopotamus was transferred to Surat Municipal Corporation Zoo.
- In an exchange with Jaipur Zoo, National Zoological Park gave 1:0 Hamadryas Baboon and received 1:0 Hyena and 1:1 Chinkara.
- During the year, Giraffe, Rhino, Jaguar, Panther, Swamp Deer, Sangai, Chinkara,Cape Buffalo and Black Swan gave birth to new babies.
- Birds Aviary was provided with tree for providing enrichmint in enclosure plants and grasses were planted for better aesthetic. Special drive was undertaken to eradicate parthenium.
- The zoo continued to follow pre-drawn veterinary schedule for periodic screening of diseases and nutritional supplement. The Zoo Health Committee continued to give their valuable advise for maintaining the animals in good health and monitored the same periodically. In a novel experiment, the National Zoological Park tried to put some of its herbivore species on fast once a week. This has yielded very good results.

- Students from veterinary college, Hissar, Haryana were given training in treatment of wildlife in captivity as a part of their activities during internship.
- Strict Sanitary Schedule was maintained by periodic application of disinfectants inside and outside the animal houses, and around the animal enclosures.

The enclosure moats were maintained dry. The incinerator was maintained in working condition and dead animals were disposed off by burning in incinerator. The Zoo remained committed to provide its animals a better environment by continuing its ban on:

- Plastic entry
- Food entry
- Vehicle entry

To generate awareness about conservation, the zoo organised an orientation programme for school teachers and trolley drivers. Several competitions were held like on the spot painting competition, essay competition, amateur photography competition, during the Wildlife Week. Several theme programmes like — teachers for tigers, primates in peril, bear day, etc. were held at different time of the year. Animal Welfare fortnight was celebrated from 14th to 31st January, 2004, wherein an exhibition of paintings on wildlfie was held. The paintings were prepared by a pair of brother and sister. In the month of February, six groups from different school were invited for different theme programme. Ninety new signages prepared for various enclosures, giving directions and requesting visitors for not teasing and feeding the zoo animals. Educatioin centre was renovated by providing false ceiling, new fans and air condition, chairs etc. – A Network of Closed Circuit Television was established to monitor the visitors to check vandalism and for research and education.

3

Reforestation

Reforestation is the restocking of existing forests and woodlands which have been depleted, an effect of deforestation. Reforestation can be used to improve the quality of human life by soaking up pollution and dust from the air, rebuild natural habitats and ecosystems, mitigate global warming since forests facilitate biosequestration of atmospheric carbon dioxide, and harvest for resources, particularly timber.

The term reforestation is similar to afforestation, the process of restoring and recreating areas of woodlands or forests that may have existed long ago but were deforested or otherwise removed at some point in the past.

Reforestation of large areas can be done through the use of measuring rope (for accurate plant spacing) and ribbeds, (or wheeled augers for planting the larger trees) for making the hole in which a seedling or plant can be inserted. Indigenous soil inoculates (e.g., Zaccaria bi color) can optionally be used to increase survival rates in hardy environments.

A debatable issue in managed reforestation is whether or not the succeeding forest will have the same biodiversity as the original forest. If the forest is replaced with only one species of tree and all other vegetation is prevented from growing back, a monoculture forest similar to agricultural crops would be the result. However, most reforestation involves the planting of different feedlots of seedlings taken from the area often of multiple species. Another important factor is the natural regeneration of a wide variety of plant and animal species that can occur on a clear cut. In some areas the suppression of forest fires for hundreds of years has resulted in large single aged and single species forest stands. The logging of small clear cuts and or prescribed burning, actually increases the biodiversity in these areas by creating a greater variety of tree stand ages and species.

Reforestation need not be only used for recovery of accidentally destroyed forests. In some countries, such as Finland, the forests are *managed* by the wood products and pulp and paper industry. In such an arrangement, like other crops, trees are replanted wherever they are cut. In such circumstances, the industry can cut the trees in a way to allow easier reforestation. In Canada, the wood product and pulp and paper industry systematically replaces many of the trees it cuts, employing large numbers of summer workers for tree planting work.

In just 20 years, a teak plantation in Costa Rica can produce up to about 400 m of wood per hectare. As the natural teak forests of Asia become more scarce or difficult to obtain, the prices commanded by plantation-grown teak grow higher every year. Other species such as mahogany grow slower than teak in Tropical America but are also extremely valuable. Faster growers include pine, eucalyptus, and Emelina.

Reforestation, if several native species are used, can provide other benefits in addition to financial returns, including restoration of the soil, rejuvenation of local flora and fauna, and the capturing and sequestering of 38 tons of carbon dioxide per hectare per year.

The reestablishment of forests is not just simple tree planting. Forests are made up of a diversity of species and they build dead organic matter into soils over time. A major tree-planting programme in a place like this would enhance the local climate and reduce the demands of burning large amounts of fossil fuels for cooling in the summer.

For Climate Change Mitigation

Forests absorb carbon dioxide through their photosynthesis cycle, and by using this idea, increasing forests with reforestation and discouraging deforestation will help mitigate global warming. Forest ecosystems are especially important to the global carbon cycle in two ways. First, they are responsible for moving around three billion tons of anthropogenic carbon every year. This amounts to about 30 per cent of all carbon dioxide emissions from fossil fuels. Second, forest ecosystems are terrestrial carbon sinks in that they store large amounts of carbon which accounts for as much as double the amount of carbon in the atmosphere.

Canadell and Raupach (2008) believe that there are four major strategies available to mitigate carbon emissions through forestry activities: increase the amount of forested land through a reforestation process; increase the carbon density of existing forests at a stand and landscape scale; expand the use of forest products that will sustainably replace fossil-fuel emissions; and reduce carbon emissions that are caused from deforestation and degradation.

However, achieving the first strategy requires great effort of land transformation. For example, China has used 24 million ha of new forest plantation and natural forest regrowth to offset 21 per cent of Chinese fossil fuel emissions in 2000. In theory, any tree would cover more forest area and absorb more carbon dioxide from the atmosphere. On the other hand, a genetically modified tree specimen might grow much faster than any other regular tree. Some of these trees are already being developed in the lumber and biofuel industries. These fast-growing trees would not only be planted for those industries but they can also be planted to help absorb carbon dioxide faster than regular trees. There are many projects around the world that use tree-planting as a way to offset carbon emissions, fighting climate change. For example, in China, Shanghai Roots and Shoots, a division of the Jane Goodall Institute launched The Million Tree Project in Kulun Qi, Inner Mongolia to plant one million trees to stop desertification and help curb climate change.

Mitigating the rate of deforestation has huge potential toward a cost-effective contribution to protect the atmosphere's climate. At this point, there are 13 million ha of tropical regions that are deforested every year. These regions can reduce rates of deforestation by 50 per cent by 2050.

A study from the National Center for Atmospheric Research in Boulder, Colorado, USA, found that, unlike previous belief that forests in higher latitudes soak up a vast amount of carbon dioxide, more carbon dioxide is absorbed in tropical climates. Trees in temperate latitudes have a net warming effect on the climate. The heat that dark leaves absorb outweighs the carbon they soak up, therefore, tropical trees absorb carbon dioxide as well as being able to cool the planet by up to 0.7° C.

Trees in tropical climates have, on average, larger, brighter, and more abundant leaves than non-tropical climates. The advantage of planting trees in a tropical setting is the quicker growth rate due to the longer rainy seasons. There is no need for the trees to hibernate and can therefore grow year-round.

An incredible portion of the Earth's biodiversity is situated in tropical areas. The lack of reforestation in tropical climates is putting a larger portion of species at risk of becoming endangered.

A study of the girth of 70,000 trees across Africa has shown that tropical forests are soaking up more carbon dioxide pollution than previously realized. The research suggests almost one fifth of fossil fuel emissions are absorbed by forests across Africa, Amazonia and Asia.

Simon Lewis, a climate expert at the University of Leeds, who led the study, said: "Tropical forest trees are absorbing about 18 per cent of the carbon dioxide added to the atmosphere each year from burning fossil fuels, substantially buffering the rate of change".

Extensive forest resources placed anywhere in the world will not always have a positive impact. For example, large reforestation programmes in boreal regions have a limited impact on climate mitigation. This is because it substitutes a bright snow-dominated region that reflects the sunlight with dark forest canopies. On the other hand, a positive example would be reforestation projects in tropical regions, which would lead to a positive biophysical change such as the formation of clouds. These clouds would then reflect the sunlight, creating a positive impact on climate mitigation.

Some incentives for reforestation can be as a simple as a financial compensation. Streck and Scholz (2006) explain how a group of scientists from various institutions have developed a compensated reduction of deforestation approach which would reward developing countries that disrupt any further act of deforestation. Countries that participate and take the option to reduce their emissions from deforestation during a committed period of time would receive financial compensation for the carbon dioxide emissions that they avoided . To raise the payments, the host country would issue government bonds or negotiate some kind of loan with a financial institution that would want to take part in the compensation promised to the other country. The funds received by the country could be invested to help find alternatives to the extensive cutdown of forests. This whole process of cutting emissions would be voluntary, but once the country has agreed to lower they emissions they would be obligated to reduce their emissions. However, if a country was not able to meet their obligation, their target would get added to their next commitment period. The authors of these proposals see this as a solely government-to-government agreement; private entities would not participate in the compensation trades.

Indonesia

In Java, Indonesia each newlywed couple is to give whoever is sermonizing their wedding 5 seedlings to combat global warming. Each couple that wishes to have a divorce has to give 25 seedlings to whoever divorces them.

Germany

In Germany car forestation is required as part of the federal forest law. 31 per cent of Germany are forests according to the second forest inventory of 2001-03. The size of the forest area in Germany increased between the first and the second forest inventory due to forestation of degenerated bogs and agricultural areas.

Criticism

Reforestation competes with other land uses such as food production, livestock grazing, and living space for further economic growth.

There is also the risk that through a forest fire or insect outbreak much of the stored carbon in a reforested area could make its way back to the atmosphere. Reduced harvesting rates and fire suppression have caused an increase in the forest biomass in the western United States over the past century. This causes an increase of about a factor of four in the frequency of fires due to longer and hotter dry seasons.

Afforestation

Afforestation is the establishment of a forest or stand of trees in an area where the preceding vegetation or land use was not forest. Reforestation is the reestablishment of forest cover either naturally (by natural seeding, coppice, or root suckers) or artificially (by direct seeding or planting), usually maintaining a same or similar forest type, and done promptly after the previous stand or forest was removed. Many governments and non-governmental organizations directly engage in programmes of *afforestation* to restore forests, increase carbon capture and sequestration, and assist in preservation of biodiversity. (In the UK afforestation may mean legally converting land into a royal forest).

In some places, forests need help to reestablish themselves because of environmental factors. For example, once forest cover is destroyed in arid zones, the land may dry and become inhospitable to new tree growth. Other factors include overgrazing by livestock, especially animals such as goats, and over-harvesting of forest resources. Together these may lead to desertification and the loss of topsoil; without soil, forests cannot grow until the long process of soil creation has been completed — if erosion allows this. In some tropical areas, forest cover removal may result in a duricrust or duripan that effectively seal off the soil to water penetration and root growth. In many areas, reforestation is impossible because people are using the land. In other areas, mechanical breaking up of duripans or duricrusts is necessary, careful and continued watering may be essential, and special protection, such as fencing, may be needed.

World Regions

Brazil

Because of the extensive Amazon deforestation during the last decades and ongoing, the small efforts of afforestation are insignificant on a national scale of the Amazon Rainforest.

China

China has deforested most of its historically wooded areas. China reached the point where timber yields declined far below historic levels, due to over-harvesting of trees beyond sustainable yield. Although it has set official goals for reforestation, these goals were set for an 80 year time horizon and are not significantly met by 2008. China is trying to correct these problems by projects as the Green Wall of China, which aims to replant a great deal of forests and halt the expansion of the Gobi desert. A law promulgated in 1981 requires that every citizen over the age of 11 plant at least one tree per year. As a result, China currently has the highest afforestation rate of any country or region in the world, with 47,000 square kilometers of afforestation in 2008. However, the forest area per capita is still far lower than the international average. An ambitious proposal for China is the Aerially Delivered Re-forestation and Erosion Control System.

North Africa

In North Africa, the sahara forest project coupled with the Seawater Greenhouse has been proposed. Some projects have also been launched in countries as Senegal to revert desertification. At present (2010) African leaders are discussing the combining of national countries in their continent to increase effectiveness. In addition, other projects as the Keita project in Niger have been launched in the past, and have been able to locally revert damage done by desertification.

Europe

Europe has deforested the majority of its historical forests. The European Union has paid farmers for afforestation since 1990, offering grants to turn farmland back into forest and payments for the management of forest. Between 1993 and 1997, EU afforestation policies made possible the re-forestation of over 5,000 square kilometres of land. A second programme, running between 2000 and 2006, afforested in excess of 1000 square kilometres of land (precise statistics not yet available). A third such programme began in 2007.

In Poland, the National Programme of Afforestation was introduced by the government after World War II, when total area of forests shrank to 20 per cent of country's territory. Consequently, forested areas of Poland grew year by year, and on December 31, 2006, forests covered 29 per cent of the country. It is planned that by 2050, forests will cover 33 per cent of Poland.

According to FAO statistics, Spain had the fastest afforestation rate in Europe in the 1990-2005 period . In those years, a total of 44,360 square kilometres were afforested, and the total forest cover rose from 13,5 to 17,9 million hectares. In 1990, forests covered 26.6 per cent of the Spanish territory. As of 2005, that figure had risen to 35.4 per cent. Spain today has the third largest forest area in the European Union, after Sweden and Finland.

Iran

Iran is considered a low forest cover region of the world with present cover approximating seven per cent of the land area. This is a value reduced by an estimated six million hectares of virgin forest, which includes oak, almond and pistacio. Due to soil substrates, it is difficult to achieve afforestation on a large scale compared to other temperate areas endowed with more fertile and less rocky and arid soil conditions. Consequently, most of the afforestation is conducted with non-native species, leading to habitat destruction for native flora and fauna, and resulting in an accelerated loss of biodiversity.

4

Ecosystem

An ecosystem is a biological environment consisting of all the organisms living in a particular area, as well as all the nonliving, physical components of the environment with which the organisms interact, such as air, soil, water, and sunlight. It is all the organisms in a given area, along with the non-living (abiotic) factors with which they interact; a biological community and its physical environment.

The entire array of organisms inhabiting a particular ecosystem is called a community. In a typical ecosystem, plants and other photosynthetic organisms are the producers that provide the food. Ecosystems can be permanent or temporary. Ecosystems usually form a number of food webs.

Ecosystems are functional units consisting of living things in a given area, non-living chemical and physical factors of their environment, linked together through nutrient cycle and energy flow.

- Natural
- Terrestrial ecosystem
- Aquatic ecosystem
- Lentic, the ecosystem of a lake, pond or swamp
- Lotic, the ecosystem of a river, stream or spring
- Artificial, ecosystems created by humans.

Central to the ecosystem concept is the idea that living organisms interact with every other element in their local environment. Eugene Odum, a founder of ecology, stated: "Any unit that includes all of the organisms (ie:

the "community") in a given area interacting with the physical environment so that a flow of energy leads to clearly defined trophic structure, biotic diversity, and material cycles (i.e.: exchange of materials between living and non-living parts) within the system is an ecosystem".

Biomes

Biomes are a classification of globally similar areas, including ecosystems, such as ecological communities of plants and animals, soil organisms and climatic conditions. Biomes are in part defined based on factors such as plant structures (such as trees, shrubs and grasses), leaf types (such as broadleaf and needleleaf), plant spacing (forest, woodland, savanna) and climate. Unlike ecozones, biomes are not defined by genetic, taxonomic or historical similarities. Biomes are often identified with particular patterns of ecological succession and climax vegetation.

A fundamental classification of biomes is:

- Terrestrial (land) biomes
- Freshwater biomes
- Marine biomes

Ecosystems have become particularly important politically, since the Convention on Biological Diversity (CBD) — ratified by 192 countries — defines "the protection of ecosystems, natural habitats and the maintenance of viable populations of species in natural surroundings" as a commitment of ratifying countries. This has created the political necessity to spatially identify ecosystems and somehow distinguish among them. The CBD defines an 'ecosystem' as a "dynamic complex of plant, animal and micro-organism communities and their non-living environment interacting as a functional unit".

With the need of protecting ecosystems, the political need arose to describe and identify them efficiently. Vreugdenhil et al. argued that this could be achieved most effectively by using a physiognomic-ecological classification system, as ecosystems are easily recognizable in the field as well as on satellite images. They argued that the structure and seasonality of the associated vegetation, or flora, complemented with ecological data (such as elevation, humidity, and drainage), are each determining modifiers that separate partially distinct sets of species. This is true not only for plant species, but also for species of animals, fungi and bacteria. The degree of ecosystem distinction is subject to the physiognomic modifiers that can be identified on an image and/or in the field. Where necessary, specific fauna elements can be added, such as seasonal concentrations of animals and the distribution of coral reefs.

Several physiognomic-ecological classification systems are available:

- Physiognomic-Ecological Classification of Plant Formations of the Earth: a system based on the 1974 work of Mueller-Dombois and Heinz Ellenberg, and developed by UNESCO. This classificatie "describes the above-ground or underwater vegetation structures and cover as observed in the field, described as plant life forms. This classification is fundamentally a species-independent physiognomic, hierarchical vegetation classification system which also takes into account ecological factors such as climate, elevation, human influences such as grazing, hydric regimes and survival strategies such as seasonality. The system was expanded with a basic classification for open water formations".
- Land Cover Classification System (LCCS), developed by the Food and Agriculture Organization (FAO).
- Forest-Range Environmental Study Ecosystems (FRES) developed by the United States Forest Service for use in the United States.

Several aquatic classification systems are available, and an effort is being made by the United States Geological Survey (USGS) and the Inter-American Biodiversity Information Network (IABIN) to design a complete ecosystem classification system that will cover both terrestrial and aquatic ecosystems.

From a philosophy of science perspective, ecosystems are not discrete units of nature that simply can be identified using the most 'correct' type of classification approach. In agreement with the definition by Tansley ('mental isolates'), any attempt to delineate or classify ecosystems should be explicit about the observer/analyst input in the classification including its normative rationale.

Ecosystem Services

Ecosystem services are "fundamental life-support services upon which human civilization depends,"[i] and can be direct or indirect. Examples of direct ecosystem services are: pollination, wood and erosion prevention. Indirect services could be considered climate moderation, nutrient cycles and detoxifying natural substances.

The services and goods an ecosystem provides are often undervalued as many of them are without market value. Broad examples include:

- regulating (climate, floods, nutrient balance, water filtration)
- provisioning (food, medicine, fur)
- cultural (science, spiritual, ceremonial, recreation, aesthetic)
- supporting (nutrient cycling, photosynthesis, soil formation).

Ecosystem Legal Rights

Ecuador's new constitution of 2008 is the first in the world to recognize legally enforceable Rights of Nature, or ecosystem rights.

The borough of Tamaqua, Pennsylvania passed a law giving ecosystems legal rights. The ordinance establishes that the municipal government or any Tamaqua resident can file a lawsuit on behalf of the local ecosystem. Other townships, such as Rush, followed suit and passed their own laws.

This is part of a growing body of legal opinion proposing 'wild law'. Wild law, a term coined by Cormac Cullinan (a lawyer based in South Africa), would cover birds and animals, rivers and deserts.

From an anthropocentric point of view, some people perceive ecosystems as production units that produce goods and services, such as wood by forest ecosystems and grass for cattle by natural grasslands. Meat from wild animals, often referred to as bush meat in Africa, has proven to be extremely successful under well-controlled management schemes in South Africa and Kenya. Much less successful has been the discovery and commercialization of substances of wild organism for pharmaceutical purposes. Services derived from ecosystems are referred to as ecosystem services. They may include:

- facilitating the enjoyment of nature, which may generate many forms of income and employment in the tourism sector, often referred to as eco-tourisms;
- water retention, thus facilitating a more evenly distributed release of water; and
- soil protection, open-air laboratory for scientific research, etc.

A greater degree of species or biological diversity - commonly referred to as Biodiversity - of an ecosystem may contribute to greater resilience of an ecosystem, because there are more species present at a location to respond to change and thus 'absorb' or reduce its effects. This reduces the effect before the ecosystem's structure is fundamentally changed to a different state. This is not universally the case and there is no proven relationship between the species diversity of an ecosystem and its ability to provide goods and services on a sustainable level: Humid tropical forests produce very few goods and direct services and are extremely vulnerable to change, while many temperate forests readily grow back to their previous state of development within a lifetime after felling or a forest fire. Some grasslands have been sustainably exploited for thousands of years (Mongolia, Africa, European peat and mooreland communities).

Introduction of new elements, whether biotic or abiotic, into an ecosystem tend to have a disruptive effect. In some cases, this can lead to ecological collapse or 'trophic cascading' and the death of many species within the ecosystem. Under this deterministic vision, the abstract notion of ecological health attempts to measure the robustness and recovery capacity for an ecosystem; i.e. how far the ecosystem is away from its steady state.

Often, however, ecosystems have the ability to rebound from a disruptive agent. The difference between collapse or a gentle rebound is determined by two factors–the toxicity of the introduced element and the resiliency of the original ecosystem.

Ecosystems are primarily governed by stochastic (chance) events, the reactions these events provoke on non-living materials and the responses by organisms to the conditions surrounding them. Thus, an ecosystem results from the sum of individual responses of organisms to stimuli from elements in the environment.The presence or absence of populations merely depends on reproductive and dispersal success, and population levels fluctuate in response to stochastic events. As the number of species in an ecosystem is higher, the number of stimuli is also higher. Since the beginning of life organisms have survived continuous change through natural selection of successful feeding, reproductive and dispersal behaviour. Through natural selection the planet's species have continuously adapted to change through variation in their biological composition and distribution. Mathematically it can be demonstrated that greater numbers of different interacting factors tend to dampen fluctuations in each of the individual factors.

Given the great diversity among organisms on earth, most ecosystems only changed very gradually, as some species would disappear while others would move in. Locally, sub-populations continuously go extinct, to be replaced later through dispersal of other sub-populations. Stochastists do recognize that certain intrinsic regulating mechanisms occur in nature. Feedback and response mechanisms at the species level regulate population levels, most notably through territorial behaviour. Andrewatha and Birch suggest that territorial behaviour tends to keep populations at levels where food supply is not a limiting factor. Hence, stochastists see territorial behaviour as a regulatory mechanism at the species level but not at the ecosystem level. Thus, in their vision, ecosystems are not regulated by feedback and response mechanisms from the ecosystem itself and there is no such thing as a balance of nature.

If ecosystems are governed primarily by stochastic processes, through which its subsequent state would be determined by both predictable and random actions, they may be more resilient to sudden change than each species individually. In the absence of a balance of nature, the species composition of ecosystems would undergo shifts that would depend on the nature of the change, but entire ecological collapse would probably be infrequent events.

The theoretical ecologist Robert Ulanowicz has used information theory tools to describe the structure of ecosystems, emphasizing mutual information (correlations) in studied systems. Drawing on this methodology and prior observations of complex ecosystems, Ulanowicz depicts approaches to determining the stress levels on ecosystems and predicting system reactions to defined types of alteration in their settings (such as increased or reduced energy flow, and eutrophication.

In addition, Eric Sanderson has developed the Muir web, based on experience on the Mannahatta project. This graphical schematic shows how different species are connected to each other, not only regarding their position in the food chain, but also regarding other services, i.e. provisioning of shelter.

Ecosystem Ecology

Ecosystem ecology is the integrated study of biotic and abiotic components of ecosystems and their interactions within an ecosystem framework. This science examines how ecosystems work and relates this to their components such as chemicals, bedrock, soil, plants, and animals. Ecosystem ecology examines physical and biological structure and examines how these ecosystem characteristics interact.

5

Ecology

Ecology is the scientific study of the relation of living organisms to each other and their surroundings. Ecosystems are defined by a web, community, or network of individuals that arrange into a self-organized and complex hierarchy of pattern and process. Ecosystems create a biophysical feedback between living (biotic) and non-living (abiotic) components of an environment that generates and regulates the biogeochemical cycles of the planet. Ecosystems provide goods and services that sustain human societies and general well-being. Ecosystems are sustained by biodiversity within them. Biodiversity is the full-scale of life and its processes, including genes, species and ecosystems forming lineages that integrate into a complex and regenerative spatial arrangement of types, forms, and interactions.

Ecology is a sub-discipline of biology, the study of life. The word 'ecology' ('oekologie') was coined in 1866 by the German scientist Ernst Haeckel (1834-1919). Haeckel was a zoologist, artist, writer, and later in life a professor of comparative anatomy. Ancient philosophers of Greece, including Hippocrates and Aristotle, were among the earliest to record notes and observations on the natural history of plants and animals; the early rudiments of modern ecology. Modern ecology mostly branched out of natural history science that flourished in the late 19th century. Charles Darwin's evolutionary treatise and the concept of adaptation as it was introduced in 1859 is a pivotal cornerstone in modern ecological theory.

Ecology is not synonymous with environment, environmentalism, natural history or environmental science. Ecology is closely related to the biological disciplines of physiology, evolution, genetics and behaviour. An understanding of how biodiversity affects ecological function is an important focus area in ecological studies. Ecosystems sustain every life-supporting function on the planet, including climate regulation, water filtration, soil formation (pedogenesis), food, fibres, medicines, erosion control, and many other natural features of historical, spiritual or scientific value.

There are many practical applications of ecology in conservation biology, wetland management, natural resource management (agriculture, forestry, fisheries), city planning (urban ecology), community health, economics, basic and applied science and it provides a conceptual framework for understanding and researching human social interaction (human ecology).

Ecosystems are forever confronted with a range of natural environmental fluctuations that vary transiently in magnitude through space and time. It can take thousands of years for ecological processes to mature; the life-span of a tree, for example, can encompass different successional stages. The ecological process is extended even further through time as trees die, decay and provide habitat as nurse logs or coarse woody debris. The area of an ecosystem can vary greatly from tiny to vast. A single tree is of little consequence to the classification of a forest ecosystem, but critically relevant to the smaller organisms living in and on it. Several generations of an aphid population can exist over the lifespan of a single leaf. Each of those aphids, in turn, support diverse bacterial communities. Fine scale structure of aphid populations can be constrained by top-down influences of tree growth that is related to site specific variables, such as soil type, moisture content, slope of the land, and forest canopy closure. Like-wise, finer scale dynamics operating in the aphid populations can impart bottom-up influence on tree growth rates. The scale of ecological dynamics can operate as a closed island with respect to local site variables, such as aphids migrating on a tree, while at the same time remain open with regard to broader scale influences, such as atmosphere or climate. Hence, ecologists have devised means of hierarchically classifying ecosystems by analyzing data collected from finer scale units, such as vegetation associations, climate, and soil types, and integrate this information to identify larger emergent patterns of uniform organization and processes that operate on regional, local, and chronological scales.

There are different views on complexity and how it relates to ecology. One perspective lumps things that we do not understand into this category by virtue of the computational effort it would require to piece together the numerous interacting parts. Alternatively, complexity in life sciences can be viewed as emergent self-organized systems with multiple possible outcomes directed by random accidents of history; an extension of the first perspective. Global patterns of biological diversity are complex. This biocomplexity stems from the interplay among ecological processes that operate and influence patterns that grade into each other, such as transitional areas or ecotones that stretch across different scales. "Complexity in ecology is of at least six distinct types: spatial, temporal, structural, process, behavioural, and geometric." Small scale patterns do not necessarily explain large scale phenomena, otherwise captured in the expression 'the sum is greater than the parts'. Ecologists have identified emergent and self-organizing phenomena that operate at different environmental scales of influence, ranging from molecular to planetary, and these require different sets of scientific explanation. Long-term ecological studies provide important track records to better understand the complexity of ecosystems over longer temporal and broader spatial scales. The International Long Term Ecological Network manages and exchanges scientific information among research sites. The longest experiment in existence is the Park Grass Experiment that was initiated in 1856. Another example includes the Hubbard Brook study in operation since 1960.

To structure the study of ecology into a manageable framework of understanding, the biological world is conceptually organized as a nested hierarchy of organization, ranging in scale from genes, to cells, to tissues, to organs, to organisms, to species and up to the level of the biosphere. Together these hierarchical scales of life form a panarchy. Ecosystems are primarily researched at three key levels of organization—organisms, populations, and communities. Ecologists study ecosystems by sampling a certain number of individuals that are representative of a population. Ecosystems consist of communities interacting with each other and the environment. In ecology, communities are created by the interaction of the populations of different species in an area.

Biodiversity is the variety of life and its processes. It includes the variety of living organisms, the genetic differences among them, the communities and ecosystems in which they occur, and the ecological and evolutionary processes that keep them functioning, yet ever changing and adapting.

Biodiversity (an abbreviation of biological diversity) describes the diversity of life from genes to ecosystems and spans every level of biological organization. Biodiversity means different things to different people and there are many ways to index, measure, characterize, and represent its complex organization. Biodiversity includes species diversity, ecosystem diversity, genetic diversity and the complex processes operating at and among these respective levels. Biodiversity plays an important role in ecological health as much as it does for human health. Preventing or prioritizing species extinctions is one way to preserve biodiversity, but populations, the genetic diversity within them and ecological processes, such as migration, are being threatened on global scales and disappearing rapidly as well.

Conservation priorities and management techniques require different approaches and considerations to address the full ecological scope of biodiversity. Populations and species migration, for example, are more sensitive indicators of ecosystem services that sustain and contribute natural capital toward the well-being of humanity. An understanding of biodiversity has practical application for ecosystem-based conservation planners as they make ecologically responsible decisions in management recommendations to consultant firms, governments and industry.

Ecological Niche and Habitat

There are many definitions of the niche dating back to 1917, but G. Evelyn Hutchinson made conceptual advances in 1957 and introduced the most widely accepted definition: "The niche is the set of biotic and abiotic conditions in which a species is able to persist and maintain stable population sizes." The ecological niche is a central concept in the ecology of organisms and is sub-divided into the *fundamental* and the *realized* niche. The fundamental niche is the set of environmental conditions under which a species is able to persist. The realized niche is the set of environmental plus ecological conditions under which a species persists. The Hutchisonian niche is defined more technically as an "euclidean hyperspace whose *dimensions* are defined as environmental variables and whose *size* is a function of the number of values that the environmental values may assume for which an organism has *positive fitness*".

The habitat of a species is a related but distinct concept that describes the environment over which a species is known to occur and the type of community that is formed as a result. More specifically, "habitats can be defined as regions in environmental space that are composed of multiple dimensions, each representing a biotic or abiotic environmental variable; that is, any component or characteristic of the environment related directly (e.g. forage biomass and quality) or indirectly (e.g. elevation) to the use of a location by the animal." For example, the habitat might refer to an aquatic or terrestrial environment that can be further categorized as montane or alpine ecosystems.

Biogeographical patterns and range distributions are explained or predicted through knowledge and understanding of a species traits and niche requirements. Species have functional traits that are uniquely adapted to the ecological niche. A trait is a measurable property, phenotype, or characteristic of an organism that influences its performance. Genes play an important role in the development and expression of traits. Resident species evolve traits that are fitted to their local environment. This tends to afford them a competitive advantage and discourages similarly adapted species from having an overlapping geographic range. The competitive exclusion principle suggests that two species cannot coexist indefinitely by living off the same limiting resource. When similarly adapted species are found to overlap geographically, closer inspection reveals subtle ecological differences in their habitat or dietary requirements.

Niche Construction

Organisms are subject to environmental pressures, but they are also modifiers of their habitats. The regulatory feedback between organisms and their environment can modify conditions from local (e.g., a beaver pond) to global scales (e.g., Gaia), over time and even after death, such as decaying logs or silica skeleton deposits from marine organisms. The process and concept of ecosystem engineering has also been called niche construction. Ecosystem engineers are defined as: "... organisms that directly or indirectly modulate the availability of resources to other species, by causing physical state changes in biotic or abiotic materials. In so doing they modify, maintain and create habitats".

The ecosystem engineering concept has stimulated a new appreciation for the degree of influence that organisms have on the ecosystem and evolutionary process. The terms niche construction are more often used in reference to the under appreciated feedback mechanism of natural selection imparting forces on the abiotic niche. An example of natural selection through ecosystem engineering occurs in the nests of social insects, including ants, bees, wasps, and termites. There is an emergent homeostasis or homeorhesis in the structure of the nest that regulates, maintains and defends the physiology of the entire colony. Termite mounds, for example, maintain a constant internal temperature through the design of air-conditioning chimneys. The structure of the nests themselves are subject to the forces of natural selection. Moreover, the nest can survive over successive generations, which means that ancestors inherit both genetic material and a legacy niche that was constructed before their time.

Populations are also studied and modeled according to the metapopulation concept. The metapopulation concept was introduced in 1969: "as a population of populations which go extinct locally and recolonize." Metapopulation ecology is another statistical approach that is often used in conservation research. Metapopulation research simplifies the landscape into patches of varying levels of quality.

In metapopulation terminology there are emigrants (individuals that leave a patch), immigrants (individuals that move into a patch) and sites are classed either as sources or sinks. A site is a generic term that refers to places where ecologists sample populations, such as ponds or defined sampling areas in a forest. Source patches are productive sites that generate a seasonal supply of juveniles that migrate to other patch locations. Sink patches are unproductive sites that only receive migrants and will go extinct unless rescued by an adjacent source patch or environmental conditions become more favorable. Metapopulation models examine patch dynamics over time to answer questions about spatial and demographic ecology. The ecology of metapopulations is a dynamic process of extinction and colonization. Small patches of lower quality (i.e., sinks) are maintained or rescued by a seasonal influx of new immigrants. A dynamic metapopulation structure evolves from year to year, where some patches are sinks in dry years and become sources when conditions are more favorable. Ecologists use a mixture of computer models and field studies to explain metapopulation structure.

Community ecology is the study of the interactions among a collection of interdependent species that cohabitate the same geographic area. An example of a study in community ecology might measure primary production in a wetland in relation to decomposition and consumption rates. This requires an understanding of the community connections between plants (i.e., primary producers) and the decomposers (e.g., fungi and bacteria). or the analysis of predator-prey dynamics affecting amphibian biomass. Food webs and trophic levels are two widely employed conceptual models used to explain the linkages among species.

Food Webs

A food web is the archetypal ecological network. They are a type of concept map that illustrate pathways of energy flows in an ecological community, usually starting with solar energy being used by plants during photosynthesis. As plants grow, they accumulate carbohydrates and are eaten by grazing herbivores. Step by step lines or relations are drawn until a web of life is illustrated.

There are different ecological dimensions that can be mapped to create more complicated food webs, including: species composition (type of species), richness (number of species), biomass (the dry weight of plants and animals), productivity (rates of conversion of energy and nutrients into growth), and stability (food webs over time). A food web diagram illustrating species composition shcws how change in a single species can directly and indirectly influence many others. Microcosm studies are used to simplify food web research into semi-isolated units such as small springs, decaying logs, and laboratory experiments using organisms that reproduce quickly, such as daphnia feeding on algae grown under controlled environments in jars of water.

Principles gleaned from food web microcosm studies are used to extrapolate smaller dynamic concepts to larger systems. Food webs are limited because they are generally restricted to a specific habitat, such as a cave or a pond. The food web illustration (right) only shows a small part of the complexity connecting the aquatic system to the adjacent terrestrial land. Many of these species migrate into other habitats to distribute their effects on a larger scale. In other words, food webs are incomplete, but are nonetheless a valuable tool in understanding community ecosystems.

Trophic Dynamics

The Greek root of the word *troph*, t??f?, trophe, means food or feeding. Links in food-webs primarily connect feeding relations or trophism among species. Biodiversity within ecosystems can be organized into vertical and horizontal dimensions. The vertical dimension represents feeding relations that become further removed from the base of the food chain up toward top predators. The horizontal dimension represents the abundance or biomass at each level. When the relative abundance or biomass of each functional feeding group is stacked into their respective trophic levels they naturally sort into a 'pyramid of numbers'. Functional groups are broadly categorized as autotrophs (or primary producers), heterotrophs (or consumers), and detrivores (or decomposers). Heterotrophs can be further sub-divided into different functional groups, including: primary consumers (strict herbivores), secondary consumers (predators that feed exclusively on herbivores) and tertiary consumers (predators that feed on a mix of herbivores and predators). Omnivores do not fit neatly into a functional category because they eat both plant and animal tissues. It has been suggested that omnivores have a greater functional influence as predators because relative to herbivores they are comparatively inefficient at grazing.

The decomposition of dead organic matter, such as leaves falling on the forest floor, turns into soils that feed plant production. The total sum of the planet's soil ecosystems is called the pedosphere where a very large proportion of the Earth's biodiversity sorts into other trophic levels. Invertebrates that feed and shred larger leaves, for example, create smaller bits for smaller organisms in the feeding chain. Collectively, these are the detrivores that regulate soil formation. Tree roots, fungi, bacteria, worms, ants, beetles, centipedes, spiders, mammals, birds, reptiles, amphibians and other less familiar creatures all work to create the trophic web of life in soil ecosystems. As organisms feed and migrate through soils they physically displace materials, which is an important ecological process called bioturbation. Biomass of soil microorganisms are influenced by and feed back into the trophic dynamics of the exposed solar surface ecology. Paleoecological studies of soils places the origin for bioturbation to a time before the Cambrian period. Other events, such as the evolution of trees and amphibians moving into land in the Devonian period played a significant role in the development of soils and ecological trophism.

Functional trophic groups sort out hierarchically into pyramidic trophic levels because it requires specialized adaptations to become a photosynthesizer or a predator, so few organisms have the adaptations needed to combine both abilities. This explains why functional adaptations to trophism (feeding) organizes different species into emergent functional groups. Trophic levels are part of the holistic or complex systems view of ecosystems. Each trophic level contains unrelated species that grouped together because they share common ecological functions. Grouping functionally similar species into a trophic system gives a macroscopic image of the larger functional design.

Keystone Species

A keystone species is a species that is disproportionately connected to more species in the food-web. Keystone species have lower levels of biomass in the trophic pyramid relative to the importance of their role. The many connections that a keystone species holds means that it maintains the organization and structure of entire communities. The loss of a keystone species results in a range of dramatic cascading effects that alters trophic dynamics, other food-web connections and can cause the extinction of other species in the community.

Sea otters (*Enhydra lutris*) are commonly cited as an example of a keystone species because they limit the density of sea urchins that feed on kelp. If sea otters are removed from the system, the urchins graze until the kelp beds disappear and this has a dramatic effect on community structure. Hunting of sea otters, for example, is thought to have indirectly led to the extinction of the Steller's Sea Cow (*Hydrodamalis gigas*). While the keystone species concept has been used extensively as a conservation tool, it has been criticized for being poorly defined from an operational stance. It is very difficult to experimentally determine in each different ecosystem what species may hold a keystone role. Furthermore, food-web theory suggests that keystone species may not be all that common. It is therefore unclear how generally the keystone species model can be applied.

The concept of the ecosystem was first introduced in 1935 to describe habitats within biomes that form an integrated whole and a dynamically responsive system having both physical and biological complexes. Within an ecosystem there are inseparable ties that link organisms to the physical and biological components of their environment to which they are adapted. Ecosystems are complex adaptive systems where the interaction of life processes form self-organizing patterns across different scales of time and space. This section introduces key areas of ecosystem ecology that are used to inquire, understand and explain observed patterns of biodiversity and ecosystem function across different scales of organization.

Biome

Ecological units of organization are defined through reference to any magnitude of space and time on the planet. Communities of organisms, for example, are somewhat arbitrarily defined, but the processes of life integrate at different levels and organize into more complex wholes. Biomes, for example, are a larger unit of organization that categorize regions of the Earth's ecosystems mainly according to the structure and composition of vegetation. Different researchers have applied different methods to define continental boundaries of biomes dominated by different functional types of vegetative communities that are limited in distribution by climate, precipitation, weather and other environmental variables. Examples of biome names include: tropical rainforest, temperate broadleaf and mixed forests, temperate deciduous forest, taiga, tundra, hot desert, and polar desert. Other researchers have recently started to categorize other types of biomes, such as the human and oceanic microbiomes. To a microbe, the human body is a habitat and a landscape. The microbiome has been largely discovered through advances in molecular genetics that have revealed a hidden richness of microbial diversity on the planet. The oceanic microbiome plays a significant role in the ecological biogeochemistry of the planet's oceans.

Biosphere

Ecological theory has been used to explain self-emergent regulatory phenomena at the planetary scale. The largest scale of ecological organization is the biosphere: the total sum of ecosystems on the planet. Ecological relations regulate the flux of energy, nutrients, and climate all the way up to the planetary scale. For example, the dynamic history of the planetary CO_2 and O_2 composition of the atmosphere has been largely determined by the biogenic flux of gases coming from respiration and photosynthesis, with levels fluctuating over time and in relation to the ecology and evolution of plants and animals. When sub-component parts are organized into a whole there are oftentimes emergent properties that describe the nature of the system. This the Gaia hypothesis, and is an example of holism applied in ecological theory. The ecology of the planet acts as a single regulatory or holistic unit called Gaia. The Gaia hypothesis states that there is an emergent feedback loop generated by the metabolism of living organisms that maintains the temperature of the Earth and atmospheric conditions within a narrow self-regulating range of tolerance.

Relation to Evolution

Ecology and evolution are considered sister disciplines of the life sciences. Natural selection, life history, development, adaptation, populations, and inheritance are examples of concepts that thread equally into ecological and evolutionary theory. Morphological, behavioural and/or genetic traits, for example, can be mapped onto evolutionary trees to study the historical development of a species in relation to their functions and roles in different ecological circumstances. In this framework, the analytical tools of ecologists and evolutionists overlap as they organize, classify and investigate life through common systematic principals, such as phylogenetics or the Linnaean system of taxonomy. The two disciplines often appear together, such as in the title of the journal *Trends in Ecology and Evolution*. There is no sharp boundary separating ecology from evolution and they differ more in their areas of applied focus. Both disciplines discover and explain emergent and unique properties and processes operating across different spatial or temporal scales of organization. While the boundary between ecology and evolution is not always clear, it is understood that ecologists study the abiotic and biotic factors that influence the evolutionary process.

All organisms are motile to some extent. Even plants express complex behaviour, including memory and communication. Behavioural ecology is the study of ethology and its ecological and evolutionary implications. Ethology is the study of observable movement or behaviour in nature. This could include investigations of motile sperm of plants, mobile phytoplankton, zooplankton swimming toward the female egg, the cultivation of fungi by weevils, the mating dance of a salamander, or social gatherings of amoeba.

Adaptation is the central unifying concept in behavioural ecology. 'International Society for Behavioural Ecology'. Behaviours can be recorded as traits and inherited in much the same way that eye and hair colour can. Behaviours evolve and become adapted to the ecosystem because they are subject to the forces of natural selection. Hence, behaviours can be adaptive, meaning that they evolve functional utilities that increases reproductive success for the individuals that inherit such traits. This is also the technical definition for fitness in biology, which is a measure of reproductive success over successive generations.

Predator-prey interactions are an introductory concept into food-web studies as well as behavioural ecology. Prey species can exhibit different kinds of behavioural adaptations to predators, such as avoid, flee or defend. Many prey species are faced with multiple predators that differ in the degree of danger posed. To be adapted to their environment and face predatory threats, organisms must balance their energy budgets as they invest in different aspects of their life history, such as growth, feeding, mating, socializing, or modifying their habitat. Hypotheses posited in behavioural ecology are generally based on adaptive principals of conservation, optimization or efficiency. For example:

- "The threat-sensitive predator avoidance hypothesis predicts that prey should assess the degree of threat posed by different predators and match their behaviour according to current levels of risk".
- "The optimal flight initiation distance occurs where expected postencounter fitness is maximized, which depends on the prey's initial fitness, benefits obtainable by not fleeing, energetic escape costs, and expected fitness loss due to predation risk"

Symbiosis: Leafhoppers (*Eurymela fenestrata*) are protected by ants (*Iridomyrmex purpureus*) in a symbiotic relationship. The ants protect the leafhoppers from predators and in return the leafhoppers feeding on plants exude honeydew from their anus that provides energy and nutrients to tending ants.

Elaborate sexual displays and posturing are encountered in the behavioural ecology of animals. The birds of paradise, for example, display elaborate ornaments and song during courtship. These displays serve a dual purpose of signaling healthy or well-adapted individuals and desirable genes. The elaborate displays are driven by sexual selection as an advertisement of quality of traits among male suitors.

Social Ecology

Social ecological behaviours are notable in the social insects, slime moulds, social spiders, human society, and naked mole rats where eusocialism has evolved. Social behaviours include reciprocally beneficial behaviours among kin and nest mates. Social behaviours evolve from kin and group selection. Kin selection explains altruism through genetic relationships, whereby an altruistic behaviour leading to death is rewarded by the survival of genetic copies distributed among surviving relatives. The social insects, including ants, bees and wasps are most famously studied for this type of relationship because the male drones are clones that share the same genetic make-up as every other male in the colony. In contrast, group selectionists find examples of altruism among non-genetic relatives and explain this through selection acting on the group, whereby it becomes selectively advantageous for groups if their members express altruistic behaviours to one another. Groups that are predominantly altruists beat groups that are predominantly selfish.

Coevolution

Ecological interactions can be divided into host and associate relationships. A host is any entity that harbors another that is called the associate. Host and associate relationships among species that are mutually or reciprocally beneficial are called mutualisms. If the host and associate are physically connected, the relationship is called symbiosis. Approximately 60 per cent of all plants, for example, have a symbiotic relationship with arbuscular mycorrhizal fungi. Symbiotic plants and fungi exchange carbohydrates for mineral nutrients. Symbiosis differs from indirect mutualisms where the organisms live apart. For example, tropical rainforests regulate the Earth's atmosphere. Trees living in the equatorial regions of the planet supply oxygen into the atmosphere that sustains species living in distant polar regions of the planet. This relationship is called commensalism because many other host species receive the benefits of clean air at no cost or harm to the associate tree species supplying the oxygen. The host and associate relationship is called parasitism if one species benefits while the other suffers. Competition among species or among members of the same species is defined as reciprocal antagonism, such as grasses competing for growth space.

Parasites: A harvestman arachnid is parasitized by mites. This is parasitism because the harvestman is being consumed as its juices are slowly sucked out while the mites gain all the benefits travelling on and feeding off of their host.

Popular ecological study systems for mutualism include, fungus-growing ants employing agricultural symbiosis, bacteria living in the guts of insects and other organisms, the fig wasp and yucca moth pollination complex, lichens with fungi and photosynthetic algae, and corals with photosynthetic algae.

Biogeography

The word *biogeography* is an amalgamation of *biology* and *geography*. Biogeography is the comparative study of the geographic distribution of organisms and the corresponding evolution of their traits in space and time. The Journal of Biogeography was established in 1974. Biogeography and ecology share many of their disciplinary roots. For example, the theory of island biogeography, published by the mathematician Robert MacArthur and ecologist Edward O. Wilson in 1967 is considered one of the fundamentals of ecological theory.

Biogeography has a long history in the natural sciences where questions arise concerning the spatial distribution of plants and animals. Ecology and evolution provide the explanatory context for biogeographical studies. Biogeographical patterns result from ecological processes that influence range distributions, such as migration and dispersal. and from historical processes that split populations or species into different areas. The biogeographic processes that result in the natural splitting of species explains much of the modern distribution of the Earth's biota. The splitting of lineages in a species is called vicariance biogeography and it is a sub-discipline of biogeography. There are also practical applications in the field of biogeography concerning ecological systems and processes. For example, the range and distribution of biodiversity and invasive species responding to climate change is a serious concern and active area of research in context of global warming.

r/K-Selection Theory

A population ecology concept (introduced in MacArthur and Wilson's (1967) book, *The Theory of Island Biogeography*) is r/K selection theory, one of the first predictive models in ecology used to explain life-history evolution. The premise behind the r/K selection model is that natural selection pressures change according to population density. For example, when an island is first colonized, density of individuals is low. The initial increase in population size is *not* limited by competition, leaving an abundance of available resources for rapid population growth. These early phases of population growth experience *density-independent* forces of natural selection, which is called *r*-selection. As the population becomes more crowded, it approaches the island's carrying capacity, thus forcing individuals to compete more heavily for fewer available resources. Under crowded conditions the population experiences density-dependent forces of natural selection, called *K*-selection.

In the *r/K*-selection model, the first variable *r* is the intrinsic rate of natural increase in population size and the second variable *K* is the carrying capacity of a population. Different species evolve different life-history strategies spanning a continuum between these two selective forces. An *r*-selected species is one that has high birth rates, low levels of parental investment, and high rates of mortality before individuals reach maturity. Evolution favors high rates of fecundity in *r*-selected species. Many kinds of insects and invasive species exhibit *r*-selected characteristics. In contrast, a *K*-selected species has low rates of fecundity, high levels of parental investment in the young, and low rates of mortality as individuals mature. Humans and elephants are examples of species exhibiting *K*-selected characteristics, including longevity and efficiency in the conversion of more resources into fewer offspring.

Molecular Ecology

The important relationship between ecology and genetic inheritance predates modern techniques for molecular analysis. Molecular ecological research became more feasible with the development of rapid and accessible genetic technologies, such as the polymerase chain reaction (PCR). The rise of molecular technologies and influx of research questions into this new ecological field resulted in the publication *Molecular Ecology* in 1992. Molecular ecology uses various analytical techniques to study genes in an evolutionary and ecological context. In 1994, John Avise also played a leading role in this area of science with the publication of his book, *Molecular Markers, Natural History and Evolution*. Newer technologies opened a wave of genetic analysis into organisms once difficult to study from an ecological or evolutionary standpoint, such as bacteria, fungi and nematodes.

Molecular ecology engendered a new research paradigm to investigate ecological questions considered otherwise intractable. Molecular investigations revealed previously obscured details in the tiny intricacies of nature and improved resolution into probing questions about behavioural and biogeographical ecology. For example, molecular ecology revealed promiscuous sexual behaviour and multiple male partners in tree swallows previously thought to be socially monogamous. In a biogeographical context, the marriage between genetics, ecology and evolution resulted in a new sub-discipline called phylogeography.

Relation to the Environment

The environment is dynamically interlinked, imposed upon and constrains organisms at any time throughout their life cycle. Like the term ecology, environment has different conceptual meanings and to many these terms also overlap with the concept of *nature*. Environment "... includes the physical world, the social world of human relations and the built world of human creation." The environment in ecosystems includes both physical parameters and biotic attributes. The physical environment is external to the level of biological organization under investigation, including abiotic factors such as temperature, radiation, light, chemistry, climate and geology. The biotic environment includes genes, cells, organisms, members of the same species (conspecifics) and other species that share a habitat. The laws of thermodynamics applies to ecology by means of its physical state. Armed with an understanding of metabolic and thermodynamic principles a complete accounting of energy and material flow can be traced through an ecosystem.

Environmental and ecological relations are studied through reference to conceptually manageable and isolated parts. Once the effective environmental components are understood they conceptually link back together as a *holocoenotic* system. In other words, the organism and the environment form a dynamic whole (or umwelt). Change in one ecological or environmental factor can concurrently affect the dynamic state of an entire ecosystem.

Ecological studies are necessarily holistic as opposed to reductionistic. Holism has three scientific meanings or uses that identify with:

1. the mechanistic complexity of ecosystems;
2. the practical description of patterns in quantitative reductionist terms where correlations may be identified but nothing is understood about the causal relations without reference to the whole system;
3 a metaphysical hierarchy whereby the causal relations of larger systems are understood without reference to the smaller parts.

An example of the metaphysical aspect to holism is the trend of increased exterior thickness in shells of different species. The reason for a thickness increase can be understood through reference to principals of natural selection via predation without any reference to the biomolecular properties of the exterior shells.

Metabolism and the Early Atmosphere

Metabolism — the rate at which energy and material resources are taken up from the environment, transformed within an organism, and allocated to maintenance, growth and reproduction – is a fundamental physiological trait.

The Earth formed approximately 4.5 billion years ago and environmental conditions were too extreme for life to form for the first 500 million years. During this early Hadean period, the Earth started to cool, allowing a crust and oceans to form. Environmental conditions were unsuitable for the origins of life for the first billion years after the Earth formed. The Earth's atmosphere transformed from being dominated by hydrogen, to one composed mostly of methane and ammonia. Over the next billion years the metabolic activity of life transformed the atmosphere to higher concentrations of carbon dioxide, nitrogen, and water vapor. These gases changed the way that light from the sun hit the Earth's surface and greenhouse effects trapped heat. There were untapped sources of free energy within the mixture of reducing and oxidizing gasses that set the stage for primitive ecosystems to evolve and, in turn, the atmosphere also evolved.

The biology of life operates within a certain range of temperatures. Heat is a form of energy that regulates temperature. Heat affects growth rates, activity, behaviour and primary production. Temperature is largely dependent on the incidence of solar radiation. The latitudinal and longitudinal spatial variation of temperature greatly affects climates and consequently the distribution of biodiversity and levels of primary production in different ecosystems or biomes across the planet. Heat and temperature relate importantly to metabolic activity. Poikilotherms, for example, have a body temperature that is largely regulated and dependent on the temperature of the external environment. In contrast, homeotherms regulate their internal body temperature by expending metabolic energy.

There is a relationship between light, primary production, and ecological energy budgets. Sunlight is the primary input of energy into the planet's ecosystems. Light is composed of electromagnetic energy of different wavelengths. Radiant energy from the sun generates heat, provides photons of light measured as active energy in the chemical reactions of life, and also acts as a catalyst for genetic mutation. Plants, algae, and some bacteria absorb light and assimilate the energy through photosynthesis. Organisms capable of assimilating energy by photosynthesis or through inorganic fixation of H_2S are autotrophs. Autotrophs–responsible for primary production–assimilate light energy that becomes metabolically stored as potential energy in the form of biochemical enthalpic bonds.

Water

Wetland conditions such as shallow water, high plant productivity, and anaerobic substrates provide a suitable environment for important physical, biological, and chemical processes. Because of these processes, wetlands play a vital role in global nutrient and element cycles.

The rate of diffusion of carbon dioxide and oxygen is approximately 10,000 times slower in water than it is in air. When soils become flooded, they quickly lose oxygen and transform into a low-concentration (hypoxic - with less than 2 mg O_2l^{-1}) environment and eventually become completly (anoxic) environment where anaerobic bacteria thrive among the roots. Water also influences the spectral composition and amount of light as it reflects off the water surface and submerged particles. Aquatic plants exhibit a wide variety of morphological and physiological adaptations that allow them to survive, compete and diversify these environments. For example, the roots and stems develop large air spaces (Aerenchyma) that regulate the efficient transportation gases (for example, CO_2 and O_2) used in respiration and photosynthesis. In drained soil, microorganisms use oxygen during respiration. In aquatic environments, anaerobic soil microorganisms use nitrate, manganese ions, ferric ions, sulfate, carbon dioxide and some organic compounds. The activity of soil microorganisms and the chemistry of the water reduces the oxidation-reduction potentials of the water. Carbon dioxide, for example, is reduced to methane (CH_4) by methanogenic bacteria. Salt water plants (or halophytes) have specialized physiological adaptations, such as the development of special organs for shedding salt and osmoregulate their internal salt (NaCl) concentrations, to live in estuarine, brackish, or oceanic environments. The physiology of fish is also specially adapted to deal with high levels of salt through osmoregulation. Their gills form electrochemical gradients that mediate salt excresion in saline environments and uptake in fresh water.

Gravity

The shape and energy of the land is affected to a large degree by gravitational forces. On a larger scale, the distribution of gravitational forces on the earth are uneven and influence the shape and movement of tectonic plates as well as having an influence on geomorphic processes such as orogeny and erosion. These forces govern many of the geophysical properties and distributions of ecological biomes across the Earth. On a organism scale, gravitational forces provide directional cues for plant and fungal growth (gravitropism), orientation cues for animal migrations, and influence the biomechanics and size of animals. Ecological traits, such as allocation of biomass in trees during growth are subject to mechanical failure as gravitational forces influence the position and structure of branches and leaves. The cardiovascular systems of all animals are functionally adapted to overcome pressure and gravitational forces that change according to the features of organisms (e.g., height, size, shape), their behaviour (e.g., diving, running, flying), and the habitat occupied (e.g., water, hot deserts, cold tundra).

Pressure

Climatic and osmotic pressure places physiological constraints on organisms, such as flight and respiration at high altitudes, or diving to deep ocean depths. These constraints influence vertical limits of ecosystems in the biosphere as organisms are physiologically sensitive and adapted to atmospheric and osmotic water pressure differences. Oxygen levels, for example, decrease with increasing pressure and are a limiting factor for life at higher altitudes. Water transportation through trees is another important ecophysiological parameter where osmotic pressure gradients factor in. Water pressure in the depths of oceans requires that organisms adapt to these conditions. For example, mammals, such as whales, dolphins and seals are specially adapted to deal with changes in sound due to water pressure differences. Different species of hagfish provide another example of adaptation to deep-sea pressure through specialized protein adaptations.

Wind and Turbulence

Turbulent forces in air and water have significant effects on the environment and ecosystem distribution, form and dynamics. On a planetary scale, ecosystems are affected by circulation patterns in the global trade winds. Wind power and the turbulent forces it creates can influence heat, nutrient, and biochemical profiles of ecosystems. For example, wind running over the surface of a lake creates turbulence, mixing the water column and influencing the environmental profile to create thermally layered zones, partially governing how fish, algae, and other parts of the aquatic ecology are structured. Wind speed and turbulence also exert influence on rates of evapotranspiration rates and energy budgets in plants and animals. Wind speed, temperature and moisture content can vary as winds travel across different landfeatures and elevations. The westerlies, for example, come into contact with the coastal and interior mountains of western North America to produce a rain shadow on the leeward side of the mountain. The air expands and moisture condenses as the winds move up in elevation which can cause precipitation; this is called orographic lift. This environmental process produces spatial divisions in biodiversity, as species adapted to wetter conditions are range-restricted to the coastal mountain valleys and unable to migrate across the xeric ecosystems of the Columbia Basin to intermix with sister lineages that are segregated to the interior mountain systems.

Plants convert carbon dioxide into biomass and emit oxygen into the atmosphere. Approximately 350 million years ago (near the Devonian period) the photosynthetic process brought the concentration of atmospheric oxygen above 17 per cent, which allowed combustion to occur. Fire releases CO_2 and converts fuel into ash and tar. Fire is a significant ecological parameter that raises many issues pertaining to its control and suppression in management. While the issue of fire in relation to ecology and plants has been recognized for a long time, Charles Cooper brought attention to the issue of forest fires in relation to thc ecology of forest fire suppression and management in the 1960s.

Fire creates environmental mosaics and a patchiness to ecosystem age and canopy structure. Native North Americans were among the first to influence fire regimes by controlling their spread near their homes or by lighting fires to stimulate the production of herbaceous foods and basketry materials. The altered state of soil nutrient supply and cleared canopy structure also opens new ecological niches for seedling establishment. Most ecosystem are adapted to natural fire cycles. Plants, for example, are equipped with a variety of adaptations to deal with forest fires. Some species (e.g., *Pinus halepensis*) cannot germinate until after their seeds have lived through a fire. This environmental trigger for seedlings is called serotiny. Some compounds from smoke also promote seed germination. Fire plays a major role in the persistence and resilience of ecosystems.

Biogeochemistry

Ecologists study and measure nutrient budgets to understand how these materials are regulated and flow through the environment. This research has led to an understanding that there is a global feedback between ecosystems and the physical parameters of this planet including minerals, soil, pH, ions, water and atmospheric gases. There are six major elements, including H (hydrogen), C (carbon), N (nitrogen), O (oxygen), S (sulfur), and P (phosphorus) that form the constitution of all biological macromolecules and feed into the Earth's geochemical processes. From the smallest scale of biology the combined effect of billions upon billions of ecological processes amplify and ultimately regulate the biogeochemical cycles of the Earth. Understanding the relations and cycles mediated between these elements and their ecological pathways has significant bearing toward understanding global biogeochemistry.

The ecology of global carbon budgets gives one example of the linkage between biodiversity and biogeochemistry. For starters, the Earth's oceans are estimated to hold 40,000 gigatonnes (Gt) carbon, vegetation and soil is estimated to hold 2070 Gt carbon, and fossil fuel emissions are estimated to emit an annual flux of 6.3 Gt carbon. At different times in the Earth's history there has been major restructuring in these global carbon budgets that was regulated to a large extent by the ecology of the land. For example, through the early-mid Eocene volcanic outgassing, the oxidation of methane stored in wetlands, and seafloor gases increased atmospheric CO_2 concentrations to levels as high as 3500 ppm. In the Oligocene, from 25 to 32 million years ago, there was another significant restructuring in the global carbon cycle as grasses evolved a special type of C4 photosynthesis and expanded their ranges. This new photosynthetic pathway evolved in response to the drop in atmospheric CO_2 concentrations below 550 ppm. Ecosystem functions such as these feed back significantly into global atmospheric models for carbon cycling. Loss in the abundance and distribution of biodiversity causes global carbon cycle feedbacks that are expected to increase rates of global warming in the next century. The effect of global warming melting large sections of permafrost creates a new mosaic of flooded areas where decomposition results in the emission of methane (CH_4). Hence, there is a relationship between global warming, decomposition and respiration in soils and wetlands producing significant climate feedbacks and altered global biogeochemical cycles. There is concern over increases in atmospheric methane in the context of the global carbon cycle, because methane is also a greenhouse gas that is 23 times more effective at absorbing long-wave radiation than CO_2 on a 100 year time scale.

Early Beginnings

Ecology has a complex origin due in large part to its interdisciplinary nature. Ancient philosophers of Greece, including Hippocrates and Aristotle were among the first to record their observations on natural history. However, philosophers in ancient Greece viewed life as a static element that did not require an understanding of adaptation, a modern cornerstone of ecological theory. Topics more familiar in the modern context, including food chains, population regulation, and productivity, did not develop until the 1700s through the published works of microscopist Antoni van Leeuwenhoek (1632-1723) and botanist Richard Bradley . Biogeographer Alexander von Humbolt (1769-1859) was another early pioneer in ecological thinking and was among the first to recognize ecological gradients. Humbolt alluded to the modern ecological law of species to area relationships.

In the early 20th century, ecology was an analytical form of natural history. Following in the traditions of Aristotle, the descriptive nature of natural history examined the interaction of organisms with both their environment and their community. Natural historians, including James Hutton and Jean-Baptiste Lamarck, contributed significant works that laid the foundations of the modern ecological sciences. The term 'ecology' (German: *Oekologie*) is of a more recent origin and was first coined by the German biologist Ernst Haeckel in his book *Generelle Morphologie der Organismen* (1866).

Opinions differ on who was the founder of modern ecological theory. Some mark Haeckel's definition as the beginning, others say it was Eugenius Warming with the writing of Oecology of Plants: An Introduction to the Study of Plant Communities (1895). Ecology may also be thought to have begun with Carl Linnaeus' research principals on the economy of nature that matured in the early 18th century. He founded an early branch of ecological study he called the economy of nature The works of Linnaeus influenced Darwin in *The Origin of Species* where he adopted the usage of Linnaeus' phrase on the *economy or polity of nature.* Linnaeus was the first to frame *the balance of nature* as a testable hypothesis. Haeckel, who admired Darwin's work, defined ecology in reference to the economy of nature which has led some to question if ecology is synonymous with Linnaeus' concepts for the economy of nature.

The modern synthesis of ecology is a young science, which first attracted substantial formal attention at the end of the 19th century (around the same time as evolutionary studies) and become even more popular during the 1960s environmental movement, though many observations, interpretations and discoveries relating to ecology extend back to much earlier studies in natural history. For example, the concept on the balance or regulation of nature can be traced back to Herodotos (died *c.* 425 BC) who described an early account of mutualism along the Nile river where crocodiles open their mouths to beneficially allow sandpipers safe access to remove leeches. In the broader contributions to the historical development of the ecological sciences, Aristotle is considered one of the earliest naturalists who had an influential role in the philosophical development of ecological sciences. One of Aristotle's students, Theophrastus, made astute ecological observations about plants and posited a philosophical stance about the autonomous relations between plants and their environment that is more in line with modern ecological thought. Both Aristotle and Theophrastus made extensive observations on plant and animal migrations, biogeography, physiology, and their habits in what might be considered an analog of the modern ecological niche. Hippocrates, another Greek philosopher, is also credited with referrence to ecological topics in its earliest developments.

From Aristotle to Darwin the natural world was predominantly considered static and unchanged since its original creation. Prior to *The Origin of Species* there was little appreciation or understanding of the dynamic and reciprocal relations between organisms, their adaptations and their modifications to the environment. While Charles Darwin is most notable for his treatise on evolution, he is also one of the founders of soil ecology. In *The Origin of Species* Darwin also made note of the first ecological experiment that was published in 1816. In the science leading up to Darwin the notion of evolving species was gaining popular support. This scientific paradigm changed the way that researchers approached the ecological sciences.

Nowhere can one see more clearly illustrated what may be called the sensibility of such an organic complex, —expressed by the fact that whatever affects any species belonging to it, must speedily have its influence of some sort upon the whole assemblage. He will thus be made to see the impossibility of studying any form completely, out of relation to the other forms, —the necessity for taking a comprehensive survey of the whole as a condition to a satisfactory understanding of any part.

After the Turn of 20th Century

Some suggest that the first ecological text (*Natural History of Selborne*) was published in 1789, by Gilbert White (1720-1793). The first American ecology book was published in 1905 by Frederic Clements. In his book, Clements forwarded the idea of plant communities as a superorganism. This publication launched a debate between ecological holism and individualism that lasted until the 1970s. The Clements superorganism concept proposed that ecosystems progress through regular and determined stages of seral development that are analogous to developmental stages of an organism whose parts function to maintain the integrity of the whole. The Clementsian paradigm was challenged by Henry Gleason. According to Gleason, ecological communities develop from the unique and coincidental association of individual organisms. This perceptual shift placed the focus back onto the life histories of individual organisms and how this relates to the development of community associations.

The Clementsian superorganism theory has not been completely rejected, but some suggest it was an overextended application of holism. Holism remains a critical part of the theoretical foundation in contemporary ecological studies. Holism was first introduced in 1926 by a polarizing historical figure, a South African General named Jan Christian Smuts. Smuts was inspired by Clement's superorganism theory as he developed and published on the concept of holism, which contrasts starkly against his racial political views as the father of apartheid. Around the same time, Charles Elton pioneered the concept of food chains in his classical book 'Animal Ecology'. Elton defined ecological relations using concepts of food chains, food cycles, food size, and described numerical relations among different functional groups and their relative abundance. Elton's 'food cycle' was replaced by 'food web' in a subsequent ecological text.

Ecology has developers in many nations, including Russia's Vladimir Vernadsky and his founding of the biosphere concept in the 1920s or Japan's Kinji Imanishi and his concepts of harmony in nature and habitat segregation in the 1950s. The scientific recognition or importance of contributions to ecology from other cultures is hampered by language and translation barriers.

The ecosystems of planet Earth are coupled to human environments. Ecosystems regulate the global geophysical cycles of energy, climate, soil nutrients, and water that in turn support and grow natural capital (including the environmental, physiological, cognitive, cultural, and spiritual dimensions of life). Ultimately, every manufactured product in human environments comes from natural systems. Ecosystems are considered common-pool resources because ecosystems do not exclude beneficiaries and they can be depleted or degraded. For example, green space within communities provides sustainable health services that reduces mortality and regulates the spread of vector borne disease. Research shows that people who are more engaged with regular access to natural areas have lower rates of diabetes, heart disease and psychological disorders. These ecological health services are regularly depleted through urban development projects that do not factor in the common-pool value of ecosystems.

The ecological commons delivers a diverse supply of community services that sustains the well-being of human society. The Millennium Ecosystem Assessment, an international UN initiative involving more than 1,360 experts worldwide, identifies four main ecosystem service types having 30 sub-categories stemming from natural capital. The ecological commons includes provisioning (e.g., food, raw materials, medicine, water supplies), regulating (e.g., climate, water, soil retention, flood retention), cultural (e.g., science and education, artistic, spiritual), and supporting (e.g., soil formation, nutrient cycling, water cycling) services.

Policy and human institutions should rarely assume that human enterprise is benign. A safer assumption holds that human enterprise almost always exacts an ecological toll - a debit taken from the ecological commons.

Sixth Mass Extinction

Global assessments of biodiversity indicate that the current epoch, the Holocene (or Anthropocene) is a sixth mass extinction. Species loss is accelerating at 100-1000 times faster than average background rates in the fossil record. The field of conservation biology involves ecologists that are researching, confronting, and searching for solutions to sustain the planet's ecosystems for future generations.

"Human activities are associated directly or indirectly with nearly every aspect of the current extinction spasm".

Nature is a resilient system. Ecosystems regenerate, withstand, and are forever adapting to fluctuating environments. Ecological resilience is an important conceptual framework in conservation management and it is defined as the preservation of biological relations in ecosystems that persevere and regenerate in response to disturbance over time. Disturbances, such as fire, are both cause and product of natural fluctuations in death rates, species assemblages, and biomass densities within an ecological community. These disturbances create places of renewal where new directions emerge out of the patchwork of natural experimentation and opportunity. However, persistent, systematic, large and nonrandom disturbance caused by the niche constructing behaviour of human beings, habitat conversion and land development, has pushed many of the Earth's ecosystems to the extent of their resilient thresholds. Three planetary thresholds have already been crossed, including:

1. biodiversity loss;
2. climate change; and
3. nitrogen cycles.

These biophysical systems are ecologically interrelated and naturally resilient, but human civilization has transitioned the planet to the Anthropocene epoch, where the threshold for planetary scale resilience has been crossed and the ecological state of the Earth is deteriorating rapidly to the detriment of humanity. The world's fisheries and oceans, for example, are facing dire challenges as the threat of global collapse appears imminent, with serious ramifications for the well-being of humanity. The ecology of the planet is further threatened by global warming, but investments in nature conservation can provide a regulatory feedback to store and regulate carbon and other greenhouse gases.

Ecological Footprint

While we are used to thinking of cities as geographically discrete places, most of the land 'occupied' by their residents lies far beyond their borders. The total area of land required to sustain an urban region (its 'ecological footprint') is typically at least an order of magnitude greater than that contained within municipal boundaries or the associated built-up area.

In 1992, William Rees developed the ecological footprint concept. The ecological footprint and its close analog the water footprint has become a popular way of accounting for the level of impact that human society is imparting on the Earth's ecosystems. All indications are that the human enterprise is unsustainable as the footprint of society is placing too much stress on the ecology of the planet.

The WWF 2008 living planet report and other researchers report that human civilization has exceeded the bio-regenerative capacity of the planet. This means that the footprint of human consumption is extracting more natural resources than can be replenished by ecosystems around the world

Ecological Economics

Ecological economics is an economic science that extends its methods of valuation onto nature in an effort to address the inequity between market growth and biodiversity loss. Natural capital is the stock of materials or information stored in biodiversity that generates services that can enhance the welfare of communities. Population losses are the more sensitive indicator of natural capital than are species extinction in the accounting of ecosystem services.

The prospect for recovery in the economic crisis of nature is grim. Populations, such as local ponds and patches of forest are being cleared away and lost at rates that exceed species extinctions. The mainstream growth-based economic system adopted by governments worldwide does not include a price or markets for natural capital. This type of economic system places further ecological debt onto future generations.

Many human-nature interactions occur indirectly due to the production and use of human-made (manufactured and synthesized) products, such as electronic appliances, furniture, plastics, airplanes, and automobiles. These products insulate humans from the natural environment, leading them to perceive less dependence on natural systems than is the case, but all manufactured products ultimately come from natural systems.

Human societies are increasingly being placed under stress as the ecological commons is diminished through an accounting system that has incorrectly assumed "... that nature is a fixed, indestructible capital asset". The current wave of threats, including massive extinction rates and concurrent loss of natural capital to the detriment of human society, is happening rapidly.

This is called a biodiversity crisis, because 50 per cent of the worlds species are predicted to go extinct within the next 50 years. Conventional monetary analyses are unable to detect or deal with these sorts of ecological problems. Multiple global ecological economic initiatives are being promoted to solve this problem. For example, governments of the G8 met in 2007 and set forth The Economics of Ecosystems and Biodiversity (TEEB) initiative.

In a global study we will initiate the process of analyzing the global economic benefit of biological diversity, the costs of the loss of biodiversity and the failure to take protective measures versus the costs of effective conservation.

6

Prairie Restoration

Prairie restoration is an ecologically friendly way to restore some of the prairie land that was lost to industry, farming and commerce. For example, the U.S. state of Illinois alone once held over 22 million acres (89,000 km^2) of prairie land and now just 2,000 acres (8 km^2) of *original* prairie land exist.

Purpose

Ecologically, prairie restoration aids in conservation of earth's topsoil, which is often exposed to erosion from wind and rain when prairies are plowed under to make way for new commerce. Conversely, much more of the prairie lands have become the fertile fields on which cereal crops of corn, barley and wheat are grown.

Many prairie plants are also highly resistant to drought, temperature extremes, disease, and native insect pests. They are frequently used for xeriscaping projects in arid regions of the American West.

A restoration project of prairie lands can be large or small. A backyard prairie restoration will enrich soil, help with erosion and take up extra water in excessive rainfalls. Prairie flowers are attractive to native butterflies and other pollinators. On a larger scale, communities and corporations are creating areas of restored prairies which in turn will store organic carbon in the soil and help maintain the biodiversity of the 3000 plus species that count on the grasslands for food and shelter.

Types of Plants

Prairie plants consist of grasses and forbs. Grasses, which are monocots, are similar to what may be in a yard, but grasses in the prairie will be of a broader leaf. Some prominent tallgrass prairie grasses include Big Bluestem, Indiangrass, and Switchgrass. Midgrass and shortgrass species include Little Bluestem and Buffalograss. Forbs fall into an unusual category. They are not grasses, trees or shrubs, but are herbaceous and share the field with the less diverse grasses. Most wildflowers and legumes are forbs. Forbs are structurally specialized to resist herbaceous grazers such as American bison, and their commonly hairy leaves help deter the cold and prevent excessive evaporation. Many of the forbs contain secondary compounds that were discovered by the American Natives and are still used widely today. One particular forb, the purple coneflower, is recognized more readily by its scientific name *Echinacea purpurea*, or just *Echinacea*, which is used as an herbal remedy for colds.

Early prairie restoration efforts tended to focus largely on a few dominant species, typically grasses, with little attention to seed source. With experience, later restorers have realized the importance of obtaining a broad mix of species and using local ecotype seed.

Care of Prairies

Fire is a big component to the success of grasslands, large or small. Controlled burns, with a permit, are recommended every 4-8 years (after two growth seasons) to burn away dead plants; prevent certain other plants from encroaching (such as trees) and release nutrients into the ground to encourage new growth. A much more wildlife habitat friendly alternative to burning every 4-8 years is to burn 1/4th to 1/8th of a tract every year. This will leave wildlife a home every year and still accomplish the task of burning. The Native Americans may also have used the burns to control pests such as ticks.

If controlled burns are not possible, rotational mowing is recommended as a substitute.

Prairie Contributors

Some popular prairie restoration projects have been completed and maintained by conservation departments, such as Midewin National Tallgrass Prairie, located in Wilmington, Illinois. This restoration project is administered by the U.S. Department of Agriculture Forest Service and the Illinois Department of Natural Resources. It sits on part of the Joliet Army Ammunitions Plant, specifically on an area once contaminated from TNT manufacturing. Since 1997, the project has opened some 15,000 acres (61 km^2) of restored prairie to the public.

Another large restoration project finds its home on the ample area of Fermilab; a U.S. governmental atomic accelerator laboratory located in

Batavia, Illinois. Fermilab's 6,800 acres (28 km^2) sit a top fertile farmland and the prairie restoration project consists of approximately 1000 acres (4 km^2) of that. This project began in 1971 and continues today with the help of Fermilab employees and many community teachers, botanists and volunteers.

Prairies are considered part of the temperate grasslands, savannas, and shrublands biome by ecologists, based on similar temperate climates, moderate rainfall, and grasses, herbs, and shrubs, rather than trees, as the dominant vegetation type. Temperate grassland regions include the Pampas of Argentina, and the steppes of Eurasia.

Lands typically referred to as 'prairie' tend to be in North America. The term encompasses the area referred to as the Interior Lowlands of the United States, Canada and Mexico, which includes all of the Great Plains as well as the wetter, somewhat hillier land to the east. In the U.S., the area is constituted by most or all of the states of North Dakota, South Dakota, Nebraska, Kansas, and Oklahoma, and sizable parts of the states of Montana, Wyoming, Colorado, New Mexico, Texas, Missouri, Iowa, Illinois, Indiana, Wisconsin, and western and southern Minnesota. The Central Valley of California is also a prairie. The Canadian Prairies occupy vast areas of Manitoba, Saskatchewan, and Alberta.

The formation of the North American Prairies started with the upwelling of the Rocky Mountains. The mountains created a rain shadow that killed most of the trees.

Most prairie soil was deposited during the last glacial advance that began about 110,000 years ago. The glaciers expanding southward scraped the soil, picking up material and leveling the terrain. As the glaciers retreated about 10,000 years ago, it deposited this material in the form of till.

Tallgrass Prairie evolved over tens of thousands of years with the disturbances of grazing and fire. Native ungulates such as bison, elk, and white-tailed deer, roamed the expansive, diverse, plentiful grassland before European colonization of the Americas. For 10,000-20,000 years native people used fire annually as a tool to assist in hunting, transportation and safety. Evidence of ignition sources of fire in the tallgrass prairie are overwhelmingly human as opposed to lightning. Humans, and grazing animals, were active participants in the process of prairie formation and the establishment of the diversity of graminoid and forbs species. Fire has the effect on prairies of removing trees, clearing dead plant matter, and changing the availability of certain nutrients in the soil from the ash produced. Fire kills the vascular tissue of trees, but not prairie, as up to 75 per cent (depending on the species) of the total plant biomass is below the soil surface and will re-grow from its deep (up to 6 feet) roots. Without disturbance, trees will encroach on a grassland, cast shade, which suppresses the understory. Prairie and widely spaced Oak trees evolved to coexist in the oak savanna ecosystem.

Fertility

In spite of long recurrent droughts and occasional torrential rains, the grasslands of the Great Plains are not subject to great soil erosion. The deep, interconnected root systems of prairie grasses firmly hold the soil in place and prevent run-off of soil. When a plant dies, the fungi, bacteria and the other decomposers slowly eat the roots and leaves, returning nutrients to the soil.

These deep roots also help prairie plants to reach water in even the driest conditions. The grass suffers much less damage from dry conditions than the farm crops that have replaced many former prairies.

Types

The types of prairies in North America are usually split into three groups: wet, mesic, and dry.

Wet

In this type of prairie, the soil is usually very moist most of the growing season, and has poor water drainage. This can possibly contain a bog or fen, since it often has plentiful stagnant water. Has the best type of farming soil.

Mesic

Mesic prairies have good drainage, but have good soil during the growing season. This type of prairie is the most often converted for agricultural usage, consequently it is one of the more endangered types of prairie.

Dry

Dry Prairie is a prairie which has somewhat wet to very dry soil during the growing season because of good drainage in the soil. Often, this prairie can be found on uplands or slopes.

Farming

The very dense soil plagued the first settlers who were using wooden plows, which were more suitable for loose forest soil. On the prairie the plows bounced around and the soil stuck to them. This problem was solved in 1837 by an Illinois blacksmith named John Deere who developed a steel moldboard plow that was stronger and cut the roots, making the fertile soils ready for farming.

The tallgrass prairie has been converted into one of the most intensive crop producing areas in North America. Less than one tenth of one per cent (<0.09%) of the original landcover of the tallgrass prairie biome remains. States formerly with landcover in native tallgrass prairie such as Iowa, Illinois, Minnesota, Wisconsin, Nebraska, and Missouri have became valued for their highly productive soils and are included in the Corn Belt. As an example of this land use intensity, Illinois and Iowa for the United States, rank 49th and 50th out of 50 states in total uncultivated land remaining.

Biofuels

Research, by David Tilman, ecologist at the University of Minnesota, suggests that "biofuels made from high-diversity mixtures of prairie plants can reduce global warming by removing carbon dioxide from the atmosphere. Even when grown on infertile soils, they can provide a substantial portion of global energy needs, and leave fertile land for food production." Unlike corn and soybeans which are major food crops, prairie grasses are not used for human consumption. Prairie grasses can be grown in infertile soil, eliminating the cost of adding nutrients to the soil. Tilman and his colleagues estimate that prairie grass biofuels would yield 51 per cent more energy per acre than ethanol from corn grown on fertile land. Some grasses commonly used are lupine, big bluestem (turkey foot), blazing star, switchgrass, and prairie clover.

Preservation

Only one per cent of tallgrass prairie remains in the U.S. today.

Significant preserved areas of prairie include:

- University of Wisconsin–Madison Arboretum, University of Wisconsin–Madison, Wisconsin
- Ceresco Prairie Conservancy, Ripon College, Wisconsin
- Grasslands National Park, Saskatchewan
- Cypress Hills Interprovincial Park, Alberta and Saskatchewan
- Midewin National Tallgrass Prairie, in Will County, Illinois
- Neal Smith National Wildlife Refuge, Iowa
- Konza Prairie, Manhattan, Kansas
- Tallgrass Prairie National Preserve, Kansas

- Tallgrass Prairie Preserve 32,000 acres (130 km^2), Oklahoma
- Nine-Mile Prairie, Nebraska
- Zumwalt Prairie, Wallowa County, Oregon
- Richard Bong State Recreation Area, in Kenosha County, Wisconsin
- Hoosier Prairie, Lake County, Indiana
- Jacobsburg Environmental Education Centre, Pennsylvania
- Clymer Meadow Preserve, Hunt County, Texas
- Tallgrass Aspen Parkland, Manitoba and Minnesota
- Kissimmee Prairie Preserve State Park, Okeechobee County, Florida
- Paynes Prairie Preserve State Park, Alachua County, Florida
- American Prairie Foundation, Phillips and Blaine Counties, Montana

Virgin Prairies

Virgin prairie refers to prairie land that has never been plowed. Small virgin prairies exist in the American Midwestern states and in Canada. Restored prairie refers to a prairie that has been reseeded after plowing or other disturbance.

Prairie Garden

A prairie garden is a garden primarily consisting of plants from a prairie.

7

Riparian Zone Restoration

Riparian zone restoration is the ecological restoration of riparian zone habitats of streams, rivers, springs, lakes, floodplains, and other hydrologic ecologies.

Riparian Zone Restoration

Riparian zones have been degraded throughout much of the world. The unique biodiversity of riparian ecosystems and the importance of riparian zones in preventing erosion, protecting water quality, providing habitat and wildlife corridors, and maintaining the health of in-stream biota (Aquatic organisms) has led to a surge of restoration activities aimed at riparian ecosystems in the last few decades. Restoration efforts are typically guided by an ecological understanding of riparian zone processes and knowledge of the causes of degradation. They are often interdependent with stream restoration projects.

Causes of Riparian Zone Degradation

Riparian zone disturbance falls into two main categories: hydrologic modifications that indirectly impact riparian communities through changes in stream morphology and hydrologic processes, and habitat alterations that result in direct modification of riparian communities through land clearing or disturbance.

HYDROLOGIC MODIFICATIONS

Dams and Diversions

Dams are built on rivers primarily to store water for human use, generate hydroelectric power, and/or control flooding. Natural riparian ecosystems upstream of dams can be destroyed when newly-created reservoirs inundate riparian habitat. Dams can also cause substantial changes in downstream riparian communities by altering the magnitude, frequency, and timing of flood events and reducing the amount of sediment and nutrients delivered from upstream. Diverting water from stream channels for agricultural, industrial, and human use reduces the volume of water flowing downstream, and can have similar effects.

In a natural riparian system, periodic flooding can remove sections of riparian vegetation. This leaves portions of the floodplain available for regeneration and effectively 'resets' the successional timeline Frequent disturbance naturally favours many early-successional (pioneer) riparian species. Many studies show that a reduction in flooding due to dams and diversions can allow community succession to progress beyond a typical stage, causing changes in community structure.

Changing flood regimes can be especially problematic when exotic species are favoured by altered conditions. For example, dam regulation changes floodplain hydrology in the southwest U.S. by impeding annual flooding cycles. This modification has been implicated in the dominance of saltcedar (Tamarix chinensis) over the native cottonwood (Populus deltoids). Cottonwoods were found to be competitively superior to saltcedar when flooding allowed seeds of both species to cogerminate. However, the lack of flooding caused by altered hydrology creates more favourable conditions for the germination of saltcedar over cottonwoods.

Groundwater Withdrawals

Riparian zones are characterized by a distinct community of plant species that are physiologically adapted to a greater amount of freshwater than upland species. In addition to having frequent direct contact with surface water through periodic rises in stream water levels and flooding, riparian zones are also characterized by their proximity to groundwater. Particularly in arid regions, shallow groundwater, seeps, and springs provides a more constant source of water to riparian vegetation than occasional flooding. By reducing the availability of water, groundwater withdrawals can impact the health of riparian vegetation. For example, Fremont cottonwood (*Populus fremontii*), and San Joaquin willow (*Salix gooddingii*), common riparian species in Arizona, were found to have more dead branches and experienced greater mortality with decreasing groundwater levels.

Plant community composition can change dramatically over a gradient of groundwater depth: plants that can only survive in wetland conditions can be replaced by plants that are tolerant of drier conditions as groundwater levels are reduced, causing habitat community shifts and in some cases complete loss of riparian species. Studies have also shown that decreases in groundwater levels may favour the invasion and persistence of certain exotic invasive species such as Saltcedar (*Tamarix chinensis*), which do not appear to show the same degree of physiologic water stress as native species when subjected to lower groundwater levels.

Stream Channelization and Levee Construction

Stream channelization is the process of engineering straighter, wider, and deeper stream channels, usually for improved navigation, wetland drainage, and/or faster transport of flood waters downstream. Levees are often constructed in conjunction with channelization to protect human development and agricultural fields from flooding. Riparian vegetation can be directly removed or damaged during and after the channelization process. In addition, channelization and levee construction modify the natural hydrology of a stream system. As water flows through a natural stream, meanders are created when faster flowing water erodes outer banks and slower flowing water deposits sediment on inner banks. Many riparian plant species depend on these areas of new sediment deposition for germination and establishment of seedlings. Channel straightening and levee construction eliminate these areas of deposition, creating unfavorable conditions for riparian vegetation recruitment.

By preventing overbank flooding, levees reduce the amount of water available to riparian vegetation in the floodplain, which alters the types of vegetation that can persist in these conditions. A lack of flooding has been shown to decrease the amount of habitat heterogeneity in riparian ecosystems as wetland depressions in the floodplain no longer fill and hold water. Because habitat heterogeneity is correlated with species diversity, levees can cause reductions in the overall biodiversity of riparian ecosystems.

HABITAT ALTERATION

Land Clearing

In many places around the world, riparian zones have been completely eliminated as humans have cleared land for raising crops, growing timber, and developing land for commercial or residential purposes. Removing riparian vegetation increases the erodibility of stream banks, and can also speed the rate of channel migration. In addition, removal of riparian vegetation fragments the remaining riparian ecosystem, which can prevent or hinder dispersal of species between habitat patches. This can diminish riparian plant diversity, as well as decrease abundances and diversity of migratory birds or other species that depend on large, undisturbed areas of habitat Fragmentation can also prevent gene flow between isolated riparian patches, reducing genetic diversity.

Livestock Grazing

Cattle have a propensity to aggregate around water, which can be detrimental to riparian ecosystems. While native ungulates such as deer are commonly found in riparian zones, livestock may trample or graze down native riparian vegetation, creating an unnatural amount and type of disturbance that riparian species have not evolved to tolerate. Livestock grazing has been shown to reduce areal cover of native plant species, create disturbance frequencies that favour exotic annual weeds, and alter plant community composition. For example, in an arid South African ecosystem, grazing was found to cause a reduction of grasses, sedges, and tree species and an increase in non-succulent shrubs.

Mining

Mining stream channels for sand and gravel can impact riparian zones by destroying habitat directly, removing groundwater through pumping, altering stream channel morphology, and changing sediment flow regimes. Conversely, mining activities in the floodplain can create favourable areas for the establishment of riparian vegetation (e.g., cottonwoods) along streams where natural recruitment processes have been impacted through other forms of human activity. Mining for metals can impact riparian zones when toxic materials accumulate in sediments.

Invasive Exotics

The number and diversity of invasive exotic species in riparian ecosystems is increasing worldwide. Riparian zones may be particularly vulnerable to invasion due to frequent habitat disturbance (both natural and anthropogenic) and the efficiency of rivers and streams in dispersing propagules. Invasive species can greatly impact the ecosystem structure and function of riparian zones. For example, the higher biomass of dense stands of the invasive Acacia mearnsii and Eucalyptus species causes greater water consumption and thus lower water levels in streams in South Africa. Invasive plants can also cause changes in the amount of sediment that is trapped by vegetation, altering channel morphology, and can increase the flammability of the vegetation, increasing fire frequency. Exotic animals can also impact riparian zones. For example, feral burros along the Santa Maria river strip bark and cambium off native cottonwoods, causing tree mortality.

Methods of Riparian Zone Restoration

Methods for restoring riparian zones are often determined by the cause of degradation. Two main approaches are used in riparian zone restoration: restoring hydrologic processes and geomorphic features, and reestablishing native riparian vegetation.

Restoring Hydrologic Processes and Geomorphic Features

When altered flow regimes have impacted riparian zone health, re-establishing natural streamflow may be the best solution to effectively restore riparian ecosystems. The complete removal of dams and flow-altering structures may be required to fully restore historic conditions, but this is not always realistic or feasible. An alternative to dam removal is for periodic flood pulses consistent with historical magnitude and timing to be simulated by releasing large amounts of water at once instead of maintaining more consistent flows throughout the year. This would allow overbank flooding, which is vital for maintaining the health of many riparian ecosystems. However, simply restoring a more natural flow regime also has logistical constraints, as legally appropriated water rights may not include the maintenance of such ecologically important factors. Reductions in groundwater pumping may also help restore riparian ecosystems by reestablishing groundwater levels that favour riparian vegetation; however, this too can be hampered by the fact that groundwater withdrawal regulations do not usually incorporate provisions for riparian protection.

The negative effects of channelization on stream and riparian health can be lessened through physical restoration of the stream channel. This can be accomplished by restoring flow to historic channels, or through the creation of new channels. In order for restoration to be successful, particularly for the creation of entirely new channels, restoration plans must take into account the geomorphic potential of the individual stream and tailor restoration methods accordingly. This is typically done through examination of reference streams (physically and ecologically similar streams in stable, natural condition) and by methods of stream classification based on morphological features. Stream channels are typically designed to be narrow enough to overflow into the floodplain on a 1.5 to 2 year timescale. The goal of geomorphic restoration is to eventually restore hydrologic processes important to riparian and instream ecosystems. However, this type of restoration can be logistically difficult: in many cases, the initial straightening or modification of the channel has resulted in humans encroaching into the former floodplain through development, agriculture, etc. In addition, stream channel modification can be extremely costly.

One well-known example of a large-scale stream restoration project is the Kissimmee River Restoration Project in central Florida. The Kissimmee River was channelized between 1962 and 1971 for flood control, turning a meandering 167-km of river into a 90-km drainage canal. This effectively eliminated seasonal inundation of the floodplain, causing a conversion from wetland to upland communities A restoration plan began in 1999 with the goals of reestablishing ecological integrity of the river-floodplain system. The project involves dechannelizing major sections of the river, directing water into reconstructed channels, removing water control structures, and changing flow regimes to restore seasonal flooding to the floodplain. Since the completion of the first phase of restoration, a number of improvements in vegetation and wildlife communities have been documented as the conversion from uplands back to wetlands has begun to take place. Breaching levees to reconnect streams to their floodplains can be an effective form of restoration as well. On the Cosumnes River in central California, for example, the return of seasonal flooding to the floodplain as a result of levee breaching was found to result in the reestablishment of primarily native riparian plant communities.

Stream channels will often recover from channelization without human intervention, provided that humans do not continue to maintain or modify the channel. Gradually, channel beds and stream banks will begin to accumulate sediment, meanders will form, and woody vegetation will take hold, stabilizing the banks. However, this process may take decades: a study found stream channel regeneration took approximately 65 years in channelized streams in West Tennessee. More active methods of restoration may speed the process along.

Restoration of Riparian Vegetation

The revegetation of degraded riparian zones is a common practice in riparian restoration. Revegetation can be accomplished through active or passive means, or a combination of the two.

Active Vegetation Restoration

A lack of naturally-available propagules can be a major limiting factor in restoration success. Therefore, actively planting native vegetation is often crucial for the successful establishment of riparian species. Common methods for actively restoring vegetation include broadcast sowing seed and directly planting seeds, plugs, or seedlings. Reestablishing clonal species such as willows can often be accomplished by simply putting cuttings directly into the ground. To increase survival rates, young plants may need to be protected from herbivory with fencing or some form of exclosure.

Reference sites are often used to determine appropriate species to plant and may be used as sources for seeds or cuttings. Reference communities serve as models for what restoration sites should ideally look like after restoration is complete. Concerns about using reference sites have been raised however, as conditions at the restored and reference sites may not be similar enough to support the same species. Also, restored riparian zones may be able to support a variety of possible species combinations, therefore the Society for Ecological Restoration recommends using multiple reference sites to formulate restoration goals.

A practical question in active vegetation restoration is whether certain plants facilitate the recruitment and persistence of other plants (as predicted by theories of succession), or whether initial community composition determines long-term community composition (priority effects). If the former applies, it may be more effective to plant facilitative species first, and wait to plant dependent species as conditions become appropriate (e.g., when enough shade is provided by overstory species). If the latter applies, it is probably best to plant all desired species at the outset.

As a critical component of restoring native riparian communities, restoration practitioners often have to remove invasive species and prevent them from reestablishing. This can be accomplished through herbicide application, mechanical removal, etc. When restoration is to be done on long stretches of rivers and streams, it is often useful to begin the project upstream and work downstream so that propagules from exotic species upstream will not hamper restoration attempts. Ensuring the establishment of native species is considered vital in preventing future colonizations of exotic plants.

Passive Vegetation Restoration

Active planting of riparian vegetation may be the fastest way to reestablish riparian ecosystems, but methods may be prohibitively resource-intensive. Riparian vegetation may come back on its own if human-induced disturbances are stopped and/or hydrologic processes are restored. For example, many studies show that preventing cattle grazing in riparian zones through exclusion fencing can allow riparian vegetation to rapidly increase in robustness and cover, and also shift to a more natural community composition. By simply restoring hydrologic processes such as periodic flooding that favor riparian vegetation, native communities may regenerate on their own (e.g., the Cosumnes River floodplain). The successful recruitment of native species will depend on whether local or upstream seed sources can successfully disperse propagules to the restoration site, or whether a native seed bank is present. One potential hindrance to passive vegetation restoration is that exotic species may preferentially colonize the riparian zone. Active weeding may improve the chances that the desired native plant community will reestablish.

Restoring Animal Life

Restoration often focuses on reestablishing plant communities, probably because plants form the foundation for other organisms within the community. Restoration of faunal communities often follows the 'Field of Dreams' hypothesis: "if you build it, they will come". Many animal species have been found to naturally recolonize areas where habitat has been restored. For example, abundances of several bird species showed marked increases after riparian vegetation had been reestablished in a riparian corridor in Iowa. Some riparian restoration efforts may be aimed at conserving particular animal species of concern, such as the Valley elderberry longhorn beetle in central California, which is dependent on a riparian tree species (blue elderberry, *Sambucus mexicana*) as its sole host plant. When restoration efforts target key species, consideration for individual species' needs (e.g., minimum width or extent of riparian vegetation) are important for ensuring restoration success.

Ecosystem Perspectives

Restoration failures may occur when appropriate ecosystem conditions are not reestablished, such as soil characteristics (e.g., salinity, pH, beneficial soil biota, etc.), surface water and groundwater levels, and flow regimes. Therefore, successful restoration may be dependent on taking a number of both biotic and abiotic factors into account. For example, restoration of soil biota, including symbiotic myccorhizae, invertebrates, and microorganisms may improve nutrient cycling dynamics. Restoration of physical processes may be a prerequisite to the reestablishment of healthy riparian communities. Ultimately, a combination of approaches taking into account causes for degradation and targeting both hydrology and the reestablishment of vegetation and other life forms may be most effective in riparian zone restoration.

8

Stream Restoration

Stream restoration or river restoration, sometimes called river reclamation in the UK, describes a set of activities that help improve the environmental health of a river or stream. Improved health may be indicated by expanded habitat for diverse species (e.g. fish, aquatic insects, other wildlife) and reduced stream bank erosion. Enhancements may also include improved water quality (i.e. reduction of pollutant levels and increased dissolved oxygen levels) and achieving a self-sustaining, functional flow regime in the stream system that does not require periodic human intervention, such as dredging or construction of flood control structures. Stream restoration projects can also yield increased property values in adjacent areas.

Stream restoration differs from:

- river engineering, a term which typically refers to alteration of a water body for a non-environmental benefit such as navigation, flood control or water supply diversion;
- waterway restoration, a term used in the United Kingdom describing alterations to a canal or river to improve navigability and related recreational amenities.

Restoration activities may range from a simple removal of a disturbance which inhibits natural stream function (e.g. repairing a damaged culvert), to stabilization of stream banks, to more active intervention such as installation of stormwater management facilities, such as riparian zone restoration and constructed wetlands.

IN-STREAM TECHNIQUES

Channel Modification

Modifications to a stream channel may be appropriate to address degradation. Channel modifications may yield improved habitat for wildlife and plants in a stream corridor, but can result in flooding, excessive erosion or other damage if not carefully planned. Design of modifications involves a careful analysis of a complex fluvial processes. Alterations may include channel shape (in terms of sinuosity and meander characteristics), cross-section and channel profile (slope along the channel bed). Alterations affect the dissipation of energy through the channel, which has an impact on stream velocity and turbulence, sediment volume and size distribution, scour, and water surface elevations, among other characteristics.

Cross-vanes and Related Structures

A cross-vane is a 'U'-shaped structure of boulders or logs, built across the channel to reduce velocity and energy near the stream banks. It reduces bank erosion, maintains channel capacity and provides other benefits such as improved habitat for aquatic species. Similar structures used to dissipate stream energy include the W-Weir and J-Hook Vane.

Engineered Log Jams

An emerging stream restoration technique is the installation of *engineered log jams.* Reintroduction of large woody debris into a stream is a fairly recent method that is being experimented with in streams such as Thornton Creek, in Seattle, WA. Because of channelization and removal of woody debris, many streams now lack the hydraulic complexity that is necessary to maintain bank stabilization and a healthy plant/animal habitat. Engineered log jams are individually designed to meet the needs of specific restoration projects, but there are overarching design elements. One element is to anchor logs along the stream bank in order to create a physical blockade against erosion. A second element of engineered log jams is to improve fish habitat. Log jams add diversity to the water flow by creating ripples, pools, and temperature variations. This is vital to fish because it provides the right circumstances to spawn, rest, feed, hunt, and hide.

Off-line Techniques

As part of a stream restoration project, stormwater management facilities may be installed in the immediate corridor or in upland areas. These facilities, which reduce the velocity and/or the volume of stormwater entering the stream channel, can also improve water quality, and include:

- Bioretention systems and rain gardens

- Constructed wetlands
- Infiltration basins
- Retention basins.

Monitoring of Restoration Projects

Sponsors of restoration projects may conduct monitoring of stream conditions after construction, to evaluate effectiveness. In some projects it may take considerable time before there is evidence of desired biological activity, such as fish spawning, therefore monitoring efforts may be conducted for several years after a restoration project has completed.

Daylighting (Streams)

In urban design and urban planning, daylighting is the redirection of a stream into an above-ground channel. Typically, the goal is to restore a stream of water to a more natural state. Daylighting is intended to improve the riparian environment for a stream which had been previously diverted into a culvert, pipe, or a drainage system.

The term also refers to the public process toward such projects. A general consensus has developed that protecting and restoring natural creeks' functions is achievable over time in an urban environment while recognizing the importance of property rights.

Natural Drainage Systems (NDS) are stormwater management features that include infiltration and slowing of stormwater flow, filtering and bioremediation of pollutants by soils and plants, reducing impervious surfaces, using porous paving, increasing vegetation, and improving related pedestrian amenities. Natural features—open, vegetated swales, stormwater cascades, and small wetland ponds—mimic the functions of nature lost to urbanization. At the heart are plants, trees, and the deep, healthy soils that support them. All three combine to form a 'living infrastructure' that, unlike pipes and vaults, increase in functional value over time.

One implementation is an S.E.A. (Street Edge Alternatives) street demonstration project in the Pipers Creek watershed, (see Pipers Creek, below). S.E.A. use innovative drainage design and landscaping instead of traditional curbs and gutters, pipes and vaults, more like the natural landscape prior to development than traditional piped systems. The final constructed design reduced imperviousness, or resistance, by more than 18 per cent, surface detention was provided with bioswales, (landscape elements intended to remove silt and pollution from surface runoff water), and 100 evergreen trees and 1100 shrubs were planted, according to FEMA . The seemingly-modest change can have dramatic effect. Two years of monitoring

(c. 2003) show that the SEA Street has reduced the total volume of stormwater leaving the street by 98 per cent for a 2-year storm event (a not-uncommon severe high precipitation). That reduction in abruptly high runoff flow can significantly moderate the rush of flow volume and turbidity that is so detrimental to water quality and habitat restoration for species survival—species like the iconic salmon. Unfortunately, the engineering alternatives have a relatively expensive initial price, since they are usually replacing existing structures, albeit life-limited ones. Further, conventional systems generally do not consider full cost accounting. The NDS alternatives can also provide returns on investment with amelioration of urban environments. Restoring stream habitat alone is clearly not enough to sustain the few determined but diminishing species of salmon.

The SEA Street breaks most of the conventions of 150 years of standard American street design. Narrow, curved streets, open drainage swales, and an abundance of diverse plants and trees welcome pedestrians as well as diverse species. Adjacent residents maintain city infrastructure in the form of street 'gardens' in front of their homes, visually integrating the neighborhood along the street. The NDS (Natural Drainage Systems) united the community visually, environmentally, and socially. The 110th Cascades SEA (2002-2003) are a creek-like cascade of stair-stepped natural, seasonal pools that intercept, infiltrate, slow and filter over 21 acres (85,000 m^2) of stormwater draining through the project.

Example Projects

Viable, daylighted streams can exist only in intimate connection with restoration and stewardship by the neighbourhoods of their watersheds in a long run, since the good health of an urban stream could not long survive carelessness or neglect. With impervious surfaces having replaced most of the natural ground cover in urban environments, both the sheer volume and flow rate from unmoderated stormwater and the carrying of non-point pollution converge through urban creeks. Effective solutions include the entire urban watershed, far beyond the riparian channel itself.

UNITED STATES

California

- Codornices Creek and Strawberry Creek, Berkeley, California
- Islais Creek, San Francisco, California

New York (State)

Yonkers, New York, the fourth largest city in the state, is moving forward with the daylighting of the Saw Mill River. Now running under the Yonkers downtown, daylighting is the cornerstone of a $3.1 billion redevelopment programme. The state government will be contributing $34 million just to the daylighting component.

Pipers Creek

Pipers Creek in the central to north Greenwood area is joined by Venema and Mohlendorph Creeks in Carkeek Park on Puget Sound. Pipers is one of the four largest streams in urban Seattle, together with Longfellow, Taylor, and Thornton creeks, (in boldface in these Urban Seattle, Metro Seattle sections). Pipers Creek drains a 1,835-acre (7 km^2) watershed into Puget Sound, from a residential upper plateau that is most of the watershed, through the steep ravines of the 216 acres (0.9 km^2) of Carkeek Park. The headwaters begin in the north Greenwood neighbourhood. Outside the park, the creek can be seen at N 90th Street between Greenwood and Palatine avenues N.

Years of hard work by neighbors and volunteers have brought salmon back to Pipers Creek, Venema, and Mohlendorph creeks in the mid 2000s after there were none for 50 years. The latter is named for the late Ted Mohlendorph, a biologist who spearheaded efforts to restore the watershed as salmon habitat.

Though still plagued by problems endemic to urban streams, Piper's Creek today is a scintillating example of the possible. Though augmented by hatchery fish, anywhere from 200 to 600 chum salmon return each November, along with a few coho in the fall and fewer occasional winter steelhead. Inspirationally, several hundred small resident cutthroat trout live in the watershed, believed to be native fish that survived decades of urban assault. Popularity of the Carkeek Park beach sees it being loved to death. An environmental learning centre and programmes are part of comprehensive restoration. More than four miles (6 km) of trail are maintained by neighbourhood volunteers who put in 4,000 hours of work in 2003, for example. The creek waters are pretty in their impressively restored settings, but the watershed is the surrounding neighbourhoods and streets, laced with petrochemicals, pesticides, fertilizers, wandering pets, and such. Along with steeply high volume during storm runoff and resulting turbidity, water quality is the remaining big issue in restoring salmon.

The north fork of Pipers Creek is the site for the 110th Cascades, an S.E.A. (Street Edge Alternatives) street demonstration project . The 110th Cascades are a creek-like cascade of stair-stepped natural, seasonal pools that intercept, infiltrate, slow and filter over 21 acres (85,000 m^2) of stormwater draining through the project. The cascades are a part of an

NDS (Natural Drainage Systems) project; together these united the community visually, environmentally, and socially, toward integrating the neighbourhood as a community.

Pipers Creek was renamed Piper's Creek by 19th century settlers; the apostrophe is becoming less common today.

Taylor Creek

- Taylor Creek flows from Deadhorse Canyon (west of Rainier Avenue S at 68th Avenue S and northwest of Skyway Park), through Lakeridge Park to Lake Washington. With volunteer effort and some city matching grants, restoration has been underway since 1971. Volunteers have planted thousands of indigenous trees and plants, removed tons of garbage, removed invasive plants, and had city help removing fish-blocking culverts and improving trails. A deer has been spotted and sightings of raccoons, opossum and birds are common. By about 2050, the area will be looking like a young version of what it looked like before being disrupted. Taylor is one of the four largest streams in urban Seattle.
- Skyway and Bryn Mawr in unincorporated King County
- Rainier View-Lakeridge
- Thornton Creek, Seattle and Shoreline
- Matthews Beach, where the creek flows into Lake Washington
- Meadowbrook
- Northgate
- Adjacent, formerly suburban city of Shoreline; southeastern neighbourhoods.

Other Areas

- Neighbourhoods of the Pipers Creek watershed
- Greenwood
- South Broadview

Northeast Blue Ridge

Fauntleroy Creek in the Fauntleroy neighbourhood of West Seattle flows about a mile (1.6 km) from as far east as 38th Avenue SW in the modest 33 acre (130,000 m^2) Fauntleroy Park at SW Barton Street, through a fish ladder at its outlet near the Fauntleroy ferry terminal (the creek drops a moderately steep 300 ft (91 m) in that one mile). Coho salmon and cutthroat trout returned as soon as barriers were removed, after concerted effort and pressure by citizen groups of activist neighbors (1989-1998). A further culvert blocks fish passage to Kilbourne Park and so on up to the headwaters in Fauntleroy Park. The 98 acre (400,000 m^2) watershed is about two-thirds residential development, from 1900s summer colony to post-World War II urban, with the rest natural space, primarily Fauntleroy Park.

Longfellow Creek is one of the four largest in urban Seattle. It flows north from Roxhill Park for several miles along the valley of the Delridge neighbourhood of West Seattle, turning east to reach the Duwamish Waterway via a 3,300 ft (1000 m) pipe beneath the Bethlehem Steel plant (now Nucor). Salmon returned without intervention as soon as toxic input was ended and barriers were removed, after having been extinguished for 60 years. Construction of a fish ladder at the north end of the West Seattle Golf Course will allow spawning salmon up along the fairways. Farther upstream the city has been enlarging and building more storm-detention ponds, recreation areas, and an outdoor-education centre at Camp Long. An area of 3 acres (12,000 m^2) of open upland, wetland and wooded space just east of Chief Sealth High School in Westwood is the first daylight of Longfellow Creek. It has been the location of some plant and tree restoration since 1997. After more than a decade of preparation by hundreds of neighbourhood volunteers, a restoration and 4.2 mile (6.7 km) legacy trail was completed in 2004. Further improvement by removal of invasive vegetation is ongoing as native species retake hold. Blue heron and coyote can be seen. The creek first emerges at the 10,000-year-old Roxhill Bog, south of the Westwood Village shopping centre.

Madrona Creek, Seattle Madrona Citizens of neighbourhoods initiated a daylighting project in 2001, encompassing from above 38th Avenue into Lake Washington. Daylighting will return the creek to a new bed and replace the sloping lawn between Lake Washington Boulevard and Lake Washington with native plantings, and with the mouth of the creek at a restored 48,000 sq ft (4,500 m^2) wetland cove on the lake. New culverts under 38th, the boulevard, and under a permeable pedestrian path will allow fish passage. Native plantings will restore about 1.5 acres (6,100 m^2), with plantings three to four feet in height at three key view corridors. Planning continued through 2004, followed by design (2205) and construction (2006). The completion celebration is scheduled for spring, 2007. The $450,000 cost is funded by community-initiated grants and private donations.

Citizen stewards of the creek and woods are represented by the Friends of Madrona Woods (1996). The urban forest encompasses about 9 acres

(36,000 m^2), largely in a couple ravines. The park area was built 1891-1893, officially no longer maintained since the 1930s with the demise of streetcars and pedestrian lifestyles. Persistent efforts began (1995) with informal removal of ivy smothering trees, then invasive species like holly, laurel and blackberries, and realization that effective restoration would require comprehensive stewardship.

With a 'Small and Simple' Department of Neighborhoods grant, the neighborhood started a formal effort. Neighbourhood groups, planning with naturalists and landscape architects brought an effective early step rebuilding trails, promoting access and building constituency. Further priorities were protection for habitat, restoration of stream beds, rehabilitation as a natural area using native plants, and using the Madrona Woods as a setting for environmental education programmes at local schools. A hired landscape architect became a team member, experimental plots were set up to test different methods for revegetating with native plants. (Plants adapt to microclimates; experimentation is required to jumpstart the otherwise very long natural processes.)

Friends of Madrona Woods earned a much larger Department of Neighbourhoods matching grant in 2000, funding the creation of a Master Action Plan, and major trail restoration work. The community match for the grant was nearly 2500 hours of volunteer labour by community members and school children from St. Therese and Epiphany schools. After many decades of urban use without formal maintenance, substantial trail engineering was required. EarthCorps was contracted to do the actual construction, which included 86 steps, two landings and a bridge.

Earth corps is a local programme to foster environmental responsibility and global cooperation among young people around the world. Two thirds the corps members come from King County and the U.S., one third are recruited from partner organizations around the world. They combine the best elements of the 1930's Civilian Conservation Corps with those of the Peace Corps. Participants learn resource management skills by completing restoration projects throughout King County. This work has included restoring stream banks and salmon habitat, reclaiming logging roads, and building trails. They completed 30,000 hours of work in 1999 alone.

In the process of clearing, volunteers found substantial erosion in the wetland hillside, leading to a grant from a Parks Department fund to stabilize it with a water cascade of natural materials. Neighbours did a little trail-building of their own with Volunteers for Outdoor Washington and an all-day trail building workshop. Local school children learn about restoration by working with Madrona Woods volunteers throughout the year. Work parties continue monthly through much of the year.

- Mapes Creek, accessible at Kubota Garden, flows from a ridge to Lake Washington.
- Rainier Beach
- Puget Creek flows into the Duwamish River from Puget Park on SW Dawson Street near 19th Avenue SW, near the Delridge neighbourhood of West Seattle.
- East Delridge
- Industrial District
- Ravenna Creek, Seattle
- Ravenna and Ravenna-Bryant
- The remaining watershed includes Roosevelt and parts of the University District.
- The creek flows past the Union Bay Natural Area into Lake Washington.
- Schmitz Creek in the Alki neighborhood of West Seattle flows to the sound from Schmitz Park, SW 55th Avenue at SW Admiral Way. Apart from the paved entrance and a parking lot at the northwest corner, the park has remained essentially unchanged since its 53 acres (210,000 m^2) were protected 1908-1912 from complete logging. Fragmentary old growth forest remains. Daylighting and drainage rebuilding to handle seasonal and storm flow was done 2001-2003.
- Alki Friends of Schmittz Park are neighborhood citizen stewards of the park (and creek).

In Other Countries

Seoul provides one example of a major world city rediscovering its river. Mayor Lee Myung Bak, formerly a construction magnate with the Hyundai chaebol involved in burying the river during the 1960s boom, ran for office promising to daylight it, and achieved in 2005 a 5.8 km (3.6 mi) greenspace in a city without very many parks or playgrounds. Although this is not a true daylighting project—the original seasonal and polluted stream runs below the stunningly engineered and landscaped new, artificial waterway—the Cheonggyecheon, 'pristine stream', is hugely popular, alleviating fears that opening the river would cause nearby businesses to lose customers.

9

Bioremediation

Bioremediation is the use of microorganismal metabolism to remove pollutants. Technologies can be generally classified as *in situ* or *ex situ*. *In situ* bioremediation involves treating the contaminated material at the site, while *ex situ* involves the removal of the contaminated material to be treated elsewhere. Some examples of bioremediation technologies are bioventing, landfarming, bioreactor, composting, bioaugmentation, rhizofiltration, and biostimulation.

Bioremediation can occur on its own (natural attenuation or intrinsic bioremediation) or can be spurred on via the addition of fertilizers to increase the bioavailability within the medium (biostimulation). Recent advancements have also proven successful via the addition of matched microbe strains to the medium to enhance the resident microbe population's ability to break down contaminants. Microorganisms used to perform the function of bioremediation are known as bioremediators.

Not all contaminants, however, are easily treated by bioremediation using microorganisms. For example, heavy metals such as cadmium and lead are not readily absorbed or captured by organisms. The assimilation of metals such as mercury into the food chain may worsen matters. Phytoremediation is useful in these circumstances because natural plants or transgenic plants are able to bioaccumulate these toxins in their above-ground parts, which are then harvested for removal. The heavy metals in the harvested biomass may be further concentrated by incineration or even recycled for industrial use.

The elimination of a wide range of pollutants and wastes from the environment requires increasing our understanding of the relative importance of different pathways and regulatory networks to carbon flux in particular environments and for particular compounds, and they will certainly accelerate the development of bioremediation technologies and biotransformation processes.

The use of genetic engineering to create organisms specifically designed for bioremediation has great potential. The bacterium *Deinococcus radiodurans* (the most radioresistant organism known) has been modified to consume and digest toluene and ionic mercury from highly radioactive nuclear waste.

Most commonly, the process is misunderstood. The microbes are ever-present in any given context and are generally referred to as 'normal microbial flora'. During bioremediation (biodegradation) processes, fertilizer/ nutrient supplementation is introduced to the environments in efforts to maximize growth and production potential. Common misbelief is that microbes are transported and dispersed into an unadulterated environment.

Mycoremediation

Mycoremediation is a form of bioremediation in which fungi are used to decontaminate the area. The term *mycoremediation* refers specifically to the use of fungal mycelia in bioremediation.

One of the primary roles of fungi in the ecosystem is decomposition, which is performed by the mycelium. The mycelium secretes extracellular enzymes and acids that break down lignin and cellulose, the two main building blocks of plant fiber. These are organic compounds composed of long chains of carbon and hydrogen, structurally similar to many organic pollutants. The key to mycoremediation is determining the right fungal species to target a specific pollutant. Certain strains have been reported to successfully degrade the nerve gases VX and sarin.

In one conducted experiment, a plot of soil contaminated with diesel oil was inoculated with mycelia of oyster mushrooms; traditional bioremediation techniques (bacteria) were used on control plots. After four weeks, more than 95 per cent of many of the PAH (polycyclic aromatic hydrocarbons) had been reduced to non-toxic components in the mycelial-inoculated plots. It appears that the natural microbial community participates with the fungi to break down contaminants, eventually into carbon dioxide and water. Wood-degrading fungi are particularly effective in breaking down aromatic pollutants (toxic components of petroleum), as well as chlorinated compounds.

Mycofiltration is a similar process, using fungal mycelia to filter toxic waste and microorganisms from water in soil.

Advantages

There are a number of cost/efficiency advantages to bioremediation, which can be employed in areas that are inaccessible without excavation. For example, hydrocarbon spills (specifically, petrol spills) or certain chlorinated solvents may contaminate groundwater, and introducing the appropriate electron acceptor or electron donor amendment, as appropriate, may significantly reduce contaminant concentrations after a long time allowing for acclimation. This is typically much less expensive than excavation followed by disposal elsewhere, incineration or other *ex situ* treatment strategies, and reduces or eliminates the need for 'pump and treat', a practice common at sites where hydrocarbons have contaminated clean groundwater.

Monitoring Bioremediation

The process of bioremediation can be monitored indirectly by measuring the *Oxidation Reduction Potential* or redox in soil and groundwater, together with pH, temperature, oxygen content, electron acceptor/donor concentrations, and concentration of breakdown products (e.g. carbon dioxide). This table shows the (decreasing) biological breakdown rate as function of the redox potential.

This, by itself and at a single site, gives little information about the process of remediation.

It is necessary to sample enough points on and around the contaminated site to be able to determine contours of equal redox potential. Contouring is usually done using specialised software, e.g. using Kriging interpolation.

If all the measurements of redox potential show that electron acceptors have been used up, it is in effect an indicator for total microbial activity. Chemical analysis is also required to determine when the levels of contaminants and their breakdown products have been reduced to below regulatory limits.

Biotransformation

Biotransformation is the chemical modification (or modifications) made by an organism on a chemical compound. If this modification ends in mineral compounds like CO_2, NH_4^+ or H_2O, the biotransformation is called mineralisation. Biotransformation means chemical alteration of chemicals such as (but not limited to) nutrients, amino acids, toxins, or drugs in the body. It is also needed to render nonpolar compounds polar so that they are not reabsorbed in renal tubules and are excreted.

Biotransformation of various pollutants is a sustainable way to clean up contaminated environments. These bioremediation and biotransformation methods harness the naturally occurring, microbial catabolic diversity to degrade, transform or accumulate a huge range of compounds including hydrocarbons (e.g. oil), polychlorinated biphenyls (PCBs), polyaromatic hydrocarbons (PAHs), pharmaceutical substances, radionuclides and metals. Major methodological breakthroughs in recent years have enabled detailed genomic, metagenomic, proteomic, bioinformatic and other high-throughput analyses of environmentally relevant microorganisms providing unprecedented insights into biotransformation and biodegradative pathways and the ability of organisms to adapt to changing environmental conditions.

Biological processes play a major role in the removal of contaminants and pollutants from the environment. Some microorganisms possess an astonishing catabolic versatility to degrade or transform such compounds. New methodological breakthroughs in sequencing, genomics, proteomics, bioinformatics and imaging are producing vast amounts of information. In the field of Environmental Microbiology, genome-based global studies open a new era providing unprecedented *in silico* views of metabolic and regulatory networks, as well as clues to the evolution of biochemical pathways relevant to biotransformation and to the molecular adaptation strategies to changing environmental conditions. Functional genomic and metagenomic approaches are increasing our understanding of the relative importance of different pathways and regulatory networks to carbon flux in particular environments and for particular compounds and they are accelerating the development of bioremediation technologies and biotransformation processes. Also there is other approach of biotransformation called enzymatic biotransformation.

Oil Biodegradation

Petroleum oil is toxic for most life forms and episodic and chronic pollution of the environment by oil causes major ecological perturbations. Marine environments are especially vulnerable since oil spills of coastal regions and the open sea are poorly containable and mitigation is difficult. In addition to pollution through human activities, millions of tons of petroleum enter the marine environment every year from natural seepages. Despite its toxicity, a considerable fraction of petroleum oil entering marine systems is eliminated by the hydrocarbon-degrading activities of microbial communities, in particular by a remarkable recently discovered group of specialists, the so-called hydrocarbonoclastic bacteria (HCB). *Alcanivorax borkumensis*, a paradigm of HCB and probably the most important global oil degrader, was the first to be subjected to a functional genomic analysis. This analysis has yielded important new insights into its capacity for:

(*i*) n-alkane degradation including metabolism, biosurfactant production and biofilm formation;

(*ii*) scavenging of nutrients and cofactors in the oligotrophic marine environment, as well as;

(*iii*) coping with various habitat-specific stresses.

The understanding thereby gained constitutes a significant advance in efforts towards the design of new knowledge-based strategies for the mitigation of ecological damage caused by oil pollution of marine habitats. HCB also have potential biotechnological applications in the areas of bioplastics and biocatalysis.

Metabolic Engineering and Biocatalytic Applications

The study of the fate of persistent organic chemicals in the environment has revealed a large reservoir of enzymatic reactions with a large potential in preparative organic synthesis, which has already been exploited for a number of oxygenases on pilot and even on industrial scale. Novel catalysts can be obtained from metagenomic libraries and DNA sequence based approaches. Our increasing capabilities in adapting the catalysts to specific reactions and process requirements by rational and random mutagenesis broadens the scope for application in the fine chemical industry, but also in the field of biodegradation. In many cases, these catalysts need to be exploited in whole cell bioconversions or in fermentations, calling for system-wide approaches to understanding strain physiology and metabolism and rational approaches to the engineering of whole cells as they are increasingly put forward in the area of systems biotechnology and synthetic biology.

Yellow Fungus, A Mushroom that Assists in Organic Decay

Drip Irrigation System in New Mexico

A Conifer Forest in the Swiss Alps (National Park)

The Douglas Squirrel (*Tamiasciurus douglasii*)
is an Example of Wildlife

Image of the Entire Surface Water Flow of the Alapaha River near Jennings, Florida going into a Sink-hole Leading to the Floridan Aquifer Groundwater

Recently Constructred Wetland Regeneration in Australia on a site Previously used for Agriculture

Parts of the San Francisco
Bay were Reclaimed from Wetlands for Urban Use

Erosion Barriers on Disturbed Slope, Marin County, California

Forest on San Juan Island

Prairie in Effigy Mounds National Monument, Iowa, United States

Prairie Grasses

Robinson Creek Restoration Project (2005) included Re-shaping of Stream Bank Slopes, Addition of Live Willow and Large Rock Baffles, Removal of Invasive Species and Revegetation with Indigenous Species

Crissy Field After Restoration

Tropical Tree Nursery at Planeta Verde Reforestación S.A.'s Plantation in Vichada, Colombia

Rainforests Often have a Great Deal of Biodiversity with Many Plant and Animal Species. This is the Gambia River in Senegal's Niokolo-Koba National Park

Two Giant Sequoias, Sequoia National Park. Note the large fire scar at the base of the right-hand tree; Fires do not kill the trees but do remove competing thin-barked species and aid Giant Sequoia Regeneration

10

Groundwater Remediation

Groundwater remediation is the process that is used to remove pollution from groundwater. Groundwater is water present below the ground surface that saturates the pore space in the subsurface. At least one half of the population of the United States depends upon groundwater as a source of drinking water. Groundwater is also used by farmers to irrigate crops and by industries to produce everyday goods. Most groundwater is clean, but groundwater can become polluted, or contaminated as a result of human activities or as a result of natural conditions. The many and diverse activities of man produce innumerable waste materials and by-products; before the 1980s, the regulation of these wastes was less stringent and waste materials were often disposed of or stored on land surfaces where they percolated into the underlying soil and eventually were carried downward, contaminating the underlying groundwater and therefore jeopardizing the natural quality of it. As a result, contaminated groundwater became unsuitable for use. Current practices can still impact groundwater, such as the over application of fertilizer or pesticides, spills from industrial operations, infiltration from urban runoff, and leaking from landfills. Using contaminated groundwater causes hazards to public health through poisoning or the spread of disease, and the practice of groundwater remediation has been developed to address these issues. Contaminants found in groundwater cover a broad range of physical, inorganic chemical, organic chemical, bacteriological, and radioactive parameters. Pollutants and contaminants can be removed from groundwater by applying various techniques thereby making it safe for use.

Groundwater remediation techniques span biological, chemical, and physical treatment technologies. Most ground water treatment techniques utilize a combination of technologies. Some of the biological treatment techniques include bioaugmentation, bioventing, biosparging, bioslurping, and phytoremediation. Some chemical treatment techniques include ozone and oxygen gas injection, chemical precipitation, membrane separation, ion exchange, carbon absorption, aqueous chemical oxidation, and surfactant enhanced recovery. Physical treatment techniques include, but not limited to, pump and treat, air sparging, and dual phase extraction.

BIOLOGICAL TREATMENT TECHNOLOGIES

Bioaugmentation

If a treatability study shows no degradation (or an extended lab period before significant degradation is achieved) in contamination contained in the groundwater, then inoculation with strains known to be capable of degrading the contaminants may be helpful. This process increases the reactive enzyme concentration within the bioremediation system and subsequently may increase contaminant degradation rates over the non-augmented rates, at least initially after inoculation.

Bioventing

Bioventing is an *in situ* remediation technology that uses microorganisms to biodegrade organic constituents adsorbed in the groundwater. Bioventing enhances the activity of indigenous bacteria and simulates the natural *in situ* biodegradation of hydrocarbons by inducing air or oxygen flow into the unsaturated zone and, if necessary, by adding nutrients. During bioventing, oxygen may be supplied through direct air injection into residual contamination in soil. Bioventing primarily assists in the degradation of adsorbed fuel residuals, but also assists in the degradation of volatile organic compounds (VOCs) as vapours move slowly through biologically active soil.

Biosparging

Biosparging is an *in situ* remediation technology that uses indigenous microorganisms to biodegrade organic constituents in the saturated zone. In biosparging, air (or oxygen) and nutrients (if needed) are injected into the saturated zone to increase the biological activity of the indigenous microorganisms. Biosparging can be used to reduce concentrations of petroleum constituents that are dissolved in groundwater, adsorbed to soil below the water table, and within the capillary fringe.

Bioslurping

Bioslurping combines elements of bioventing and vacuum-enhanced pumping of free-product that isnlighter than water (light non-aqueous phase liquid or LNAPL) to recover free-product from the groundwater and soil, and to bioremediate soils. The bioslurper system uses a 'slurp' tube that extends into the free-product layer. Much like a straw in a glass draws liquid, the pump draws liquid (including free-product) and soil gas up the tube in the same process stream. Pumping lifts LNAPLs, such as oil, off the top of the water table and from the capillary fringe (i.e., an area just above the saturated zone, where water is held in place by capillary forces). The LNAPL is brought to the surface, where it is separated from water and air. The biological processes in the term 'bioslurping' refer to aerobic biological degradation of the hydrocarbons when air is introduced into the unsaturated zone.

Phytoremediation

In the phytoremediation process certain plants and trees are planted, whose roots absorb contaminants from ground water over time, and are harvested and destroyed. This process can be carried out in areas where the roots can tap the groundwater. Few examples of plants that are used in this process are Chinese Ladder fern Pteris vittata, also known as the brake fern, is a highly efficient accumulator of arsenic. Genetically altered cottonwood trees are good absorbers of mercury and transgenic Indian mustard plants soak up selenium well.

CHEMICAL TREATMENT TECHNOLOGIES

Chemical Precipitation

Chemical precipitation is commonly used in wastewater treatment to remove hardness and heavy metals. In general, the process involves addition of agent to an aqueous waste stream in a stirred reaction vessel, either batchwise or with steady flow. Most metals can be converted to insoluble compounds by chemical reactions between the agent and the dissolved metal ions. The insoluble compounds (precipitates) are removed by settling and/ or filtering.

Ion Exchange

Ion exchange for ground water remediation is virtually always carried out by passing the water downward under pressure through a fixed bed of granular medium (either cation exchange media and anion exchange media) or spherical beads. Cations are displaced by certain cations from the solutions and ions are displaced by certain anions from the solution. Ion exchange media most often used for remediation are zeolites (both natural and synthetic) and synthetic resins.

Carbon Absorption

The most common activated carbon used for remediation is derived from bituminous coal. Activated carbon absorbs volatile organic compounds from ground water by chemically binding them to the carbon atoms.

Chemical Oxidation

In this process chemical oxidants are delivered in the subsurface to destroy (converted to water and carbon dioxide or to nontoxic substances) the organics molecules. The oxidants are introduced as either liquids or gasses. Oxidants include air or oxygen, ozone, and certain liquid chemicals such as hydrogen peroxide, permanganate and persulfate. Ozone and oxygen gas can be generated on site from air and electricity and directly injected into soil and groundwater contamination. The process has the potential to oxidize and/or enhance naturally occurring aerobic degradation. Chemical oxidation hasnpeoven to be an effective techique for dense non-aqueous phase liquid or DNAPL when it is present.

Surfactant Enhanced Recovery

Surfactant enhanced recovery increases the mobility and solubility of the contaminants absorbed to the saturated soil matrix or present as dense non-aqueous phase liquid. Surfactant-enhanced recovery injects surfactants (surface-active agents that are primary ingredient in soap and detergent) into contaminated groundwater. A typical system uses an extraction pump to remove groundwater downstream from the injection point. The extracted groundwater is treated aboveground to separate the injected surfactants from the contaminants and groundwater. Once the surfactants have separated from the groundwater they are re-used. The surfactants used are non-toxic, food-grade, and biodegradable. Surfactant enhanced recovery is used most often when the groundwater is contaminated by dense non-aqueous phase liquids (DNAPLs). These dense compounds, such as trichloroethylene (TCE), sink in groundwater because they have a higher density than water. They then act as a continuous source for contaminant plumes that can stretch for miles within an aquifer. These compounds may biodegrade very slowly. They are commonly found in the vicinity of the original spill or leak where capillary forces have trapped them.

PHYSICAL TREATMENT TECHNOLOGIES

Pump and Treat

Pump and treat is one of the most widely used ground water remediation technologies. In this process ground water is pumped to the surface and is coupled with either biological or chemical treatments to remove the impurities.

Air Sparging

Air sparging is the process of blowing air directly into the ground water. As the bubbles rise, the contaminants are removed from the groundwater by physical contact with the air (i.e., stripping) and are carried up into the unsaturated zone (i.e., soil). As the contaminants move into the soil, a soil vapour extraction system is usually used to remove vapours.

Dual Phase Extraction

Dual-phase extraction (DPE), also known as multi-phase extraction, is a technology that uses a high-vacuum system to remove both contaminated groundwater and soil vapour. In DPE systems a high-vacuum extraction well is installed with its screened section in the zone of contaminated soils and groundwater. Fluid/vapour extraction systems depress the water table and water flows faster to the extraction well. DPE removes contaminants from above and below the water table. As the water table around the well is lowered from pumping, unsaturated soil is exposed. This area, called the capillary fringe, is often highly contaminated, as it holds undissolved chemicals, chemicals that are lighter than water, and vapors that have escaped from the dissolved groundwater below. Contaminants in the newly exposed zone can be removed by vapour extraction. Once above ground, the extracted vapours and liquid-phase organics and groundwater are separated and treated. Use of dual-phase extraction with these technologies can shorten the cleanup time at a site, because the capillary fringe is often the most contaminated area.

Monitoring-Well Oil Skimming

Monitoring-wells are often drilled for the purpose of collecting groundwater samples for analysis. These wells, which are usually six inches or fewer in diametre, can also be used to remove hydrocarbons from the contaminant plume within a groundwater aquifer by using a belt style oil skimmer. Belt oil skimmers, which are simple in design, are commonly used to remove oil and other floating hydrocarbon contaminants from industrial water systems.

A monitoring-well oil skimmer remediates various oils, ranging from light fuel oils such as petrol, light diesel or kerosene to heavy products such as No. 6 oil, creosote and coal tar. It consists of a continuously moving belt that runs on a pulley system driven by an electric motor. The belt material has a strong affinity for hydrocarbon liquids and for shedding water. The belt, which can have a vertical drop of 100+ feet, is lowered into the monitoring well past the LNAPL/water interface. As the belt moves through this interface it picks up liquid hydrocarbon contaminant, which is removed and collected at ground level as the belt passes through a wiper mechanism.

To the extent that DNAPL hydrocarbons settle at the bottom of a monitoring well, and the lower pulley of the belt skimmer reaches them, these contaminants can also be removed by a monitoring-well oil skimmer.

Typically, belt skimmers remove very little water with the contaminant, so simple weir type separators can be used to collect any remaining hydrocarbon liquid, which often makes the water suitable for its return to the aquifer. Because the small electric motor uses little electricity, it can be powered from solar panels or a wind turbine, making the system self-sufficient and eliminating the cost of running electricity to a remote location.

Groundwater

Groundwater is water located beneath the ground surface in soil pore spaces and in the fractures of rock formations. A unit of rock or an unconsolidated deposit is called an aquifer when it can yield a usable quantity of water. The depth at which soil pore spaces or fractures and voids in rock become completely saturated with water is called the water table. Groundwater is recharged from, and eventually flows to, the surface naturally; natural discharge often occurs at springs and seeps, and can form oases or wetlands. Groundwater is also often withdrawn for agricultural, municipal and industrial use by constructing and operating extraction wells. The study of the distribution and movement of groundwater is hydrogeology, also called groundwater hydrology.

Typically, groundwater is thought of as liquid water flowing through shallow aquifers, but technically it can also include soil moisture, permafrost (frozen soil), immobile water in very low permeability bedrock, and deep geothermal or oil formation water. Groundwater is hypothesized to provide lubrication that can possibly influence the movement of faults. It is likely that much of the Earth's subsurface contains some water, which may be mixed with other fluids in some instances. Groundwater may not be confined only to the Earth. The formation of some of the landforms observed on Mars may have been influenced by groundwater. There is also evidence that liquid water may also exist in the subsurface of Jupiter's moon Europa.

Aquifers

An *aquifer* is a layer of porous substrate that contains and transmits groundwater. When water can flow directly between the surface and the saturated zone of an aquifer, the aquifer is unconfined. The deeper parts of unconfined aquifers are usually more saturated since gravity causes water to flow downward.

The upper level of this saturated layer of an unconfined aquifer is called the *water table* or *phreatic surface*. Below the water table, where generally all pore spaces are saturated with water is the phreatic zone.

Substrate with low porosity that permits limited transmission of groundwater is known as an *aquitard.* An *aquiclude* is a substrate with porosity that is so low it is virtually impermeable to groundwater.

A *confined aquifer* is an aquifer that is overlain by a relatively impermeable layer of rock or substrate such as an aquiclude or aquitard. If a confined aquifer follows a downward grade from its *recharge zone*, groundwater can become pressurized as it flows. This can create artesian wells that flow freely without the need of a pump and rise to a higher elevation than the static water table at the above, unconfined, aquifer.

The characteristics of aquifers vary with the geology and structure of the substrate and topography in which they occur. Generally, the more productive aquifers occur in sedimentary geologic formations. By comparison, weathered and fractured crystalline rocks yield smaller quantities of groundwater in many environments. Unconsolidated to poorly cemented alluvial materials that have accumulated as valley-filling sediments in major river valleys and geologically subsiding structural basins are included among the most productive sources of groundwater.

The high specific heat capacity of water and the insulating effect of soil and rock can mitigate the effects of climate and maintain groundwater at a relatively steady temperature. In some places where groundwater temperatures are maintained by this effect at about 50°F/10°C, groundwater can be used for controlling the temperature inside structures at the surface. For example, during hot weather relatively cool groundwater can be pumped through radiators in a home and then returned to the ground in another well. During cold seasons, because it is relatively warm, the water can be used in the same way as a source of heat for heat pumps that is much more efficient than using air.

Groundwater makes up about twenty per cent of the world's fresh water supply, which is about 0.61 per cent of the entire world's water, including oceans and permanent ice. Global groundwater storage is roughly equal to the total amount of freshwater stored in the snow and ice pack, including the north and south poles. This makes it an important resource which can act as a natural storage that can buffer against shortages of surface water, as in during times of drought.

Groundwater is naturally replenished by surface water from precipitation, streams, and rivers when this recharge reaches the water table.

Groundwater can be a long-term 'reservoir' of the natural water cycle (with residence times from days to millennia), as opposed to short-term water reservoirs like the atmosphere and fresh surface water (which have residence times from minutes to years). The figure shows how deep groundwater (which is quite distant from the surface recharge) can take a very long time to complete its natural cycle.

The Great Artesian Basin in central and eastern Australia is one of the largest confined aquifer systems in the world, extending for almost 2 million km^2. By analysing the trace elements in water sourced from deep underground, hydrogeologists have been able to determine that water extracted from these aquifers can be more than 1 million years old.

By comparing the age of groundwater obtained from different parts of the Great Artesian Basin, hydrogeologists have found it increases in age across the basin. Where water recharges the aquifers along the Eastern Divide, ages are young. As groundwater flows westward across the continent, it increases in age, with the oldest groundwater occurring in the western parts. This means that in order to have travelled almost 1000-km from the source of recharge in 1 million years, the groundwater flowing through the Great Artesian Basin travels at an average rate of about 1 metre per year.

Certain problems have beset the use of groundwater around the world. Just as river waters have been over-used and polluted in many parts of the world, so too have aquifers. The big difference is that aquifers are out of sight. The other major problem is that water management agencies, when calculating the 'sustainable yield' of aquifer and river water, have often counted the same water twice, once in the aquifer, and once in its connected river. This problem, although understood for centuries, has persisted, partly through inertia within government agencies. In Australia, for example, prior to the statutory reforms initiated by the Council of Australian Governments water reform framework in the 1990s, many Australian States managed groundwater and surface water through separate government agencies, an approach beset by rivalry and poor communication.

The time lags inherent in the dynamic response of groundwater to development have generally been ignored by water management agencies, decades after scientific understanding of the issue was consolidated. In brief, the effects of groundwater overdraft (although undeniably real) may take decades or centuries to manifest themselves. In a classic study in 1982, Bredehoeft and colleagues modelled a situation where groundwater extraction in an intermontane basin withdrew the entire annual recharge, leaving 'nothing' for the natural groundwater-dependent vegetation community. Even when the borefield was situated close to the vegetation, 30 per cent of the original vegetation demand could still be met by the lag inherent in the system after 100 years. By year 500 this had reduced to 0 per cent, signalling complete death of the groundwater-dependent vegetation. The science has been available to make these calculations for decades; however water management agencies have generally ignored effects which will appear outside the rough timeframe of political elections (3 to 5 years). Marios Sophocleous argued strongly that management agencies must define and use appropriate timeframes in groundwater planning. This will mean calculating groundwater withdrawal permits based on predicted effects decades, sometimes centuries in the future.

As water moves through the landscape it collects soluble salts, mainly sodium chloride. Where such water enters the atmosphere through evapotranspiration, these salts are left behind. In irrigation districts, poor drainage of soils and surface aquifers can result in water tables coming to the surface in low-lying areas. Major land degradation problems of soil salinity and waterlogging result , combined with increasing levels of salt in surface waters. As a consequence, major damage has occurred to local economies and environments.

Four important effects are worthy of brief mention. First, flood mitigation schemes, intended to protect infrastructure built on floodplains, have had the unintended consequence of reducing aquifer recharge associated with natural flooding. Second, prolonged depletion of groundwater in extensive aquifers can result in land subsidence, with associated infrastructure damage — as well as (thirdly) saline intrusion. Fourth, draining acid sulphate soils, often found in low-lying coastal plains, can result in acidification and pollution of formerly freshwater and estuarine streams.

Another cause for concern is that groundwater drawdown from over-allocated aquifers has the potential to cause severe damage to both terrestrial and aquatic ecosystems — in some cases very conspicuously but in others quite imperceptibly because of the extended period over which the damage occurs.

Overdraft

Groundwater is a highly useful and often abundant resource. However, over-use, or overdraft, can cause major problems to human users and to the environment. The most evident problem (as far as human groundwater use is concerned) is a lowering of the water table beyond the reach of existing wells. Wells must consequently be deepened to reach the groundwater; in some places (e.g., California, Texas and India) the water table has dropped hundreds of feet because of extensive well pumping. In the Punjab region of India, for example, groundwater levels have dropped 10 meters since 1979, and the rate of depletion is accelerating. A lowered water table may, in turn, cause other problems such as groundwater-related subsidence and saltwater intrusion.

Groundwater is also ecologically important. The importance of groundwater to ecosystems is often overlooked, even by freshwater biologists and ecologists. Groundwaters sustain rivers, wetlands and lakes, as well as subterranean ecosystems within karst or alluvial aquifers.

Not all ecosystems need groundwater, of course. Some terrestrial ecosystems — for example, those of the open deserts and similar arid environments — exist on irregular rainfall and the moisture it delivers to the soil, supplemented by moisture in the air. While there are other terrestrial ecosystems in more hospitable environments where groundwater plays no central role, groundwater is in fact fundamental to many of the world's major ecosystems. Water flows between groundwaters and surface waters. Most rivers, lakes and wetlands are fed by, and (at other places or times) feed groundwater, to varying degrees. Groundwater feeds soil moisture through percolation, and many terrestrial vegetation communities depend directly on either groundwater or the percolated soil moisture above the aquifer for at least part of each year. Hyporheic zones (the mixing zone of streamwater and groundwater) and riparian zones are examples of ecotones largely or totally dependent on groundwater.

Subsidence

Subsidence occurs when too much water is pumped out from underground, deflating the space below the above-surface, and thus causing the ground to actually collapse. The result can look like craters on plots of land. This occurs because in its natural equilibrium state, the hydraulic pressure of groundwater in the pore spaces of the aquifer and the aquitard supports some of the weight of the overlying sediments. When groundwater is removed from aquifers by excessive pumping, pore pressures in the aquifer drop and compression of the aquifer may occur. This compression may be partially recoverable if pressures rebound, but much of it is not. When the aquifer gets compressed it may cause land subsidence, a drop in the ground surface. The city of New Orleans, Louisiana, is actually below sea level today, and its subsidence is partly caused by removal of groundwater from the various aquifer/aquitard systems beneath it. In the first half of the 20th century, the city of San Jose, California, dropped 13 feet from land subsidence caused by overpumping; this subsidence has been halted with improved groundwater management.

Seawater Intrusion

Generally, in very humid or undeveloped regions, the shape of the water table mimics the slope of the surface. The recharge zone of an aquifer near the seacoast is likely to be inland, often at considerable distance. In these coastal areas, a lowered water table may induce sea water to reverse the flow toward the land. Sea water moving inland is called a saltwater intrusion. Alternatively, salt from mineral beds may leach into the groundwater of its own accord.

Mining

Sometimes the water movement from the recharge zone to the place where it is withdrawn may take centuries. When the usage of water is greater than the recharge, it is referred to as *mining* water (the water is often called fossil water because of its geologic age). Under those circumstances it is not a renewable resource.

Pollution

Water pollution of groundwater, from pollutants released to the ground that can work their way down into groundwater, can create a contaminant plume within an aquifer. Movement of water and dispersion within the aquifer spreads the pollutant over a wider area, its advancing boundary often called a plume edge, which can then intersect with groundwater wells or daylight into surface water such as seeps and springs, making the water supplies unsafe for humans and wildlife. The interaction of groundwater contamination with surface waters is analyzed by use of hydrology transport models.

The stratigraphy of the area plays an important role in the transport of these pollutants. An area can have layers of sandy soil, fractured bedrock, clay, or hardpan. Areas of karst topography on limestone bedrock are sometimes vulnerable to surface pollution from groundwater. Earthquake faults can also be entry routes for downward contaminant entry. Water table conditions are of great importance for drinking water supplies, agricultural irrigation, waste disposal (including nuclear waste), wildlife habitat, and other ecological issues.

In the US, upon commercial real estate property transactions both groundwater and soil are the subjects of scrutiny, with a Phase I Environmental Site Assessment normally being prepared to investigate and disclose potential pollution issues. In the San Fernando Valley of California, Real estate contracts for property transfer below the Santa Susana Field Laboratory (SSFL) and eastward have clauses releasing the seller from liability for groundwater contamination consequences from existing or future water pollution of the Valley Aquifer.

Love Canal was one of the most widely known examples of groundwater pollution. In 1978, residents of the Love Canal neighbourhood in upstate New York noticed high rates of cancer and an alarming number of birth defects. This was eventually traced to organic solvents and dioxins from an industrial landfill that the neighbourhood had been built over and around, which had then infiltrated into the water supply and evaporated in basements to further contaminate the air. Eight hundred families were reimbursed for their homes and moved, after extensive legal battles and media coverage.

Another example of widespread groundwater pollution is in the Ganges Plain of northern India and Bangladesh where severe contamination of groundwater by naturally occurring arsenic affects 25 per cent of water wells in the shallower of two regional aquifers. The pollution occurs because aquifer sediments contain organic matter (dead plant material) that generates anaerobic (an environment without oxygen) conditions in the aquifer. These conditions result in the microbial dissolution of iron oxides in the sediment and thus the release of the arsenic, normally strongly bound to iron oxides, into the water. As a consequence, arsenic-rich groundwater is often iron-rich, although secondary processes often obscure the association of dissolved arsenic and dissolved iron.

11

Environmental Issues with Mining

There are a number of environmental issues with mining.

Environmental issues can include erosion, formation of sinkholes, loss of biodiversity, and contamination of soil, groundwater and surface water by chemicals from mining processes. In some cases, additional forest logging is done in the vicinity of mines to increase the available room for the storage of the created debris and soil. Besides creating environmental damage, the contamination resulting from leakage of chemicals also affect the health of the local population. Mining companies in some countries are required to follow environmental and rehabilitation codes, ensuring the area mined is returned to close to its original state. Some mining methods may have significant environmental and public health effects.

Erosion of exposed hillsides, mine dumps, tailings dams and resultant siltation of drainages, creeks and rivers can significantly impact the surrounding areas, a prime example being the giant Ok Tedi Mine in Papua New Guinea. In areas of wilderness mining may cause destruction and disturbance of ecosystems and habitats, and in areas of farming it may disturb or destroy productive grazing and croplands. In urbanised environments mining may produce noise pollution, dust pollution and visual pollution.

Mining can have adverse effects on surrounding surface and ground water if protective measures are not taken. The result can be unnaturally high concentrations of some chemicals, such as arsenic, sulfuric acid, and mercury over a significant area of surface or subsurface. Runoff of mere soil or rock debris -although non-toxic- also devastates the surrounding vegetation. The dumping of the runoff in surface waters or in forests is the worst option here. Submarine tailings disposal is regarded as a better option (if the soil is pumped to a great depth). Mere land storage and refilling of the mine after it has been depleted is even better, if no forests need to be cleared for the storage of the debris. There is potential for massive contamination of the area surrounding mines due to the various chemicals used in the mining process as well as the potentially damaging compounds and metals removed from the ground with the ore. Large amounts of water produced from mine drainage, mine cooling, aqueous extraction and other mining processes increases the potential for these chemicals to contaminate ground and surface water. In well-regulated mines, hydrologists and geologists take careful measurements of water and soil to exclude any type of water contamination that could be caused by the mine's operations. The reducing or eliminating of environmental degradation is enforced in modern American mining by federal and state law, by restricting operators to meet standards for protecting surface and ground water from contamination. This is best done through the use of non-toxic extraction processes as bioleaching. If the project site becomes nonetheless polluted, mitigation techniques such as acid mine drainage (AMD) need to be performed.

The five principal technologies used to monitor and control water flow at mine sites are diversion systems, containment ponds, groundwater pumping systems, subsurface drainage systems, and subsurface barriers. In the case of AMD, contaminated water is generally pumped to a treatment facility that neutralizes the contaminants.

Heavy Metals

Dissolution and transport of metals and heavy metals by run-off and ground water is another example of environmental problems with mining, such as the Britannia Mine, a former copper mine near Vancouver, British Columbia. Tar Creek, an abandoned mining area in Picher, Oklahoma that is now an Environmental Protection Agency superfund site, also suffers from heavy metal contamination. Water in the mine containing dissolved heavy metals such as lead and cadmium leaked into local groundwater, contaminating it. Long-term storage of tailings and dust can lead to additional problems, as they can be easily blown off site by wind, as occurred at Scouriotissa, an abandoned copper mine in Cyprus.

Deforestation

With open cast mining the overburden, which may be covered in forest, must be removed before the mining can commence. Although the deforestation due to mining may be small compared to the total amount it may lead to species extinction if there is a high level of local endemism.

To ensure completion of reclamation, or restoring mine land for future use, many governments and regulatory authorities around the world require that mining companies post a bond to be held in escrow until productivity of reclaimed land has been convincingly demonstrated, although if cleanup procedures are more expensive than the size of the bond, the bond may simply be abandoned. Since 1978 the mining industry has reclaimed more than 2 million acres (8,000 km^2) of land in the United States alone. This reclaimed land has renewed vegetation and wildlife in previous mining lands and can even be used for farming and ranching.

Mining

Mining is the extraction of valuable minerals or other geological materials from the earth, usually from an ore body, vein or (coal) seam. The term also includes the removal of soil. Materials recovered by mining include base metals, precious metals, iron, uranium, coal, diamonds, limestone, oil shale, rock salt and potash. Any material that cannot be grown through agricultural processes, or created artificially in a laboratory or factory, is usually mined. Mining in a wider sense comprises extraction of any non-renewable resource (e.g., petroleum, natural gas, or even water).

Mining of stone and metal has been done since pre-historic times. Modern mining processes involve prospecting for ore bodies, analysis of the profit potential of a proposed mine, extraction of the desired materials and finally reclamation of the land to prepare it for other uses once the mine is closed.

The nature of mining processes creates a potential negative impact on the environment both during the mining operations and for years after the mine is closed. This impact has led to most of the world's nations adopting regulations to moderate the negative effects of mining operations. Safety has long been a concern as well, though modern practices have improved safety in mines significantly. Since the beginning of civilization, people have used stone, ceramics and, later, metals found on or close to the Earth's surface. These were used to manufacture early tools and weapons, for example, high quality flint found in northern France and southern England were used to create flint tools. Flint mines have been found in chalk areas where seams of the stone were followed underground by shafts and galleries. The mines at Grimes Graves are especially famous, and like most other flint mines, are Neolithic in origin (ca 4000 BC-ca 3000 BC). Other hard rocks mined or collected for axes included the greenstone of the Langdale axe industry based in the English Lake District.

The oldest known mine on archaeological record is the "Lion Cave" in Swaziland. At this site, which by radiocarbon dating proves the mine to be about 43,000 years old, paleolithic humans mined mineral hematite, which contained iron and was ground to produce the red pigment ochre. Mines of a similar age in Hungary are believed to be sites where Neanderthals may have mined flint for weapons and tools.

Ancient Egypt

Ancient Egyptians mined malachite at Maadi. At first, Egyptians used the bright green malachite stones for ornamentations and pottery. Later, between 2,613 and 2,494 BC, large building projects required expeditions abroad to the area of Wadi Maghara in order "to secure minerals and other resources not available in Egypt itself." Quarries for turquoise and copper were also found at "Wadi Hamamat, Tura, Aswan and various other Nubian sites" on the Sinai Peninsula and at Timna.

Mining in Egypt occurred in the earliest dynasties, and the gold mines of Nubia were among the largest and most extensive of any in Ancient Egypt, and are described by the Greek author Diodorus Siculus. He mentions that fire-setting was one method used to break down the hard rock holding the gold. One of the complexes is shown in one of earliest known maps. They crushed the ore and ground it to a fine powder before washing the powder for the gold dust.

Mining in Europe has a very long history, examples including the silver mines of Laurium, which helped support the Greek city state of Athens. However, it is the Romans who developed large scale mining methods, especially the use of large volumes of water brought to the minehead by numerous aqueducts. The water was used for a variety of purposes, including using it to remove overburden and rock debris, called hydraulic mining, as well as washing comminuted or crushed ores, and driving simple machinery.

The Romans used hydraulic mining methods on a large scale to prospect for the veins of ore, especially a now obsolete form of mining known as hushing. It involved building numerous aqueducts to supply water to the minehead where it was stored in large reservoirs and tanks. When a full tank was opened, the wave of water sluiced away the overburden to expose the bedrock underneath and any gold veins. The rock was then attacked by fire-setting to heat the rock, which would be quenched with a stream of water. The thermal shock cracked the rock, enabling it to be removed, aided by further streams of water from the overhead tanks. They used similar methods to work cassiterite deposits in Cornwall and lead ore in the Pennines.

The methods had been developed by the Romans in Spain in 25 AD to exploit large alluvial gold deposits, the largest site being at Las Medulas, where seven long aqueducts were built to tap local rivers and to sluice the deposits. Spain was one of the most important mining regions, but all regions of the Roman Empire were exploited. They used reverse overshot water-wheels for dewatering their deep mines such as those at Rio Tinto. In Great Britain the natives had mined minerals for millennia, but when the Romans came, the scale of the operations changed dramatically.

The Romans needed what Britain possessed, especially gold, silver, tin and lead. Roman techniques were not limited to surface mining. They followed the ore veins underground once opencast mining was no longer feasible. At Dolaucothi they stoped out the veins, and drove adits through barren rock to drain the stopes. The same adits were also used to ventilate the workings, especially important when fire-setting was used. At other parts of the site, they penetrated the water table and dewatered the mines using several kinds of machine, especially reverse overshot water-wheels. These were used extensively in the copper mines at Rio Tinto in Spain, where one sequence comprised 16 such wheels arranged in pairs, and lifting water about 80 feet (24 m). They were worked as treadmills with miners standing on the top slats. Many examples of such devices have been found in old Roman mines and some examples are now preserved in the British Museum and the National Museum of Wales.

Mining as an industry underwent dramatic changes in medieval Europe. The mining industry in the early Middle Ages was mainly focused on the extraction of copper and iron. Other precious metals were also used mainly for gilding or coinage. Initially, many metals were obtained through open-pit mining, and ore was primarily extracted from shallow depths, rather than though the digging of deep mine shafts. Around the 14th century, the demand for weapons, armor, stirrups, and horseshoes greatly increased the demand for iron. Mediaeval knights for example were often laden with up to 100 pounds of plate or chain link armor in addition to swords, lances and other weapons. The overwhelming dependency on iron for military purposes helped to spur increased iron production and extraction processes.

These new military applications coincided with a population explosion throughout Europe in the 11th-14th centuries which enriched the demand for precious metals in order to fill a currency shortage. The silver crisis of 1465 occurred when the mines had all reached depths at which the shafts could no longer be pumped dry with the available technology. Although the increased use of bank notes and the use of credit during this period did decrease the dependence and value of precious metals, these forms of currency still remained vital to the story of mediaeval mining. Use of water power in the form of water mills was extensive; they were employed in crushing ore, raising ore from shafts and ventilating galleries by powering giant bellows. Black powder was first used in mining in Selmecbánya,

Kingdom of Hungary (present-day Banská Štiavnica, Slovakia) in 1627. Black powder allowed blasting of rock and earth to loosen and reveal ore veins, which was much faster than fire-setting, in which rock was exposed to heat and then doused with cold water. Black powder allowed the mining of previously impenetrable metals and ores. In 1762, the world's first mining academy was established in the same town.

The widespread adoption of agricultural innovations such as the iron plowshare, as well as the growing use of metal as a building material, was also a driving force in the tremendous growth of the iron industry during this period. Inventions like the arrastra were often used by the Spanish to pulverize ore after being mined. This device employed animal power and utilized mechanical principles similar to that of the ancient Middle Eastern technology of grain threshing.

Much of our knowledge of Mediaeval mining techniques comes from books such as Biringuccio's *De la pirotechnia* and probably most importantly from Georg Agricola's *De re metallica* (1556). These books detail many different mining methods used in German and Saxon mines. One of the prime issues confronting medieval miners (and one which Agricola explains in detail) was the removal of water from mining shafts. As miners dug deeper to access new veins, flooding became a very real obstacle. As a result the mining industry became dramatically more efficient and prosperous as the use of various mechanical and animal driven pump systems were implemented.

In North America there are ancient, prehistoric copper mines along Lake Superior. "Indians availed themselves of this copper starting at least 5000 years ago," and copper tools, arrowheads, and other artifacts that were part of an extensive native trade network have been discovered. In addition, obsidian, flint, and other minerals were mined, worked, and traded. While the early French explorers that encountered the sites made no use of the metals due to the difficulties in transporting it, the copper was eventually traded throughout the continent along major river routes. In Manitoba, Canada, there also are ancient quartz mines near Waddy Lake and surrounding regions.

In the early colonial history of the Americas, "native gold and silver was quickly expropriated and sent back to Spain in fleets of gold—and silver-laden galleons" mostly from mines in Central and South America. Turquoise dated at 700 A.D. was mined in pre-Columbian America; in the Cerillos Mining District in New Mexico, estimates are that "about 15,000 tons of rock had been removed from Mt Chalchihuitl using stone tools before 1700".

Mining in the United States became prevalent in the 19th century, and the General Mining Act of 1872 was passed to encourage mining of federal lands. As with the California Gold Rush in the mid 19th century, mining for minerals and precious metals, along with ranching, was a driving factor in the Westward Expansion to the Pacific coast. With the exploration of the West, mining camps were established and "expressed a distinctive spirit, an enduring legacy to the new nation;" Gold Rushers would experience the same problems as the Land Rushers of the transient West that preceded them. Aided by railroads, many travelled West for work opportunities in mining. Western cities such as Denver and Sacramento originated as mining towns.

The process of mining from discovery of an ore body through extraction of minerals and finally to returning the land to its natural state consists of several distinct steps. The first is discovery of the ore body, which is carried out through prospecting or exploration to find and then define the extent, location and value of the ore body. This leads to a mathematical resource estimation to estimate the size and grade of the deposit.

This estimation is used to conduct a pre-feasibility study to determine the theoretical economics of the ore deposit. This identifies, early on, whether further investment in estimation and engineering studies is warranted and identifies key risks and areas for further work. The next step is to conduct a feasibility study to evaluate the financial viability, technical and financial risks and robustness of the project.

This is when the mining company makes the decision to develop the mine or to walk away from the project. This includes mine planning to evaluate the economically recoverable portion of the deposit, the metallurgy and ore recoverability, marketability and payability of the ore concentrates, engineering concerns, milling and infrastructure costs, finance and equity requirements and an analysis of the proposed mine from the initial excavation all the way through to reclamation. The proportion of a deposit that is economically recoverable is dependent on the enrichment factor of the ore in the area.

Once the analysis determines a given ore body is worth recovering, development begins to create access to the ore body. The mine buildings and processing plants are built and any necessary equipment is obtained. The operation of the mine to recover the ore begins and continues as long as the company operating the mine finds it economical to do so. Once all the ore that the mine can produce profitably is recovered, reclamation begins to make the land used by the mine suitable for future use.

Mining techniques can be divided into two common excavation types: surface mining and sub-surface (underground) mining. Surface mining is much more common, and produces, for example, 85 per cent of minerals (excluding petroleum and natural gas) in the United States, including 98 per cent of metallic ores. Targets are divided into two general categories of materials: *placer deposits*, consisting of valuable minerals contained within river gravels, beach sands, and other unconsolidated materials; and *lode deposits*, where valuable minerals are found in veins, in layers, or in mineral grains generally distributed throughout a mass of actual rock. Both types of ore deposit, placer or lode, are mined by both surface and underground methods.

Processing of placer ore material consists of gravity-dependent methods of separation, such as sluice boxes. Only minor shaking or washing may be necessary to disaggregate (unclump) the sands or gravels before processing. Processing of ore from a lode mine, whether it is a surface or subsurface mine, requires that the rock ore be crushed and pulverized before extraction of the valuable minerals begins. After lode ore is crushed, recovery of the valuable minerals is done by one, or a combination of several, mechanical and chemical techniques.

Some mining, including much of the rare earth elements and uranium mining, is done by less-common methods, such as *in-situ* leaching: this technique involves digging neither at the surface nor underground. The extraction of target minerals by this technique requires that they be soluble, e.g., potash, potassium chloride, sodium chloride, sodium sulfate, which dissolve in water. Some minerals, such as copper minerals and uranium oxide, require acid or carbonate solutions to dissolve.

Surface mining is done by removing (stripping) surface vegetation, dirt, and if necessary, layers of bedrock in order to reach buried ore deposits. Techniques of surface mining include; Open-pit mining which consists of recovery of materials from an open pit in the ground, quarrying or gathering building materials from an open pit mine, strip mining which consists of stripping surface layers off to reveal ore/seams underneath, and mountaintop removal, commonly associated with coal mining, which involves taking the top of a mountain off to reach ore deposits at depth. Most (but not all) placer deposits, because of their shallowly buried nature, are mined by surface methods. Landfill mining, finally, involves sites where landfills are excavated and processed.

Sub-surface mining consists of digging tunnels or shafts into the earth to reach buried ore deposits. Ore, for processing, and waste rock, for disposal, are brought to the surface through the tunnels and shafts. Sub-surface mining can be classified by the type of access shafts used, the extraction method or the technique used to reach the mineral deposit. Drift mining utilizes horizontal access tunnels, slope mining uses diagonally sloping access shafts and shaft mining consists of vertical access shafts.

Other methods include shrinkage stope mining which is mining upward creating a sloping underground room, long wall mining which is grinding a long ore surface underground and room and pillar which is removing ore from rooms while leaving pillars in place to support the roof of the room. Room and pillar mining often leads to retreat mining which is removing the pillars which support rooms, allowing the room to cave in, loosening more ore. Additional sub-surface mining methods include hard rock mining which is mining of hard materials, bore hole mining, drift and fill mining, long hole slope mining, sub level caving and block caving.

Heavy machinery is needed in mining for exploration and development, to remove and stockpile overburden, to break and remove rocks of various hardness and toughness, to process the ore and for reclamation efforts after the mine is closed. Bulldozers, drills, explosives and trucks are all necessary for excavating the land. In the case of placer mining, unconsolidated gravel, or alluvium, is fed into machinery consisting of a hopper and a shaking screen or trommel which frees the desired minerals from the waste gravel. The minerals are then concentrated using sluices or jigs.

Large drills are used to sink shafts, excavate stopes and obtain samples for analysis. Trams are used to transport miners, minerals and waste. Lifts carry miners into and out of mines, as well as moving rock and ore out, and machinery in and out of underground mines. Huge trucks, shovels and cranes are employed in surface mining to move large quantities of overburden and ore. Processing plants can utilize large crushers, mills, reactors, roasters and other equipment to consolidate the mineral-rich material and extract the desired compounds and metals from the ore.

Extractive Metallurgy

The science of extractive metallurgy is a specialized area in the science of metallurgy that studies the extraction of valuable metals from their ores, especially through chemical or mechanical means. Mineral processing (or mineral dressing) is a specialized area in the science of metallurgy that studies the mechanical means of crushing, grinding, and washing that enable the separation (extractive metallurgy) of valuable metals or minerals from their gangue (waste material). Since most metals are present in ores as oxides or sulfides, the metal needs to be reduced to its metallic form. This can be accomplished through chemical means such as smelting or through electrolytic reduction, as in the case of aluminum. Geometallurgy combines the geologic sciences with extractive metallurgy and mining.

Environmental issues can include erosion, formation of sinkholes, loss of biodiversity, and contamination of soil, groundwater and surface water by chemicals from mining processes. In some cases, additional forest logging is done in the vicinity of mines to increase the available room for the storage of the created debris and soil. Contamination resulting from leakage of chemicals can also affect the health of the local population if not properly controlled.

Mining companies in most countries are required to follow stringent environmental and rehabilitation codes in order to minimize environmental impact and avoid impacts on human health. These codes and regulations all require the common steps of Environmental impact assessment, development of Environmental management plans, Mine closure planning (which must be done before the start of mining operations), and Environmental monitoring during operation and after closure. However, in some areas, particularly in the developing world, regulation may not be well enforced by governments.

For major mining companies, and any company seeking international financing, there are however a number of other mechanisms to enforce good environmental standards. These generally relate to financing standards such as Equator Principles, IFC environmental standards, and criteria for Socially responsible investing. Mining companies have used this financial industry oversight to argue for some level of self-policing. In 1992 a Draft Code of Conduct for Transnational Corporations was proposed at the Rio Earth Summit by the UN Centre for Transnational Corporations (UNCTC), but the Business Council for Sustainable Development (BCSD) together with the International Chamber of Commerce (ICC) argued successfully for self-regulation instead.

This was followed up by the Global Mining Initiative which was initiated by nine of the largest metals and mining companies, and led to the formation of the International Council on Mining and Metals to 'act as a catalyst' for social and environmental performance improvement in the mining and metals industry internationally. The mining industry has provided funding to various conservation groups, some of which have been working with conservation agendas that are at odds with emerging acceptance of the rights of indigenous people — particularly rights to make land-use decisions.

Ore mills generate large amounts of waste, called tailings. For example, 99 tons of waste are generated per ton of copper, with even higher ratios in gold mining . These tailings can be toxic. Tailings, which are usually produced as a slurry, are most commonly dumped into ponds made from naturally existing valleys. These ponds are secured by impoundments (dams or embankment dams). In 2000 it was estimated that 3,500 tailings impoundments existed, and that every year, 2 to 5 major failures and 35 minor failures occurred (citation needed); for example, in the Marcopper mining disaster at least 2 million tons of tailings were released into a local river. Subaqueous tailings disposal is another option. The mining industry has argued that submarine tailings disposal (STD), which disposes of tailings in the sea, is ideal because it avoids the risks of tailings ponds; although the practice is illegal in the United States and Canada, it is used in the developing world.

Certification of mines with good practices occurs through the International Organization for Standardization (ISO) such as ISO 9000 and ISO 14001, which certifies an 'auditable environmental management system'; this certification involves short inspections, although it has been accused of lacking rigor. Certification is also available through Ceres' Global Reporting Initiative, but these reports are voluntary and unverified. Miscellaneous other certification programmes exist for various projects, typically through non-profit groups.

Regulations and World Bank Relationship

The World Bank has been involved in mining since 1955, mainly through grants from its International Bank for Reconstruction and Development, with the Bank's Multilateral Investment Guarantee Agency offering political risk insurance. Between 1955 and 1990 it provided about $2 billion to fifty mining projects, broadly categorized as reform and rehabilitation, greenfield mine construction, mineral processing, technical assistance, and engineering. These projects have been criticized, particularly the Ferro Carajas project of Brazil, begun in 1981. The bank established mining codes intended to increase foreign investment, in 1988 solicited feedback from 45 mining companies on how to increase their involvement.

In 1992 the bank began to push for privatization of government-owned mining companies with a new set of codes, beginning with its report *The Strategy for African Mining*. In 1997, Latin America's largest miner Companhia Vale do Rio Doce (CVRD) was privatized. These and other movements such as the Philippines 1995 Mining Act led the World Bank to publish a third report (*Assistance for Minerals Sector Development and Reform in Member Countries*) which endorsed mandatory environment impact assessments and attention to the locals. The codes based on this report are influential in the legislation of developing nations. The new codes are intended to encourage development through tax holidays, zero custom duties, reduced income taxes, and related measures. The results of these codes were analyzed by a group from the University of Quebec, which concluded that the codes promote foreign investment but "fall very short of permitting sustainable development". The observed negative correlation between natural resources and economic development is known as the resource curse.

Mining Industry

Mining exists in many countries but Australia and Canada have a reputation for domestic mining expertise, and London is known as the capital of global "mining houses" such as Rio Tinto, BHP Billiton, and Anglo American PLC. The US mining industry is also large but it is dominated by the coal and nonmetal minerals, and the various regulations have worked to reduce the significance of mining in the United States. In 2007 the total market cap of mining companies was reported at US$962 billion, which compares to a total global market cap of publicly traded companies of about US$50 trillion in 2007.

While exploration and mining can sometimes be conducted by individual entrepreneurs or small business, most modern-day mines are large enterprises requiring large amounts of capital to establish. Consequently, the mining sector of the industry is dominated by large, often multinational companies, most of them publicly listed. It can be argued that what is referred to as the 'mining industry' is actually two sectors, one specializing in exploration for new resources, the other specializing in mining those resources. The exploration sector is typically made up of individuals and small mineral resource companies ('juniors') dependent on venture capital. The mining sector is typically large and multi-national companies sustained by mineral production from their mining operations. In addition to these two sectors, various other industries such as equipment manufacture, environmental testing and metallurgy analysis also rely on and support the mining industry throughout the world. Canadian stock exchanges have a particular focus on mining companies, particularly junior exploration companies through the TSX Venture Exchange; Canadian companies raise capital on these exchanges and then invest the money in exploration globally. Some have argued that below juniors there exists a substantial sector of illegitimate companies primarily focused on manipulating stock prices.

Mining operations can be grouped into five major categories in terms of their respective resources. These are, oil and gas extraction, coal mining, metal ore mining, nonmetallic mineral mining and quarrying, and support activities for mining. Out of all these categories, oil and gas extraction remains one of the largest in terms of its global economic importance. Prospecting potential mining sites, a vital area of concern for the mining industry is now done using sophisticated new technologies such as seismic prospecting and remote-sensing satellites.

Corporate Classifications

Mining companies can be classified based on their size and financial capabilities:

Major companies are considered to have an adjusted annual mining-related revenue of more than US$500 million, with the financial capability to develop a major mine on its own.

- Intermediate companies have at least $50 million in annual revenue but less than $500 million.
- Junior companies rely on equity financing as their principal means of funding exploration. Juniors are mainly pure exploration companies, but may also produce minimally, and do not have a revenue of US$50 million.

Safety

Safety has long been a controversial issue in the mining business especially with sub-surface mining. While mining today is substantially safer than it was in the previous decades, mining accidents are often very high profile, such as the Quecreek Mine Rescue saving 9 trapped Pennsylvania coal miners in 2002. The Courrières mine disaster, Europe's worst mining accident, caused the death of 1,099 miners (including many children) in Northern France on 10 March 1906. It seems that this disaster was surpassed only by the Benxihu Colliery accident in China on April 26, 1942, which killed 1,549 miners. Government figures indicate that 5,000 Chinese miners die in accidents each year, while other reports have suggested a figure as high as 20,000. Mining ventilation is a significant safety concern for many miners. Poor ventilation of the mines causes exposure to harmful gases, heat and dust inside sub-surface mines. These can cause harmful physiological effects, including death. The concentration of methane and other airborne contaminants underground can generally be controlled by dilution (ventilation), capture before entering the host air stream (methane drainage), or isolation (seals and stoppings).

Ignited methane gas is a common source of explosions in coal mines, or, the more violent coal dust explosions. Gases in mines can also poison the workers or displace the oxygen in the mine, causing asphyxiation. For this reason, the MHSA requires that workers have gas detection equipment in groups of miners. It must be able to detect common gases, such as CO, O_2, H_2S, and % Lower Explosive Limit. Additionally, further regulation is being requested for more gas detection as newer technology such as nanotechnology is introduced.

High temperatures and humidity may result in heat-related illnesses, including heat stroke which can be fatal. Dusts can cause lung problems, including silicosis, asbestosis and pneumoconiosis (also known as miners lung or black lung disease). A ventilation system is set up to force a stream of air through the working areas of the mine. The air circulation necessary for the effective ventilation of a mine is generated by one or more large mine fans, usually located above ground. Air flows in one direction only, making circuits through the mine such that each main work area constantly receives a supply of fresh air.

Miners utilize equipment strong enough to break through extremely hard layers of the Earth's crust. This equipment, combined with the closed workspace that underground miners work in, can cause hearing loss. For example, a roof bolter (commonly used by mine roof bolter operators) can reach sound power levels of up to 115 dB. Combined with the reverberant effects of underground mines, a miner without proper hearing protection is at a high risk for hearing loss.

Since mining entails removing dirt and rock from its natural location creating large empty pits, rooms and tunnels, cave-ins are a major concern within mines. Modern techniques for timbering and bracing walls and ceilings within sub-surface mines have reduced the number of fatalities due to cave-ins, but accidents still occur. The presence of heavy equipment in confined spaces also poses a risk to miners, and despite modern improvements to safety practices, mining remains dangerous throughout the world.

Abandoned Mines

There are upwards of 560,000 abandoned mines on public and privately owned lands in the United States alone. Abandoned mines pose a threat to anyone who may attempt to explore them without proper knowledge and safety training. Old mines are often dangerous and can contain deadly gases. Standing water in mines from seepage or infiltration poses a significant hazard as the water can hide deep pits and trap gases below the water. Additionally, since weather may have eroded the earth and rock surrounding it, the entrance to an old mine in particular can be very dangerous. Old mine workings, caves, etc. are commonly hazardous simply due to the lack of oxygen in the air, a condition in mines known as blackdamp.

As of 2008, the deepest mine in the world is TauTona in Carletonville, South Africa at 3.9 kilometres, eplacing Savuka Mine in the North West Province of South Africa at 3,774 metres. East Rand Mine in Boksburg, South Africa briefly held the record at 3,585 metres, and the first mine declared the deepest in the world was also TauTona when it was at 3,581 metres. The deepest mine in Europe is Pyhäsalmi Mine in Pyhäjärvi, Finland at 1,444 metres. The second deepest mine in Europe is Boulby Mine England at 1,400 metres (shaft depth 1,100 metres).

The deepest open pit mine in the world is Bingham Canyon Mine in Bingham Canyon, Utah, United States at over 1,200 metres. The largest and second deepest open pit copper mine in the world is Chuquicamata in Chuquicamata, Chile at 900 metres, 940,600 tons of copper and 17,700 tons of molybdenum produced annually.

The deepest open pit mine with respect to sea level is Tagebau Hambach in Germany, where the ground of the pit is 293 meters below sea level.

The largest underground mine: El Teniente, in Rancagua, Chile, 2,400 kilometres of underground drifts, 418,000 tons of copper yearly. The deepest borehole in the world is Kola Superdeep Borehole at 12,262 metres. This, however, is not a matter of mining but rather related to scientific drilling.

12

Land Rehabilitation

Land rehabilitation is the process of returning the land in a given area to some degree of its former state, after some process (industry, natural disasters etc.) has resulted in its damage. Many projects and developments will result in the land becoming degraded, for example mining, farming and forestry.

While it is rarely possible to restore the land to its original condition, the rehabilitation process usually attempts to bring some degree of restoration. Modern methods have in many cases not only restored degraded land but actually improved it, depending on what criteria are used to measure 'improvement'.

Mine Rehabilitation

Modern mine rehabilitation aims to minimize and mitigate the environmental effects of modern mining, which may in the case of open pit mining involve movement of significant volumes of rock. Rehabilitation management is an ongoing process, often resulting in open pit mines being backfilled.

After mining finishes, the mine area must undergo rehabilitation.

- Waste dumps are contoured to flatten them out, to further stabilise them against erosion.
- If the ore contains sulfides it is usually covered with a layer of clay to prevent access of rain and oxygen from the air, which can oxidise the sulfides to produce sulfuric acid.
- Landfills are covered with topsoil, and vegetation is planted to help consolidate the material.

- Dumps are usually fenced off to prevent livestock denuding them of vegetation.
- The open pit is then surrounded with a fence, to prevent access, and it generally eventually fills up with groundwater.
- Tailings dams are left to evaporate, then covered with waste rock, clay if need be, and soil, which is planted to stabilise it.

For underground mines, rehabilitation is not always a significant problem or cost. This is because of the higher grade of the ore and lower volumes of waste rock and tailings. In some situations, stopes are backfilled with concrete slurry using waste, so that minimal waste is left at surface.

The removal of plant and infrastructure is not always part of a rehabilitation programme, as many old mine plants have cultural heritage and cultural value. Often in gold mines, rehabilitation is performed by scavenger operations which treat the soil within the plant area for spilled gold using modified placer mining gravity collection plants.

Land Reclamation

Land reclamation, usually known as reclamation, is the process to create new land from sea or riverbeds. The land reclaimed is known as reclamation ground or landfill.

The creation of new land was for the need of human activities. Notable examples in the West include large parts of the Netherlands, parts of New Orleans (which is partially built on land that was once swamp); much of San Francisco's waterfront has been reclaimed from the San Francisco Bay; Mexico City (which is situated at the former site of Lake Texcoco); Helsinki (of which the major part of the city centre is built on reclaimed land); the Cape Town foreshore; the Chicago shoreline; the Manila Bay shoreline; Back Bay, Boston, Massachusetts; Battery Park City, Manhattan; Liberty State Park, Jersey City; the port of Zeebrugge in Belgium; the southwestern residential area in Brest, Belarus, the polders of the Netherlands; and the Toronto Islands, Leslie Street Spit, and the waterfront in Toronto. In the Far East, Hong Kong, Macau, Japan, the southern Chinese cities of Shenzhen, the Philippine capital Manila, and the city-state of Singapore, where land is in short supply, are also famous for their efforts on land reclamation. One of the earliest and famous project was the Praya Reclamation Scheme, which added 50 to 60 acres (240,000 m^2) of land in 1890 during the second phase of construction. It was one of the most ambitious projects ever taken during the Colonial Hong Kong era. Some 20 per cent of land in the Tokyo Bay area has been reclaimed. Monaco and the British territory of Gibraltar are also expanding due to land reclamation. The city of Rio de Janeiro was largely built on reclaimed land, as was Wellington, New Zealand.

Artificial islands are an example of land reclamation. Creating an artificial island is an expensive and risky undertaking. It is often considered in places that are densely populated and flat land is scarce. Kansai International Airport (in Osaka) and Hong Kong International Airport are examples where this process was deemed necessary. The Palm Islands, The World and hotel Burj al-Arab off Dubai in the United Arab Emirates are other examples of artificial islands.

Agriculture

Agriculture was a drive for land reclamation before industrialisation. In South China, farmers reclaimed paddy fields by enclosing an area with a stone wall on the sea shore near river mouth or river delta. The species of rice that grow on these grounds are more salt tolerant. Another use of such enclosed land is creation of fish ponds. It is commonly seen on the Pearl River Delta and Hong Kong. These reclamation also attracts species of migrating birds.

A related practice is the draining of swampy or seasonally submerged wetlands to convert them to farmland. While this does not create new land exactly, it allows commercially productive use of land that would otherwise be restricted to wildlife habitat. It is also an important method of mosquito control.

Beach Restoration

Beach rebuilding is the process of repairing beaches using materials such as sand or mud from inland. This can be used to build up beaches suffering from beach starvation or erosion from longshore drift. It stops the movement of the original beach material through longshore drift and retains a natural look to the beach. Although it is not a long-lasting solution, it is cheap compared to other types of coastal defences.

Landfill

As human overcrowding of developed areas intensified during the 20th century, it has become important to develop land re-use strategies for completed landfills. Some of the most common usages are for parks, golf courses and other sports fields. Increasingly, however, office buildings and industrial uses are made on a completed landfill. In these latter uses, methane capture is customarily carried out to minimize explosive hazard within the building.

An example of a Class A office building constructed over a landfill is the Dakin Building at Sierra Point, Brisbane, California. The underlying fill was deposited from 1965 to 1985, mostly consisting of construction debris from San Francisco and some municipal wastes. Aerial photographs prior to 1965 show this area to be tidelands of the San Francisco Bay. A clay cap was constructed over the debris prior to building approval.

A notable example is Sydney Olympic Park, the primary venue for the 2000 Summer Olympic Games, which was built atop an industrial wasteland that included landfills.

Another strategy for landfill is the incineration of landfill trash at high temperature via the plasma-arc gasification process, which is currently used at two facilities in Japan, and will be used at a planned facility in St. Lucie County, Florida.

Environmental Impact

Parts (highlighted in brown) of the San Francisco Bay were reclaimed from wetlands for urban use.

Draining wetlands for ploughing, for example, is a form of habitat destruction. In some parts of the world, new reclamation projects are restricted or no longer allowed, due to environmental protection laws.

Environmental Legislation

Hong Kong legislators passed the Protection of the Harbour Ordinance in 1996 in an effort to safeguard the increasingly threatened Victoria Harbour against encroaching land development.

Land Amounts Added

Land reclamation in Hong Kong: Grey (built), red (proposed or under development). Most of the urban area of Hong Kong is on the reclaimed land.

- *Netherlands* — about 1/5 land from land reclamation or about 7,000 km^2.
- *South Korea* — As of 2006, 38 per cent or 1,550 km^2 of coastal wetlands reclaimed, including 400 km^2 at Saemangeum.
- *Singapore* — 20 per cent of the original size or 135 km^2. As of 2003, plans for 99 km ^{2} more are to go ahead , despite the fact that disputes persist with Malaysia over Singapore's extensive land reclamation works.
- *Hong Kong* — Praya Reclamation Scheme began in the late 1860s and consisted of two stages totaling 50 to 60+ acres. Hong Kong Disneyland, Hong Kong International Airport, and its predecessor, Kai Tak Airport, were all built on reclaimed land. In addition, much reclamation has taken place in prime locations on the waterfront on both sides of Victoria Harbour. This has raised environmental issues of the protection of the harbour which was once the source of prosperity

of Hong Kong, traffic congestion in the Central district, as well as the collusion of the Hong Kong Government with the real estate developers in the territory.

In addition, as the city expands, new towns in different decades were mostly built on reclaimed land, such as Tuen Mun, Tai Po, Shatin-Ma On Shan, West Kowloon, Kwun Tong and Tseung Kwan O.

- *Macau* — 170 per cent of the original size or 17 km^2
- *Mumbai*
- *Tokyo Bay, Japan* — 249 km^2
- *Kobe, Japan* — 23 km^2 (1995)
- *Bahrain* — 76.3 per cent of original size of 410 km^2 (1931-2007).
- *New Zealand* — significant areas of land totalling several hundred hectares have been reclaimed along the harbourfront of Auckland, Wellington and Dunedin. In Dunedin - which in its early days was nicknamed 'Mudedin' — around 2.5 km^2, including much of the inner city and suburbs of Dunedin North, South Dunedin and Andersons Bay is reclaimed from the Otago Harbour, and a similar area in the suburbs of St Clair and St Kilda is reclaimed swampland.

13

Soil Conservation

Soil conservation is a set of management strategies for prevention of soil being eroded from the earth's surface or becoming chemically altered by overuse, acidification, salinization or other chemical soil contamination. It is a component of environmental soil science.

Decisions regarding appropriate crop rotation, cover crops, and planted windbreaks are central to the ability of surface soils to retain their integrity, both with respect to erosive forces and chemical change from nutrient depletion. Crop rotation is simply the conventional alternation of crops on a given field, so that nutrient depletion is avoided from repetitive chemical uptake/deposition of single crop growth.

Cover crops serve the function of protecting the soil from erosion, weed establishment or excess evapotranspiration; however, they may also serve vital soil chemistry functions . For example, legumes can be ploughed under to augment soil nitrates, and other plants have the ability to metabolize soil contaminants or alter adverse pH. The cover crop Mucuna pruriens (velvet bean) has been used in Nigeria to increase phosphorus availability after application of rock phosphate. Some of these same precepts are applicable to urban landscaping, especially with respect to ground-cover selection for erosion control and weed suppression. soil is one of the three main natural resources alongside with water and air.

Windbreaks are created by planting sufficiently dense rows or stands of trees at the windward exposure of an agricultural field subject to wind erosion . Evergreen species are preferred to achieve year-round protection; however, as long as foliage is present in the seasons of bare soil surfaces, the effect of deciduous trees may also be adequate.

Erosion Prevention

Contour plowing, Pennsylvania 1938. The rows formed slow water run-off during rainstorms to prevent soil erosion and allows the water time to settle into the soil.

Practices

There are also conventional practices that farmers have invoked for centuries. These fall into two main categories: contour farming and terracing, standard methods recommended by the U.S. Natural Resources Conservation Service, whose Code 330 is the common standard. Contour farming was practiced by the ancient Phoenicians, and is known to be effective for slopes between two and ten per cent . Contour plowing can increase crop yields from 10 to 50 per cent, partially as a result from greater soil retention.

There are many erosion control methods that can be used such as conservation tillage systems and crop rotation.

Keyline design is an enhancement of contour farming, where the total watershed properties are taken into account in forming the contour lines. Terracing is the practice of creating benches or nearly level layers on a hillside setting. Terraced farming is more common on small farms and in underdeveloped countries, since mechanized equipment is difficult to deploy in this setting.

Human overpopulation is leading to destruction of tropical forests due to widening practices of slash-and-burn and other methods of subsistence farming necessitated by famines in lesser developed countries. A sequel to the deforestation is typically large scale erosion, loss of soil nutrients and sometimes total desertification.

Perimeter Runoff Control

Trees, shrubs and groundcovers are also effective perimeter treatment for soil erosion prevention, by insuring any surface flows are impeded. A special form of this perimeter or inter-row treatment is the use of a "grassway" that both channels and dissipates runoff through surface friction, impeding surface runoff, and encouraging infiltration of the slowed surface water.

The ions responsible for salination are: Na^+, K^+, Ca^{2+}, Mg^{2+} and Cl. Salinity is estimated to affect about one third of all the earth's arable land . Soil salinity adversely affects the metabolism of most crops, and erosion effects usually follow vegetation failure. Salinity occurs on drylands from overirrigation and in areas with shallow saline water tables. In the case of over-irrigation, salts are deposited in upper soil layers as a byproduct of most soil infiltration; excessive irrigation merely increases the rate of salt deposition. The best-known case of shallow saline water table capillary action occurred in Egypt after the 1970 construction of the Aswan Dam. The change in the groundwater level due to dam construction led to high concentration of salts in the water table. After the construction, the continuous high level of the water table led to soil salination of previously arable land.

Use of humic acids may prevent excess salination, especially in locales where excessive irrigation was practiced. The mechanism involved is that humic acids can fix both anions and cations and eliminate them from root zones. In some cases it may be valuable to find plants that can tolerate saline conditions to use as surface cover until salinity can be reduced; there are a number of such saline-tolerant plants, such as saltbush, a plant found in much of North America and in the Mediterranean regions of Europe.

Soil pH

Soil pH levels in Lake Titikaka tend to crop growth can occur naturally in some regions; it can also be induced by acid rain or soil contamination from acids or bases. The role of soil pH is to control nutrient availability to vegetation. The principal macronutrients (calcium, phosphorus, nitrogen, potassium, magnesium, sulfur) prefer neutral to slightly alkaline soils. Calcium, magnesium and potassium are usually made available to plants via cation exchange surfaces of organic material and clay soil surface particles. While acidification increases the initial availability of these cations, the residual soil moisture concentrations of nutrient cations can fall to alarmingly low levels after initial nutrient uptake. Moreover, there is no simple relationship of pH to nutrient availability because of the complex combination of soil types, soil moisture regimes and meteorological factors.

Soil Organisms

Promoting the viability of beneficial soil organisms is an element of soil conservation; moreover this includes macroscopic species, notably the earthworm, as well as microorganisms. Positive effects of the earthworm are known well, as to aeration and promotion of macronutrient availability. When worms excrete egesta in the form of casts, a balanced selection of minerals and plant nutrients is made into a form accessible for root uptake. US research shows that earthworm casts are five times richer in available nitrogen, seven times richer in available phosphates and eleven times richer in available potash than the surrounding upper150 mm of soil. The weight of casts produced may be greater than 4.5 kg per worm per year. By burrowing, the earthworm is of value in creating soil porosity, creating channels enhancing the processes of aeration and drainage.

Microorganisms

Soil microorganisms play a vital role in macronutrient wildlife. For example, nitrogen fixation is carried out by free-living or symbiotic bacteria. These bacteria have the nitrogenase enzyme that combines gaseous nitrogen with hydrogen to produce ammonia, which is then further converted by the bacteria to make other organic compounds. Some nitrogen fixing bacteria such as rhizobia live in the root nodules of legumes. Here they form a mutualistic relationship with the plant, producing ammonia in exchange for carbohydrates. In the case of the carbon cycle, carbon is transferred within the biosphere as heterotrophs feed on other organisms. This process includes the uptake of dead organic material (detritus) by fungi and bacteria in the form of fermentation or decay phenomena.

Mycorrhizae

Mycorrhizae are symbiotic associations between soil-dwelling fungi and the roots of vascular plants. fungi helps increase the availability of minerals, water, and organic nutrients to the plant, while extracting sugars and amino acids from the plant. There are two main types, endomycorrhizae (which penetrate the roots) and ectomycorrhizae (which resemble 'socks', forming a sheath around the roots). They were discovered when scientists observed that certain seedlings failed to grow or prosper without soil from their native environment.

Some soil microorganisms known as extremophiles have remarkable properties of adaptation to extreme environmental conditions including temperature, pH and water deprivation.

Degradation and Contamination

The viability of soil organisms can be compromised when insecticides and herbicides are applied to planting regimes. Often there are unforeseen and unintended consequences of such chemical use in the form of death of impaired functioning of soil organisms. Thus any use of pesticides should only be undertaken after thorough understanding of residual toxicities upon soil organisms as well as terrestrial ecological components.

Killing soil microorganisms is a deleterious impact of slash and burn agricultural methods. With the surface temperatures generated, virtual annilation of soil and vegetative cover organisms are destroyed, and in many environments these effects can be virtually irreversible (at least for generations of mankind). Shifting cultivation is also a farming system that often employs slash and burn as one of its elements.

Systems, most of which have an adverse effect upon soil quality and plant metabolism. While the role of pH has been discussed above, heavy metals, solvents, petroleum hydrocarbons, herbicides and pesticides also contribute soil residues that are of potential concern. Some of these chemicals are totally extraneous to the agricultural landscape, but others (notably herbicides and pesticides) are intentionally introduced to serve a short term function. Many of these added chemicals have long half-lives in soil, and others degrade to produce derivative chemicals that may be either persistent or pernicious. One alternative to chemicals in agriculture is soil steaming. Steam sterilizes the soil by killing almost all beneficial and harmful micro organisms. However no harmful remains are left. Soil health may even increase since steam unlocks nutrients in the soil which may lead to better plant growth after the thermal treatment.

Typically the expense of soil contamination remediation cannot be justified in an agricultural economic analysis, since cleanup costs are generally quite high; often remediation is mandated by state and county environmental health agencies based upon human health risk issues.

Mineralization

To allow plants full realization of their phytonutrient potential, active mineralization of the soil is sometimes undertaken. This can be in the natural form of adding crushed rock or can take the form of chemical soil supplement. In either case the purpose is to combat mineral depletion of the soil. There are a broad range of minerals that can be added including common substances such as phosphorus and more exotic substances such as zinc and selenium. There is extensive research on the phase transitions of minerals in soil with aqueous contact.

The process of flooding can bring significant bedload sediment to an alluvial plain. While this effect may not be desirable if floods endanger life or if the eroded sediment originates from productive land, this process of addition to a floodplain is a natural process that can rejuvenate soil chemistry through mineralization and macronutrient addition.

14

Water Conservation

Water conservation refers to reducing the usage of water and recycling of waste water for different purposes such as cleaning, manufacturing, and agricultural irrigation.

Water Conservation

Water conservation can be defined as:

- Any beneficial reduction in water loss, use or waste as well as the preservation of water quality.
- A reduction in water use accomplished by implementation of water conservation or water efficiency measures; or,
- Improved water management practices that reduce or enhance the beneficial use of water.

A water conservation measure is an action, behavioural change, device, technology, or improved design or process implemented to reduce water loss, waste, or use. Water efficiency is a tool of water conservation. That results in more efficient water use and thus reduces water demand. The value and cost-effectiveness of a water efficiency measure must be evaluated in relation to its effects on the use and cost of other natural resources (e.g. energy or chemicals).

WATER EFFICIENCY

Goals

The goals of water conservation efforts include as follows:

- *Sustainability* — To ensure availability for future generations, the withdrawal of fresh water from an ecosystem should not exceed its natural replacement rate.
- *Energy Conservation* — Water pumping, delivery, and wastewater treatment facilities consume a significant amount of energy. California over 15 per cent of total electricity consumption is devoted to water management.
- *Habitat Conservation* — Minimizing human water use helps to preserve fresh water habitats for local wildlife and migrating waterfowl, as well as reducing the need to build new dams and other water diversion infrastructure.

Water conservation programmes are typically initiated at the local level, by either municipal water utilities or regional governments. Common strategies include public outreach campaigns, tiered water rates (charging progressively higher prices as water use increases), or restrictions on outdoor water use such as lawn watering and car washing. Cities in dry climates often require or encourage the installation of xeriscaping or natural landscaping in new homes to reduce outdoor water usage.

One fundamental conservation goal is universal metering. The prevalence of residential water metering varies significantly worldwide. Recent studies have estimated that water supplies are metered in less than 30 per cent of UK households, and about 61 per cent of urban Canadian homes (as of 2001). Although individual water meters have often been considered impractical in homes with private wells or in multifamily buildings, the U.S. Environmental Protection Agency estimates that metering alone can reduce consumption by 20 to 40 per cent. In addition to raising consumer awareness of their water use, metering is also an important way to identify and localize water leaks.

Some researchers have suggested that water conservation efforts should be primarily directed at farmers, in light of the fact that crop irrigation accounts for 70 per cent of the world's fresh water use. The agricultural sector of most countries is important both economically and politically, and water subsidies are common. Conservation advocates have urged removal of all subsidies to force farmers to grow more water-efficient crops and adopt less wasteful irrigation techniques.

Water-saving technology for the home includes:

- Low-flow shower heads sometimes called energy-efficient shower heads as they also use less energy.
- Low-flush toilets and composting toilets. These have a dramatic impact in the developed world, as conventional Western toilets use large volumes of water.

- Dual flush toilets created by Caroma includes two buttons or handles to flush different levels of water. Dual flush toilets use up to 67 per cent less water than conventional toilets.
- Saline water (sea water) or rain water can be used for flushing toilets.
- Faucet aerators, which break water flow into fine droplets to maintain "wetting effectiveness" while using less water. An additional benefit is that they reduce splashing while washing hands and dishes.
- Wastewater reuse or recycling systems, allowing:
  - Reuse of graywater for flushing toilets or watering gardens
  - Recycling of wastewater through purification at a water treatment plant.
  - Rainwater harvesting.
  - High-efficiency clothes washers.
  - Weather-based irrigation controllers.
  - Garden hose nozzles that shut off water when it is not being used, instead of letting a hose run.
  - using low flow taps in wash basins.
  - Automatic faucet is a water conservation faucet that eliminates water waste at the faucet. It automates the use of faucets without the use of hands.

Water can also be conserved by landscaping with native plants and by changing behaviour, such as shortening showers and not running the faucet while brushing teeth.

Commercial Applications

Many water-saving devices (such as low-flush toilets) that are useful in homes can also be useful for business water saving. Other water-saving technology for businesses includes:

- Waterless urinals
- Waterless car washes
- Infrared or foot-operated faucets, which can save water by using short bursts of water for rinsing in a kitchen or bathroom
- Pressurized waterbrooms, which can be used instead of a hose to clean sidewalks
- X-ray film processor re-circulation systems
- Cooling tower conductivity controllers
- Utilization of Lake Water and or Sea Water for Cooling Towers

- Water-saving steam sterilizers, for use in hospitals and health care facilities
- One of the method of water conservation is rain water harvesting

However, ultra-low flow sink faucets, particularly those whose flow rate is less than .75 GPM have been shown to have serious undesired consequences, including increased wash time, hands not completely cleaned, and some users choosing to forgo washing altogether to avoid the inconvenience.

Agricultural Applications

For crop irrigation, optimal water efficiency means minimizing losses due to evaporation, runoff or subsurface drainage while maximizing production. An evaporation pan in combination with specific crop correction factors can be used to determine how much water is needed to satisfy plant requirements. Flood irrigation, the oldest and most common type, is often very uneven in distribution, as parts of a field may receive excess water in order to deliver sufficient quantities to other parts. Overhead irrigation, using centre-pivot or lateral-moving sprinklers, has the potential for a much more equal and controlled distribution pattern. Drip irrigation is the most expensive and least-used type, but offers the ability to deliver water to plant roots with minimal losses.

As changing irrigation systems can be a costly undertaking, conservation efforts often concentrate on maximizing the efficiency of the existing system. This may include chiseling compacted soils, creating furrow dikes to prevent runoff, and using soil moisture and rainfall sensors to optimize irrigation schedules. Usually large gains in efficiency are possible though measurement and more effective management of the existing irrigation system.

Infiltration basins, also called recharge pits, capture rainwater and recharge ground water supplies. Use of these management practices reduces soil erosion caused by stormwater runoff and improves water quality in nearby surface waters.

Minimum Water Network Target and Design

The Cost effective minimum water network is a holistic framework/ guide for water conservation that helps in determining the minimum amount of freshwater and wastewater target for an industrial or urban system based on the water management hierarchy i.e. it considers all conceivable methods to save water. The technique ensure that the designer desired payback period is satisfied using Systematic Hierarchical Approach for Resilient Process Screening (SHARPS) technique.

15

Environmental Protection

Environmental protection is a practice of protecting the environment, on individual, organizational or governmental level, for the benefit of the natural environment and (or) humans. Due to the pressures of population and our technology the biophysical environment is being degraded, sometimes permanently. This has been recognized and governments began placing restraints on activities that caused environmental degradation. Since the 1960s activism by the environmental movement has created awareness of the various environmental issues. There is not a full agreement on the extent of the environmental impact of human activity and protection measures are occasionally criticized.

Academic institutions now offer courses such as environmental studies, environmental management and environmental engineering that study the history and methods of environmental protection. Protection of the environment is needed from various human activities. Waste, pollution, loss of biodiversity, introduction of invasive species, release of genetically modified organisms and toxics are some of the issues relating to environmental protection.

Many Constitutions acknowledge the fundamental right to environmental protection and many international treaties acknowledge the right to live in a healthy environment.

But complete environmental protection seems impossible at this current global position.

Also, many countries have organizations and agencies devoted to environmental protection. There are International environmental protection organizations, as the United Nations Environment Programme.

European Union

Environmental protection has become an important task for the institutions of the European Community after the Maastricht Treaty for the European Union ratification by all Member States. The EU is already very active in the field of environmental policy with important directives like those on environmental impact assessment and on the access to environmental information for citizens in the Member States.

New Zealand

At a national level the Ministry for the Environment is responsible for environmental policy and the Department of Conservation addresses conservation issues. At a regional level the regional councils administer the legislation and address regional environmental issues.

United States

Since 1970, the United States Environmental Protection Agency (EPA) has been working to protect the environment and human health. All U.S. states have their own state departments of environmental protection.

The EPA has drafted 'Seven Priorities for EPA's Future', which are:

- 'Taking Action on Climate Change'
- 'Improving Air Quality'
- 'Assuring the Safety of Chemicals'
- 'Cleaning Up Our Communities'
- 'Protecting America's Waters'
- 'Expanding the Conversation on Environmentalism and Working for Environmental Justice'
- 'Building Strong State and Tribal Partnerships'

In Literature

Environmental protection has become a theme in fiction as well as non-fictional literature. Books such as *Antarctica* and *Blockade* have environmental protection as a theme whereas *The Lorax* has become a popular metaphor for environmental protection.

Environmental Movement

The environmental movement, a term that includes the conservation and green politics, is a diverse scientific, social, and political movement for addressing environmental issues.

Environmentalists advocate the sustainable management of resources and stewardship of the environment through changes in public policy and individual behaviour. In its recognition of humanity as a participant in (not enemy of) ecosystems, the movement is centered on ecology, health, and human rights.

The environmental movement is represented by a range of organizations, from the large to grassroots. Due to its large membership, varying and strong beliefs, and occasionally speculative nature, the environmental movement is not always united in its goals. At its broadest, the movement includes private citizens, professionals, religious devotees, politicians, and extremists.

The roots of the modern environmental movement can be traced to attempts in nineteenth-century Europe and North America to expose the costs of environmental negligence, notably disease, as well as widespread air and water pollution, but only after the Second World War did a wider awareness begin to emerge.

The US environmental movement emerged in the late nineteenth and early twentieth century, with two key strands: protectionists such as John Muir wanted land and nature set aside for its own sake, while conservationists such as Gifford Pinchot wanted to manage natural resources for exploitation. Among the early protectionists that stood out as leaders in the movement were Henry David Thoreau, John Muir and George Perkins Marsh. Thoreau was concerned about the wildlife in Massachusetts; he wrote *Walden; or, Life in the Woods* as he studied the wildlife from a cabin. John Muir founded the Sierra Club, one of the largest conservation organizations in the United States. Marsh was influential with regards to the need for resource conservation. Muir was instrumental in the creation of the world's first national park at Yellowstone in 1872.

During the 1950s, 1960s, and 1970s, several events illustrated the magnitude of environmental damage caused by humans. In 1954, the 23 man crew of the Japanese fishing vessel *Lucky Dragon 5* was exposed to radioactive fallout from a hydrogen bomb test at Bikini Atoll. The publication of the book *Silent Spring* (1962) by Rachel Carson drew attention to the impact of chemicals on the natural environment. In 1967, the oil tanker *Torrey Canyon* went aground off the southwest coast of England, and in 1969 oil spilled from an offshore well in California's Santa Barbara Channel. In 1971, the conclusion of a law suit in Japan drew international attention to the effects of decades of mercury poisoning on the people of Minamata.

At the same time, emerging scientific research drew new attention to existing and hypothetical threats to the environment and humanity. Among them were Paul R. Ehrlich, whose book *The Population Bomb* (1968) revived concerns about the impact of exponential population growth. Biologist Barry Commoner generated a debate about growth, affluence and "flawed technology." Additionally, an association of scientists and political leaders known as the Club of Rome published their report *The Limits to Growth* in 1972, and drew attention to the growing pressure on natural resources from human activities.

Meanwhile, technological accomplishments such as nuclear proliferation and photos of the Earth from outer space provided both new insights and new reasons for concern over Earth's seemingly small and unique place in the universe.

In 1972, the United Nations Conference on the Human Environment was held in Stockholm, and for the first time united the representatives of multiple governments in discussion relating to the state of the global environment. This conference led directly to the creation of government environmental agencies and the UN Environment Programme. The United States also passed new legislation such as the Clean Water Act, the Clean Air Act, the Endangered Species Act, and the National Environmental Policy Act- the foundations for current environmental standards.

By the mid-1970s anti-nuclear activism had moved beyond local protests and politics to gain a wider appeal and influence. Although it lacked a single co-ordinating organization the anti-nuclear movement's efforts gained a great deal of attention. In the aftermath of the Three Mile Island accident in 1979, many mass demonstrations took place. The largest one was held in New York City in September 1979 and involved two hundred thousand people; speeches were given by Jane Fonda and Ralph Nader.

Since the 1970s, public awareness, environmental sciences, ecology, and technology have advanced to include modern focus points like ozone depletion, global climate change, acid rain, and the potentially harmful genetically modified organisms (GMOs). Environmental Science is the study of the interactions among the physical, chemical and biological components of the environment.

Ecology, or Ecological Science

Ecology is the scientific study of the distribution and abundance of living organisms and how these properties are affected by interactions between the organisms and their environment.

Environmental Studies

Environmental Studies is the study of the entire field of environmental issues. The scope is more broad than that of the Environmental Science degree. The ENVS degree offered at schools includes a base in sciences such as Biology, Chemistry, and Earth Sciences as well as requiring many other Social Sciences classes. This scholarly field has been established only in the past 20 years. ENVS is especially in high demand as of late since U.S. President Barack Obama has established himself as a 'green' president. The president said regarding a speech on the environment, "We can let the jobs of tomorrow be created abroad, or we can create those jobs right here in America and lay the foundation for lasting prosperity."

The major encompasses a vast range of subjects: Architecture, Atmospheric Science, Ethics, Economics, Ecology, Geology, Geography, History, and Philosophy.

There are many universities that offer this degree: University of Colorado, Dartmouth College, Emory University, University of Oregon, Western Michigan University, Santa Clara University, and U.C. Santa Cruz.

The University of Colorado is a flagship school for the environmental movement. The school offers Bachelor of Arts (BA) degrees in: Environmental Studies, Environmental Design, and Environmental Engineering. C.U. also offers Doctor of Philosophy (Ph.D) degrees in Environmental Studies as well as an Architecture Ph.D specializing in Sustainable and Healthy Environments (SHE). The university was named the #1 green school in America on Sierra Club's 2009 list.

The broad ENVS curriculum instills a range of knowledge so vast that this major is a well-rounded education for anyone entering the growing environmental workforce. The evolving workplace is being filled out by the increasing number of these ENVS graduates. The environmental field focuses on areas such as: Alternative Energy, Conservation, Green Building, Public Policy, Scientific Research, among others.

Other Focus Points

- Environmental conservation is the process in which one is involved in conserving the natural aspects of the environment. Whether through reforestation, recycling, or pollution control, environmental conservation sustains the natural quality of life.
- Environmental health movement dates at least to Progressive Era, and focuses on urban standards like clean water, efficient sewage handling, and stable population growth. Environmental health could also deal with nutrition, preventive medicine, aging, and other concerns specific to human well-being. Environmental health is also seen as an indicator for the state of the environment, or an early warning system for what may happen to humans.

- Environmental Justice is a movement that began in the U.S. in the 1980s and seeks an end to environmental racism and prevent low-income and minority communities from an unbalanced exposure to highways, garbage dumps, and factories. The Environmental Justice movement seeks to link 'social' and 'ecological' environmental concerns, while at the same time preventing de facto racism, and classism. This makes it particularly adequate for the construction of labor-environmental alliances.
- Ecology movement could involve the Gaia Theory, as well as Value of Earth and other interactions between humans, science, and responsibility.
- Deep Ecology is an ideological spinoff of the ecology movement that views the diversity and integrity of the planetary ecosystem, in and for itself, as its primary value.
- Bright green environmentalism is a currently popular sub-movement, which emphasizes the idea that through technology, good design and more thoughtful use of energy and resources, people can live responsible, sustainable lives while enjoying prosperity.
- The anti-nuclear movement opposes the use of various nuclear technologies. The initial anti-nuclear objective was nuclear disarmament and later the focus began to shift to other issues, mainly opposition to the use of nuclear power. There have been many large anti-nuclear demonstrations and protests. Major anti-nuclear groups include Campaign for Nuclear Disarmament, Friends of the Earth, Greenpeace, International Physicians for the Prevention of Nuclear War, and the Nuclear Information and Resource Service.

ENVIRONMENTAL LAW AND THEORY

Property Rights

Many environmental lawsuits question the legal rights of property owners, and whether the general public has a right to intervene with detrimental practices occurring on someone else's land. Environmental law organizations exist all across the world, such as the Environmental Law and Policy Center in the midwestern United States.

Citizens' Rights

One of the earliest lawsuits to establish that citizens may sue for environmental and aesthetic harms was Scenic Hudson Preservation Conference *vs.* Federal Power Commission, decided in 1965 by the Second Circuit Court of Appeals. The case helped halt the construction of a power plant on Storm King Mountain in New York State. See also United States environmental law and David Sive, an attorney who was involved in the case.

Nature's Rights

Christopher D. Stone's 1972 essay, "Should trees have standing?" addressed the question of whether natural objects themselves should have legal rights. In the essay, Stone suggests that his argument is valid because many current rights-holders (women, children) were once seen as objects.

Environmental Reactivism

Numerous criticisms and ethical ambiguities have led to growing concerns about technology, including the use of potentially harmful pesticides, water additives like fluoride, and the extremely dangerous ethanol-processing plants.

NIMBY syndrome refers to public outcry caused by knee-jerk reaction to an unwillingness to be exposed to even necessary developments. Some serious biologists and ecologists created the scientific ecology movement which would not confuse empirical data with visions of a desirable future world.

Today, the sciences of ecology and environmental science, rather than any aesthetic goals, provide the basis of unity to most serious environmentalists. As more information is gathered in scientific fields, more scientific issues like biodiversity, as opposed to mere aesthetics, are a concern. Conservation biology is a rapidly developing field. Environmentalism now has proponents in business: new ventures such as those to reuse and recycle consumer electronics and other technical equipment are gaining popularity. Computer liquidators are just one example.

In recent years, the environmental movement has increasingly focussed on global warming as a top issue. As concerns about climate change moved more into the mainstream, from the connections drawn between global warming and Hurricane Katrina to Al Gore's film An Inconvenient Truth, many environmental groups refocussed their efforts. In the United States, 2007 witnessed the largest grassroots environmental demonstration in years, Step It Up 2007, with rallies in over 1,400 communities and all 50 states for real global warming solutions.

Many religious organizations and individual churches now have programmes and activities dedicated to environmental issues. The religious movement is often supported by interpretation of scriptures. Most major religious groups are represented including Jewish, Islamic, Anglican, Orthodox, Evangelical, Christian and Catholic.

Radical Environmentalism

Radical environmentalism emerged out of an ecocentrism-based frustration with the co-option of mainstream environmentalism. The radical environmental movement aspires to what scholar Christopher Manes calls "a new kind of environmental activism: iconoclastic, uncompromising, discontented with traditional conservation policy, at time illegal . . ." Radical environmentalism presupposes a need to reconsider Western ideas of religion and philosophy (including capitalism, patriarchy and globalization) sometimes through 'resacralising' and reconnecting with nature. Greenpeace represents an organisation with a radical approach, but has contributed in serious ways towards understanding of critical issues, and has a science-oriented core with radicalism as a means to mediaexposure. Earth-first, takes a much more radical posture. Greenpeace, Earth-first.

16

Renewable Energy

Renewable energy is energy which comes from natural resources such as sunlight, wind, rain, tides, and geothermal heat, which are renewable (naturally replenished). In 2008, about 19 per cent of global final energy consumption came from renewables, with 13 per cent coming from traditional biomass, which is mainly used for heating, and 3.2 per cent from hydroelectricity. New renewables (small hydro, modern biomass, wind, solar, geothermal, and biofuels) accounted for another 2.7 per cent and are growing very rapidly. The share of renewables in electricity generation is around 18 per cent, with 15 per cent of global electricity coming from hydroelectricity and 3 per cent from new renewables.

Wind power is growing at the rate of 30 per cent annually, with a worldwide installed capacity of 158 gigawatts (GW) in 2009 and is widely used in Europe, Asia, and the United States. At the end of 2009, cumulative global photovoltaic (PV) installations surpassed 21 GW and PV power stations are popular in Germany and Spain. Solar thermal power stations operate in the USA and Spain, and the largest of these is the 354 megawatt (MW) SEGS power plant in the Mojave Desert. The world's largest geothermal power installation is The Geysers in California, with a rated capacity of 750 MW. Brazil has one of the largest renewable energy programmes in the world, involving production of ethanol fuel from sugar cane, and ethanol now provides 18 per cent of the country's automotive fuel. Ethanol fuel is also widely available in the USA.

While many renewable energy projects are large-scale, renewable technologies are also suited to rural and remote areas, where energy is often crucial in human development. Globally, an estimated 3 million households get power from small solar PV systems. Micro-hydro systems configured into village-scale or county-scale mini-grids serve many areas. More than 30 million rural households get lighting and cooking from biogas made in household-scale digesters. Biomass cookstoves are used by 160 million households.

Climate change concerns, coupled with high oil prices, peak oil, and increasing government support, are driving increasing renewable energy legislation, incentives and commercialization. New government spending, regulation and policies helped the industry weather the global financial crisis better than many other sectors.

Renewable energy flows involve natural phenomena such as sunlight, wind, tides, plant growth, and geothermal heat, as the International Energy Agency explains.

Renewable energy is derived from natural processes that are replenished constantly. In its various forms, it derives directly from the sun, or from heat generated deep within the earth. Included in the definition is electricity and heat generated from solar, wind, ocean, hydropower, biomass, geothermal resources, and biofuels and hydrogen derived from renewable resources.

Renewable energy replaces conventional fuels in four distinct areas: power generation, hot water/space heating, transport fuels, and rural (off-grid) energy services:

- *Power generation* — Renewable energy provides 18 per cent of total electricity generation worldwide. Renewable power generators are spread across many countries, and wind power alone already provides a significant share of electricity in some areas: for example, 14 per cent in the U.S. state of Iowa, 40 per cent in the northern German state of Schleswig-Holstein, and 20 per cent in Denmark. Some countries get most of their power from renewables, including Iceland (100%), Brazil (85%), Austria (62%), New Zealand (65%), and Sweden (54%).
- *Heating* — Solar hot water makes an important contribution in many countries, most notably in China, which now has 70 per cent of the global total (180 GWth). Most of these systems are installed on multi-family apartment buildings and meet a portion of the hot water needs of an estimated 50-60 million households in China. Worldwide, total installed solar water heating systems meet a portion of the water heating needs of over 70 million households. The use of biomass for heating continues to grow as well. In Sweden, national use of biomass energy has surpassed that of oil. Direct geothermal for heating is also growing rapidly.

- *Transport fuels*— Renewable biofuels have contributed to a significant decline in oil consumption in the United States since 2006. The 93 billion liters of biofuels produced worldwide in 2009 displaced the equivalent of an estimated 68 billion liters of gasoline, equal to about 5 per cent of world gasoline production.

Airflows can be used to run wind turbines. Modern wind turbines range from around 600 kW to 5 MW of rated power, although turbines with rated output of 1.5-3 MW have become the most common for commercial use; the power output of a turbine is a function of the cube of the wind speed, so as wind speed increases, power output increases dramatically. Areas where winds are stronger and more constant, such as offshore and high altitude sites, are preferred locations for wind farms. Typical capacity factors are 20-40 per cent, with values at the upper end of the range in particularly favourable sites.

Globally, the long-term technical potential of wind energy is believed to be five times total current global energy production, or 40 times current electricity demand. This could require large amounts of land to be used for wind turbines, particularly in areas of higher wind resources. Offshore resources experience mean wind speeds of ~90 per cent greater than that of land, so offshore resources could contribute substantially more energy.

Wind power is renewable and produces no greenhouse gases during operation, such as carbon dioxide and methane.

Energy in water can be harnessed and used. Since water is about 800 times denser than air, even a slow flowing stream of water, or moderate sea swell, can yield considerable amounts of energy. There are many forms of water energy:

- Hydroelectric energy is a term usually reserved for large-scale hydroelectric dams. Examples are the Grand Coulee Dam in Washington State and the Akosombo Dam in Ghana.
- Micro hydro systems are hydroelectric power installations that typically produce up to 100 kW of power. They are often used in water rich areas as a remote-area power supply (RAPS). There are many of these installations around the world, including several delivering around 50 kW in the Solomon Islands.
- Damless hydro systems derive kinetic energy from rivers and oceans without using a dam.
- Ocean energy describes all the technologies to harness energy from the ocean and the sea. This includes marine current power, ocean thermal energy conversion, and tidal power.

Solar energy is the energy derived from the sun through the form of solar radiation. Solar powered electrical generation relies on photovoltaics and heat engines. A partial list of other solar applications includes space heating and cooling through solar architecture, daylighting, solar hot water, solar cooking, and high temperature process heat for industrial purposes.

Solar technologies are broadly characterized as either passive solar or active solar depending on the way they capture, convert and distribute solar energy. Active solar techniques include the use of photovoltaic panels and solar thermal collectors to harness the energy. Passive solar techniques include orienting a building to the Sun, selecting materials with favourable thermal mass or light dispersing properties, and designing spaces that naturally circulate air.

Biomass

Biomass (plant material) is a renewable energy source because the energy it contains comes from the sun. Through the process of photosynthesis, plants capture the sun's energy. When the plants are burned, they release the sun's energy they contain. In this way, biomass functions as a sort of natural battery for storing solar energy. As long as biomass is produced sustainably, with only as much used as is grown, the battery will last indefinitely.

In general there are two main approaches to using plants for energy production: growing plants specifically for energy use, and using the residues from plants that are used for other things. The best approaches vary from region to region according to climate, soils and geography.

Biofuel

Liquid biofuel is usually either bioalcohol such as bioethanol or an oil such as biodiesel.

Bioethanol is an alcohol made by fermenting the sugar components of plant materials and it is made mostly from sugar and starch crops. With advanced technology being developed, cellulosic biomass, such as trees and grasses, are also used as feedstocks for ethanol production. Ethanol can be used as a fuel for vehicles in its pure form, but it is usually used as a gasoline additive to increase octane and improve vehicle emissions. Bioethanol is widely used in the USA and in Brazil.

Biodiesel is made from vegetable oils, animal fats or recycled greases. Biodiesel can be used as a fuel for vehicles in its pure form, but it is usually used as a diesel additive to reduce levels of particulates, carbon monoxide, and hydrocarbons from diesel-powered vehicles. Biodiesel is produced from oils or fats using transesterification and is the most common biofuel in Europe.

Biofuels provided 1.8 per cent of the world's transport fuel in 2008.

Geothermal Energy

Geothermal energy is energy obtained by tapping the heat of the earth itself, both from kilometers deep into the Earth's crust in some places of the globe or from some meters in geothermal heat pump in all the places of the planet. It is expensive to build a power station but operating costs are low resulting in low energy costs for suitable sites. Ultimately, this energy derives from heat in the Earth's core.

Three types of power plants are used to generate power from geothermal energy: dry steam, flash, and binary. Dry steam plants take steam out of fractures in the ground and use it to directly drive a turbine that spins a generator. Flash plants take hot water, usually at temperatures over 200 °C, out of the ground, and allows it to boil as it rises to the surface then separates the steam phase in steam/water separators and then runs the steam through a turbine. In binary plants, the hot water flows through heat exchangers, boiling an organic fluid that spins the turbine. The condensed steam and remaining geothermal fluid from all three types of plants are injected back into the hot rock to pick up more heat.

The geothermal energy from the core of the Earth is closer to the surface in some areas than in others. Where hot underground steam or water can be tapped and brought to the surface it may be used to generate electricity. Such geothermal power sources exist in certain geologically unstable parts of the world such as Chile, Iceland, New Zealand, United States, the Philippines and Italy. The two most prominent areas for this in the United States are in the Yellowstone basin and in northern California. Iceland produced 170 MW geothermal power and heated 86 per cent of all houses in the year 2000 through geothermal energy. Some 8000 MW of capacity is operational in total.

There is also the potential to generate geothermal energy from hot dry rocks. Holes at least 3 km deep are drilled into the earth. Some of these holes pump water into the earth, while other holes pump hot water out. The heat resource consists of hot underground radiogenic granite rocks, which heat up when there is enough sediment between the rock and the earths surface. Several companies in Australia are exploring this technology.

Economic Trends

All forms of energy are expensive, but as time progresses, renewable energy generally gets cheaper, while fossil fuels generally get more expensive. Al Gore has explained that renewable energy technologies are declining in price for three main reasons:

- *First*, once the renewable infrastructure is built, the fuel is free forever. Unlike carbon-based fuels, the wind and the sun and the earth itself provide fuel that is free, in amounts that are effectively limitless.
- *Second*, while fossil fuel technologies are more mature, renewable energy technologies are being rapidly improved. So innovation and ingenuity give us the ability to constantly increase the efficiency of renewable energy and continually reduce its cost.
- *Third*, once the world makes a clear commitment to shifting toward renewable energy, the volume of production will itself sharply reduce the cost of each windmill and each solar panel, while adding yet more incentives for additional research and development to further speed up the innovation process.

At the end of 2009, worldwide wind farm capacity was 157,900 MW, representing an increase of 31 per cent during the year, and wind power supplied some 1.3 per cent of global electricity consumption. Wind power accounts for approximately 19 per cent of electricity use in Denmark, 9 per cent in Spain and Portugal, and 6 per cent in Germany and the Republic of Ireland. The United States is an important growth area and installed U.S. wind power capacity reached 25,170 MW at the end of 2008. As of November 2010, the Roscoe Wind Farm (781 MW) is the world's largest wind farm.

As of September 2010, the Thanet Offshore Wind Project in United Kingdom is the largest offshore wind farm in the world at 300 MW, followed by Horns Rev II (209 MW) in Denmark. The United Kingdom is the world's leading generator of offshore wind power, followed by Denmark.

New Generation of Solar Thermal Plants

Large solar thermal power stations include the 354 megawatt (MW) Solar Energy Generating Systems power plant in the USA, Solnova Solar Power Station (Spain, 150 MW), Andasol solar power station (Spain, 100 MW), Nevada Solar One (USA, 64 MW), PS20 solar power tower (Spain, 20 MW), and the PS10 solar power tower (Spain, 11 MW).

The solar thermal power industry is growing rapidly with 1.2 GW under construction as of April 2009 and another 13.9 GW announced globally through 2014. Spain is the epicenter of solar thermal power development with 22 projects for 1,037 MW under construction, all of which are projected to come online by the end of 2010. In the United States, 5,600 MW of solar thermal power projects have been announced. In developing countries, three World Bank projects for integrated solar thermal/combined-cycle gas-turbine power plants in Egypt, Mexico, and Morocco have been approved.

Photovoltaic production has been increasing by an average of some 20 per cent each year since 2002, making it a fast-growing energy technology. At the end of 2009, the cumulative global PV installations surpassed 21,000 megawatts.

As of November 2010, the largest photovoltaic (PV) power plants in the world are the Finsterwalde Solar Park (Germany, 80.7 MW), Sarnia Photovoltaic Power Plant (Canada, 80 MW), Olmedilla Photovoltaic Park (Spain, 60 MW), the Strasskirchen Solar Park (Germany, 54 MW), the Lieberose Photovoltaic Park (Germany, 53 MW), and the Puertollano Photovoltaic Park (Spain, 50 MW). Many of these plants are integrated with agriculture and some use innovative tracking systems that follow the sun's daily path across the sky to generate more electricity than conventional fixed-mounted systems. There are no fuel costs or emissions during operation of the power stations.

Topaz Solar Farm is a proposed 550 MW solar photovoltaic power plant which is to be built northwest of California Valley in the USA at a cost of over $1 billion. High Plains Ranch is a proposed 250 MW solar photovoltaic power plant which is to be built on the Carrizo Plain, northwest of California Valley.

However, when it comes to renewable energy systems and PV, it is not just large systems that matter. Building-integrated photovoltaics or 'onsite' PV systems use existing land and structures and generate power close to where it is consumed.

Since the 1970s, Brazil has had an ethanol fuel programme which has allowed the country to become the world's second largest producer of ethanol (after the United States) and the world's largest exporter. Brazil's ethanol fuel programme uses modern equipment and cheap sugar cane as feedstock, and the residual cane-waste (bagasse) is used to process heat and power. There are no longer light vehicles in Brazil running on pure gasoline. By the end of 2008 there were 35,000 filling stations throughout Brazil with at least one ethanol pump.

Nearly all the gasoline sold in the United States today is mixed with 10 per cent ethanol, a mix known as E10, and motor vehicle manufacturers already produce vehicles designed to run on much higher ethanol blends. Ford, DaimlerChrysler, and GM are among the automobile companies that sell 'flexible-fuel' cars, trucks, and minivans that can use gasoline and ethanol blends ranging from pure gasoline up to 85 per cent ethanol (E85). By mid-2006, there were approximately six million E85-compatible vehicles on U.S. roads. The challenge is to expand the market for biofuels beyond the farm states where they have been most popular to date. Flex-fuel vehicles are assisting in this transition because they allow drivers to choose different fuels based on price and availability. The *Energy Policy Act of 2005*, which calls for 7.5 billion gallons of biofuels to be used annually by 2012, will also help to expand the market. Geothermal energy commercialization.

The International Geothermal Association (IGA) has reported that 10,715 megawatts (MW) of geothermal power in 24 countries is online, which is expected to generate 67,246 GWh of electricity in 2010. This represents a 20 per cent increase in geothermal power online capacity since 2005. IGA projects this will grow to 18,500 MW by 2015, due to the large number of projects presently under consideration, often in areas previously assumed to have little exploitable resource.

In 2010, the United States led the world in geothermal electricity production with 3,086 MW of installed capacity from 77 power plants; the largest group of geothermal power plants in the world is located at The Geysers, a geothermal field in California. The Philippines follows the US as the second highest producer of geothermal power in the world, with 1,904 MW of capacity online; geothermal power makes up approximately 18 per cent of the country's electricity generation.

Geothermal (ground source) heat pumps represented an estimated 30 GWth of installed capacity at the end of 2008, with other direct uses of geothermal heat (i.e., for space heating, agricultural drying and other uses) reaching an estimated 15 GWth. As of 2008, at least 76 countries use direct geothermal energy in some form.

Wave Farms Expansion

Portugal now has the world's first commercial wave farm, the *Agucadoura Wave Park*, officially opened in September 2008. The farm uses three Pelamis P-750 machines generating 2.25 MW. Initial costs are put at 8.5 million. A second phase of the project is now planned to increase the installed capacity to 21MW using a further 25 Pelamis machines.

Funding for a wave farm in Scotland was announced in February, 2007 by the Scottish Government, at a cost of over 4 million pounds, as part of a UK£13 million funding packages for ocean power in Scotland. The farm will be the world's largest with a capacity of 3MW generated by four Pelamis machines.

Developing Country Markets

Renewable energy can be particularly suitable for developing countries. In rural and remote areas, transmission and distribution of energy generated from fossil fuels can be difficult and expensive. Producing renewable energy locally can offer a viable alternative.

Biomass cookstoves are used by 40 per cent of the world's population. These stoves are being manufactured in factories and workshops worldwide, and more than 160 million households now use them. More than 30 million rural households get lighting and cooking from biogas made in household-scale digesters. An estimated 3 million households get power from small solar PV systems. Micro-hydro systems configured into village-scale or county-scale mini-grids serve many areas.

Kenya is the world leader in the number of solar power systems installed per capita. More than 30,000 very small solar panels, each producing 12 to 30 watts, are sold in Kenya annually.

Renewable energy projects in many developing countries have demonstrated that renewable energy can directly contribute to poverty alleviation by providing the energy needed for creating businesses and employment. Renewable energy technologies can also make indirect contributions to alleviating poverty by providing energy for cooking, space heating, and lighting. Renewable energy can also contribute to education, by providing electricity to schools.

Global revenues for solar photovoltaics, wind power, and biofuels expanded from $76 billion in 2007 to $115 billion in 2008. New global investments in clean energy technologies expanded by 4.7 per cent from $148 billion in 2007 to $155 billion in 2008. U.S. President Barack Obama's American Recovery and Reinvestment Act of 2009 includes more than $70 billion in direct spending and tax credits for clean energy and associated transportation programmes. Clean Edge suggests that the commercialization of clean energy will help countries around the world pull out of the current economic malaise. Leading renewable energy companies include First Solar, Gamesa, GE Energy, Q-Cells, Sharp Solar, Siemens, SunOpta, Suntech, and Vestas.

The International Renewable Energy Agency (IRENA) is an intergovernmental organization for promoting the adoption of renewable energy worldwide. It aims to provide concrete policy advice and facilitate capacity building and technology transfer. IRENA was formed on January 26, 2009, by 75 countries signing the charter of IRENA. As of March 2010, IRENA has 143 member states who all are considered as founding members, of which 14 have also ratified the statute.

Renewable energy policy targets exist in some 73 countries around the world, and public policies to promote renewable energy use have become more common in recent years. At least 64 countries have some type of policy to promote renewable power generation. Mandates for solar hot water in new construction are becoming more common at both national and local levels. Mandates for blending biofuels into vehicle fuels have been enacted in 17 countries.

New and emerging renewable energy technologies are still under development and include cellulosic ethanol, hot-dry-rock geothermal power, and ocean energy. These technologies are not yet widely demonstrated or have limited commercialization. Many are on the horizon and may have potential comparable to other renewable energy technologies, but still depend on attracting sufficient attention and research, development and demonstration (RD&D) funding.

Cellulosic Ethanol

Companies such as Iogen, Broin, and Abengoa are building refineries that can process biomass and turn it into ethanol, while companies such as Diversa, Novozymes, and Dyadic are producing enzymes which could enable a cellulosic ethanol future. The shift from food crop feedstocks to waste residues and native grasses offers significant opportunities for a range of players, from farmers to biotechnology firms, and from project developers to investors.

Ocean Energy

Systems to harvest utility-scale electrical power from ocean waves have recently been gaining momentum as a viable technology. The potential for this technology is considered promising, especially on west-facing coasts with latitudes between 40 and 60 degrees.

In the United Kingdom, for example, the Carbon Trust recently estimated the extent of the economically viable offshore resource at 55 TWh per year, about 14 per cent of current national demand. Across Europe, the technologically achievable resource has been estimated to be at least 280 TWh per year. In 2003, the U.S. Electric Power Research Institute (EPRI) estimated the viable resource in the United States at 255 TWh per year (6% of demand).

The world's first commercial tidal power station was installed in 2007 in the narrows of Strangford Lough in Ireland. The 1.2 megawatt underwater tidal electricity generator, part of Northern Ireland's Environment & Renewable Energy Fund scheme, takes advantage of the fast tidal flow (up to 4 metres per second) in the lough. Although the generator is powerful enough to power a thousand homes, the turbine has minimal environmental impact, as it is almost entirely submerged, and the rotors pose no danger to wildlife as they turn quite slowly.

Ocean thermal energy conversion (OTEC) uses the temperature difference that exists between deep and shallow waters to run a heat engine.

Enhanced Geothermal Systems

Enhanced geothermal system:

- Reservoir
- Pump house
- Heat exchanger
- Turbine hall
- Production well
- Injection well
- Hot water to district heating
- Porous sediments
- Observation well
- Crystalline bedrock

Enhanced Geothermal Systems are a new type of geothermal power technologies that do not require natural convective hydrothermal resources. The vast majority of geothermal energy within drilling reach is in dry and non-porous rock. EGS technologies 'enhance' and/or create geothermal resources in this 'hot dry rock (HDR)' through hydraulic stimulation.

EGS/HDR technologies, like hydrothermal geothermal, are expected to be baseload resources which produce power 24 hours a day like a fossil plant. Distinct from hydrothermal, HDR/EGS may be feasible anywhere in the world, depending on the economic limits of drill depth. Good locations are over deep granite covered by a thick (3-5 km) layer of insulating sediments which slow heat loss.

There are HDR and EGS systems currently being developed and tested in France, Australia, Japan, Germany, the U.S. and Switzerland. The largest EGS project in the world is a 25 megawatt demonstration plant currently being developed in the Cooper Basin, Australia. The Cooper Basin has the potential to generate 5,000-10,000 MW.

Nanotechnology Thin-film Solar Panels

Solar power panels that use nanotechnology, which can create circuits out of individual silicon molecules, may cost half as much as traditional photovoltaic cells, according to executives and investors involved in developing the products. Nanosolar has secured more than $100 million from investors to build a factory for nanotechnology thin-film solar panels.

Renewable Energy Debate

Renewable electricity production, from sources such as wind power and solar power, is sometimes criticized for being variable or intermittent. However, the International Energy Agency has stated that deployment of renewable technologies usually increases the diversity of electricity sources and, through local generation, contributes to the flexibility of the system and its resistance to central shocks.

There have been 'not in my back yard' (NIMBY) concerns relating to the visual and other impacts of some wind farms, with local residents sometimes fighting or blocking construction. In the USA, the Massachusetts Cape Wind project was delayed for years partly because of aesthetic concerns. However, residents in other areas have been more positive and there are many examples of community wind farm developments. According to a town councilor, the overwhelming majority of locals believe that the Ardrossan Wind Farm in Scotland has enhanced the area.

17

Wildlife Conservation

Wildlife includes all non-domesticated plants, animals and other organisms. Domesticating wild plant and animal species for human benefit has occurred many times all over the planet, and has a major impact on the environment, both positive and negative.

Wildlife can be found in all ecosystems. Deserts, rain forests, plains, and other areas including the most developed urban sites, all have distinct forms of wildlife. While the term in popular culture usually refers to animals that are untouched by human factors, most scientists agree that wildlife around the world is impacted by human activities.

Humans have historically tended to separate civilization from wildlife in a number of ways including the legal, social, and moral sense. This has been a reason for debate throughout recorded history. Religions have often declared certain animals to be sacred, and in modern times concern for the natural environment has provoked activists to protest the exploitation of wildlife for human benefit or entertainment. Literature has also made use of the traditional human separation from wildlife.

Food, Pets, Traditional Medicines

Anthropologists believe that the Stone Age peoples and hunter-gatherers relied on wildlife, both plant and animal, for their food. In fact, some species may have been hunted to extinction by early human hunters. Today, hunting, fishing, or gathering wildlife is still a significant food source in some parts of the world. In other areas, hunting and non-commercial fishing are mainly seen as a sport or recreation, with the edible meat as mostly a side benefit. Meat sourced from wildlife that is not traditionally regarded as game is known as bush meat. The increasing demand for wildlife as a source of traditional food in East Asia is decimating populations of sharks, primates, pangolins and other animals, which they believe have aphrodisiac properties.

In November 2008, almost 900 plucked and 'oven-ready' owls and other protected wildlife species were confiscated by the Department of Wildlife and National Parks in Malaysia, according to TRAFFIC. The animals were believed to be bound for China, to be sold in wild meat restaurants. Most are listed in CITES (the Convention on International Trade in Endangered Species of Wild Fauna and Flora) which prohibits or restricts such trade.

> "Malaysia is home to a vast array of amazing wildlife. However, illegal hunting and trade poses a threat to Malaysia's natural diversity".
>
> *–Chris S. Shepherd*

A November 2008 report from biologist and author Sally Kneidel, PhD, documented numerous wildlife species for sale in informal markets along the Amazon River, including wild-caught marmosets sold for as little as \$1.60 (5 Peruvian soles). Many Amazon species, including peccaries, agoutis, turtles, turtle eggs, anacondas, armadillos, etc., are sold primarily as food. Others in these informal markets, such as monkeys and parrots, are destined for the pet trade, often smuggled into the United States. Still other Amazon species are popular ingredients in traditional medicines sold in local markets. The medicinal value of animal parts is based largely on superstition.

Many wildlife species have spiritual significance in different cultures around the world, and they and their products may be used as sacred objects in religious rituals. For example, eagles, hawks and their feathers have great cultural and spiritual value to Native Americans as religious objects.

Media

Wildlife has long been a common subject for educational television shows. National Geographic specials appeared on CBS beginning in 1965, later moving to ABC and then PBS. In 1963, NBC debuted *Wild Kingdom,* a popular programme featuring zoologist Marlin Perkins as host. The BBC natural history unit in the UK was a similar pioneer, the first wildlife series LOOK presented by Sir Peter Scott, was a studio-based show, with filmed inserts. It was in this series that David Attenborough first made his appearance which led to the series Zoo Quest during which he and cameraman Charles Lagus went to many exotic places looking for elusive wildlife—notably the Komodo dragon in Indonesia and lemurs in

Madagascar. Since 1984, the Discovery Channel and its spin off Animal Planet in the USA have dominated the market for shows about wildlife on cable television, while on PBS the NATURE strand made by WNET-13 in New York and NOVA by WGBH in Boston are notable. See also Nature documentary. Wildlife television is now a multi-million dollar industry with specialist documentary film-makers in many countries including UK, USA, New Zealand NHNZ, Australia, Austria, Germany, Japan, and Canada. There are many magazines which cover wildlife including National Wildlife Magazine, Birds and Blooms, Birding (magazine), and Ranger Rick (for children).

Fuelled by media coverage and inclusion of conservation education in early school curriculum, Wildlife tourism and Ecotourism has fast become a popular industry generating substantial income for developing nations with rich wildlife specially, Africa and India. This ever growing and ever becoming more popular form of tourism is providing the much needed incentive for poor nations to conserve their rich wildlife heritage and its habitat.

Exploitation of wild populations has been a characteristic of modern man since our exodus from Africa 130,000 - 70,000 years ago. The rate of extinctions of entire species of plants and animals across the planet has been so high in the last few hundred years it is widely considered that we are in the sixth great extinction event on this planet; the Holocene Mass Extinction.

Destruction of wildlife does not always lead to an extinction of the species in question, however, the dramatic loss of entire species across Earth dominates any review of wildlife destruction as extinction is the level of damage to a wild population from which there is no return.

The four most general reasons that lead to destruction of wildlife include overkill, habitat destruction and fragmentation, impact of introduced species and chains of extinction.

Overkill

Overkill occurs whenever hunting occurs at rates greater than the reproductive capacity of the population is being exploited. The effects of this are often noticed much more dramatically in slow growing populations such as many larger species of fish. Initially when a portion of a wild population is hunted, an increased availability of resources (food, etc.) is experienced increasing growth and reproduction as Density dependent inhibition is lowered. Hunting, fishing and so on, has lowered the competition between members of a population. However, if this hunting continues at rate greater than the rate at which new members of the population can reach breeding age and produce more young, the population will begin to decrease in numbers.

Populations are confined to islands, whether literal islands or just areas of habitat that are effectively an "island" for the species concerned have also been observed to be at greater risk of dramatic population declines following unsustainable hunting.

Habitat Destruction and Fragmentation

The habitat of any given species is considered its preferred area or territory. Many processes associated human habitation of an area cause loss of this area and decrease the carrying capacity of the land for that species. In many cases these changes in land use cause a patchy break-up of the wild landscape. Agricultural land frequently displays this type of extremely fragmented, or relictual, habitat. Farms sprawl across the landscape with patches of uncleared woodland or forest dotted in-between occasional paddocks.

Examples of habitat destruction include grazing of bushland by farmed animals, changes to natural fire regimes, forest clearing for timber production and wetland draining for city expansion.

Impact of Introduced Species

Mice, cats, rabbits, dandelions and poison ivy are all examples of species that have become invasive threats to wild species in various parts of the world. Frequently species that are uncommon in their home range become out-of-control invasions in distant but similar climates. The reasons for this have not always been clear and Charles Darwin felt it was unlikely that exotic species would ever be able to grow abundantly in a place in which they had not evolved. The reality is that the vast majority of species exposed to a new habitat do not reproduce successfully. Occasionally, however, some populations do take hold and after a period of acclimation can increase in numbers significantly, having destructive effects on many elements of the native environment of which they have become part.

Chains of Extinction

This final group is one of secondary effects. All wild populations of living things have many complex intertwining links with other living things around them. Large herbivorous animals such as the hippopotamus have populations of insectivorous birds that feed off the many parasitic insects that grow on the hippo. Should the hippo die out, so too will these groups of birds, leading to further destruction as other species dependent on the birds are affected. Also referred to as a Domino effect, this series of chain reactions is by far the most destructive process that can occur in any ecological community.

Another example is the black drongos and the cattle egrets found in India. These birds feed on insects on the back of cattle, which helps to keep them disease-free. If we destroy the nesting habitats of these birds, it will result a decrease in the cattle population because of the spread of insect-borne diseases.

18

Energy Conservation

Energy conservation refers to efforts made to reduce energy consumption. Energy conservation can be achieved through increased efficient energy use, in conjunction with decreased energy consumption and/or reduced consumption from conventional energy sources.

Energy conservation can result in increased financial capital, environmental quality, national security, personal security, and human comfort. Individuals and organizations that are direct consumers of energy choose to conserve energy to reduce energy costs and promote economic security. Industrial and commercial users can increase energy use efficiency to maximize profit.

Electrical energy conservation is an important element of energy policy. Energy conservation reduces the energy consumption and energy demand per capita and thus offsets some of the growth in energy supply needed to keep up with population growth. This reduces the rise in energy costs, and can reduce the need for new power plants, and energy imports. The reduced energy demand can provide more flexibility in choosing the most preferred methods of energy production.

By reducing emissions, energy conservation is an important part of lessening climate change. Energy conservation facilitates the replacement of non-renewable resources with renewable energy. Energy conservation is often the most economical solution to energy shortages, and is a more environmentally being alternative to increased energy production.

Energy Conservation by Country

India

Petroleum Conservation Research Association (PCRA) www.pcra.org is an Indian government body created in 1976 and engaged in promoting energy efficiency and conservation in every walk of life. In the recent past PCRA has done mass media campaigns in television, radio and print media. An impact assessment survey by a third party revealed that due to these mega campaigns by PCRA, overall awareness level have gone up leading to saving of fossil fuels worth crores of rupees besides reducing pollution.

Bureau of Energy Efficiency is an Indian governmental organization created in 2002 responsible for promoting energy efficiency and conservation.

Japan

Since the 1973 oil crisis, energy conservation has been an issue in Japan. All oil based fuel is imported, so indigenous sustainable energy is being developed.

The Energy Conservation Centre promotes energy efficiency in every aspect of Japan. Private entities are implementing the efficient use of energy for industries.

Lebanon

In Lebanon and since 2002 The Lebanese Centre for Energy Conservation (LCEC) has been promoting the development of efficient and rational uses of energy and the use of renewable energy at the consumer level. It was created as a project financed by the Global Environment Facility (GEF) and the Ministry of Energy Water (MEW) under the management of the United Nations Development Programme (UNDP) and gradually established itself as an independent technical national centre although it continues to be supported by the United Nations Development Programme (UNDP) as indicated in the Memorandum of Understanding (MoU) signed between MEW and UNDP on June 18, 2007.

New Zealand

In New Zealand the Energy Efficiency and Conservation Authority is responsible for promoting energy efficiency and conservation.

European Union

At the end of 2006, the European Union-EU pledged to cut its annual consumption of primary energy by 20 per cent by 2020. The 'European

Union Energy Efficiency Action Plan' is long awaited. As part of the EU's SAVE Programme, aimed at promoting energy efficiency and encouraging energy-saving behaviour, the Boiler Efficiency Directive specifies minimum levels of efficiency for boilers fired with liquid or gaseous fuels. The European Commission is funding large-scale research projects to learn about success factors for effective energy conservation programmes.

United Kingdom

Energy conservation in the United Kingdom has been receiving increased attention over recent years. Key factors behind this are the Government's commitment to reducing carbon emissions, the projected 'energy gap' in UK electricity generation, and the increasing reliance on imports to meet national energy needs. Domestic housing and road transport are currently the two biggest problem areas.

Responsibility for energy conservation fall between three Government departments although is led by the Department for Energy and Climate Change (DECC). The Department for Communities and Local Government (CLG) is still responsible for energy standards in buildings, and the Department for Environment, Food and Rural Affairs (Defra) retains a residual interest in energy insofar as it leads to emissions of CO_2, the main greenhouse gas. The Department for Transport retains many responsibilities for energy conservation in transport. At an operational level, there are two main non-departmental governmental bodies ('quangoes') — the Energy Saving Trust, working mainly in the domestic sector with some interest in transport, and the Carbon Trust, working with industry and innovative energy technologies. In addition there are many independent NGOs working in the sector such as the Centre for Sustainable Energy in Bristol or the National Energy Foundation in Milton Keynes, and directly helping consumers make informed choices on energy efficiency sust-it

United States

The United States is currently the largest single consumer of energy. The U.S. Department of Energy categorizes national energy use in four broad sectors: transportation, residential, commercial, and industrial.

Energy usage in transportation and residential sectors, about half of U.S. energy consumption, is largely controlled by individual consumers. Commercial and industrial energy expenditures are determined by businesses entities and other facility managers. National energy policy has a significant effect on energy usage across all four sectors, and its strengthening is part of the 2010 Presidential-Congressional legislative debate.

Issues with Energy Conservation

Advocates and critics of various forms and policies of energy conservation debate some issues, such as:

- Standard economic theory suggests that technological improvements increase energy efficiency, rather than reduce energy use. This is called the *Jevons Paradox* and it is said to occur in two ways. *Firstly*, increased energy efficiency makes the use of energy relatively cheaper, thus encouraging increased use. *Secondly*, increased energy efficiency leads to increased economic growth, which pulls up energy use in the whole economy. This does not imply that increased fuel efficiency is worthless, increased fuel efficiency enables greater production and a higher quality of life. However, in order to reduce energy consumption, efficiency gains must be paired with a government intervention that reduces demand (a green tax, cap and trade).
- Some retailers argue that bright lighting stimulates purchasing. However, health studies have demonstrated that headache, stress, blood pressure, fatigue and worker error all generally increase with the common over-illumination present in many workplace and retail settings. It has been shown that natural daylighting increases productivity levels of workers, while reducing energy consumption.
- The use of telecommuting by major corporations is a significant opportunity to conserve energy, as many Americans now work in service jobs that enable them to work from home instead of commuting to work each day.
- Electric motors consume more than 60 per cent of all electrical energy generated and are responsible for the loss of 10 to 20 per cent of all electricity converted into mechanical energy.
- Consumers are often poorly informed of the savings of energy efficient products. The research one must put into conserving energy often is too time consuming and costly when there are cheaper products and technology available using today's fossil fuels. Some governments and NGOs are attempting to reduce this complexity with ecolabels that make differences in energy efficiency easy to research while shopping.
- Technology needs to be able to change behavioural patterns, it can do this by allowing energy users, business and residential, to see graphically the impact their energy use can have in their workplace or homes. Advanced real-time energy metering is able to help people save energy by their actions. Rather than become wasteful automatic energy saving technologies, real-time energy monitors and meters such as the Energy Detective, Enigin Plc's Eniscope, Ecowizard, or solutions like EDSA'a Paladin Live are examples of such solutions.

- It is frequently argued that effective energy conservation requires more than informing consumers about energy consumption, for example through smart meters at home or ecolabels while shopping. People need practical and tailored advice how to reduce energy consumption in order to make change easy and lasting. This applies to both efficiency investments, such as investment in building renovation, or behavioural change, for example turning down the heating. To provide the kind of information and support people need to invest money, time and effort in energy conservation, it is important to understand and link to people's topical concerns.
- In deregulated states commercial utility customers have the ability to compare energy rates among available electricity and natural gas providers.

Efficient Energy Use

Efficient energy use, sometimes simply called energy efficiency, is the goal of efforts to reduce the amount of energy required to provide products and services. For example, insulating a home allows a building to use less heating and cooling energy to achieve and maintain a comfortable temperature. Installing fluorescent lights or natural skylights reduces the amount of energy required to attain the same level of illumination compared to using traditional incandescent light bulbs. Compact fluorescent lights use two-thirds less energy and may last 6 to 10 times longer than incandescent lights. Improvements in energy efficiency are most often achieved by adopting a more efficient technology or production process.

There are various motivations to improve energy efficiency. Reducing energy use reduces energy costs and may result in a financial cost saving to consumers if the energy savings offset any additional costs of implementing an energy efficient technology. Reducing energy use is also seen as a key solution to the problem of reducing greenhouse gas emissions. According to the International Energy Agency, improved energy efficiency in buildings, industrial processes and transportation could reduce the world's energy needs in 2050 by one third, and help control global emissions of greenhouse gases.

Energy efficiency and renewable energy are said to be the *twin pillars* of sustainable energy policy. In many countries energy efficiency is also seen to have a national security benefit because it can be used to reduce the level of energy imports from foreign countries and may slow down the rate at which domestic energy resources are depleted.

Making homes, vehicles, and businesses more energy efficient is seen as a largely untapped solution to addressing the problems of pollution, global warming, energy security, and fossil fuel depletion. Many of these ideas have been discussed for years, since the 1973 oil crisis brought energy issues to the forefront. In the late 1970s, physicist Amory Lovins popularized the notion of a "soft energy path", with a strong focus on energy efficiency. Among other things, Lovins popularized the notion of negawatts—the idea of meeting energy needs by increasing efficiency instead of increasing energy production.

Energy efficiency has proved to be a cost-effective strategy for building economies without necessarily growing energy consumption. For example, the state of California began implementing energy-efficiency measures in the mid-1970s, including building code and appliance standards with strict efficiency requirements. During the following years, California's energy consumption has remained approximately flat on a per capita basis while national U.S. consumption doubled. As part of its strategy, California implemented a 'loading order' for new energy resources that puts energy efficiency first, renewable electricity supplies second, and new fossil-fired power plants last.

Lovins' Rocky Mountain Institute points out that in industrial settings, "there are abundant opportunities to save 70 per cent to 90 per cent of the energy and cost for lighting, fan, and pump systems; 50 per cent for electric motors; and 60 per cent in areas such as heating, cooling, office equipment, and appliances." In general, up to 75 per cent of the electricity used in the U.S. today could be saved with efficiency measures that cost less than the electricity itself. The same holds true for home-owners, leaky ducts have remained an invisible energy culprit for years. In fact, researchers at the US Department of Energy and their consortium, Residential Energy Efficient Distribution Systems (REEDS) have found that duct efficiency may be as low as 50-70 per cent. The US Department of Energy has stated that there is potential for energy saving in the magnitude of 90 Billion kWh by increasing home energy efficiency.

Other studies have emphasized this. A report published in 2006 by the McKinsey Global Institute, asserted that "there are sufficient economically viable opportunities for energy-productivity improvements that could keep global energy-demand growth at less than one per cent per annum"—less than half of the 2.2 per cent average growth anticipated through 2020 in a business-as-usual scenario. Energy productivity, which measures the output and quality of goods and services per unit of energy input, can come from either reducing the amount of energy required to produce something, or from increasing the quantity or quality of goods and services from the same amount of energy.

The Vienna Climate Change Talks 2007 Report, under the auspices of the United Nations Framework Convention on Climate Change (UNFCCC), clearly shows "that energy efficiency can achieve real emission reductions at low cost".

Appliances

Modern energy-efficient appliances, such as refrigerators, freezers, ovens, stoves, dishwashers, and clothes washers and dryers, use significantly less energy than older appliances. Current energy efficient refrigerators, for example, use 40 per cent less energy than conventional models did in 2001. Following this, if all households in Europe changed their more than ten year old appliances into new ones, 20 billion kWh of electricity would be saved annually, hence reducing CO_2 emissions by almost 18 billion kg. In the US, the corresponding figures would be 17 billion kWh of electricity and 27,000,000,000 lb (1.2×10^{10} kg) CO_2. According to a 2009 study from McKinsey & Company the replacement of old appliances is one of the most efficient global measures to reduce emissions of greenhouse gases. Modern power management systems also reduce energy usage by idle appliances by turning them off or putting them into a low-energy mode after a certain time. Many countries identify energy-efficient appliances using energy input labelling.

The impact of energy efficiency on peak demand depends on when the appliance is used. For example, an air conditioner uses more energy during the afternoon when it is hot. Therefore, an energy efficient air conditioner will have a larger impact on peak demand than off-peak demand. An energy efficient dishwasher, on the other hand, uses more energy during the late evening when people do their dishes. This appliance may have little to no impact on peak demand.

Building Design

A building's location and surroundings play a key role in regulating its temperature and illumination. For example, trees, landscaping, and hills can provide shade and block wind. In cooler climates, designing buildings with a south facing windows increases the amount of sun (ultimately heat energy) entering the building, minimizing energy use, by maximizing passive solar heating. Tight building design, including energy-efficient windows, well-sealed doors, and additional thermal insulation of walls, basement slabs, and foundations can reduce heat loss by 25 to 50 per cent.

Dark roofs may become up to 39 C° (70 F°) hotter than the most reflective white surfaces, and they transmit some of this additional heat inside the building. US Studies have shown that lightly coloured roofs use 40 per cent less energy for cooling than buildings with darker roofs. White roof systems save more energy in sunnier climates. Advanced electronic heating and cooling systems can moderate energy consumption and improve the comfort of people in the building.

Proper placement of windows and skylights and use of architectural features that reflect light into a building, can reduce the need for artificial lighting. Increased use of natural and task lighting have been shown by one study to increase productivity in schools and offices. Compact fluorescent lights use two-thirds less energy and may last 6 to 10 times longer than incandescent light bulbs. Newer fluorescent lights produce a natural light, and in most applications they are cost effective, despite their higher initial cost, with payback periods as low as a few months.

Effective energy-efficient building design can include the use of low cost Passive Infra Reds (PIRs) to switch-off lighting when areas are unnoccupied such as toilets, corridors or even office areas out-of-hours. In addition, lux levels can be monitored using daylight sensors linked to the building's lighting scheme to switch on/off or dim the lighting to pre-defined levels to take into account the natural light and thus reduce consumption. Building Management Systems (BMS) link all of this together in one centralised computer to control the whole building's lighting and power requirements.

The choice of which space heating or cooling technology to use in buildings can have a significant impact on energy use and efficiency. For example, replacing an older 50 per cent efficient natural gas furnace with a new 95 per cent one will dramatically reduce energy use, carbon emissions, and winter natural gas bills. Ground source heat pumps can be even more energy efficient and cost effective. These systems use pumps and compressors to move refrigerant fluid around a thermodynamic cycle in order to 'pump' heat against its natural flow from hot to cold, for the purpose of transferring heat into a building from the large thermal reservoir contained within the nearby ground. The end result is that heat pumps typically use four times less electrical energy to deliver an equivalent amount of heat than a direct electrical heater does. Another advantage of a ground source heat pump is that it can be reversed in summertime and operate to cool the air by transferring heat from the building to the ground. The disadvantage of ground source heat pumps is their high initial capital cost, but this is typically recouped within 5 to 10 years as a result of lower energy use.

Smart meters are slowly being adopted by the commerial sector to highlight to staff and for internal monitoring purposes the building's energy usage in a dynamic presentable format. The use of Power Quality Analysers can be introduced into an existing building to assess usage, harmonic distortion, peaks, swells and interruptions amongst others to ultimately make the building more energy-efficient. Often such meters communicate by using wireless sensor networks.

A term relevant for efficient energy use is energy use intensity, which is defined as energy consumption per floor area.

Industry

Industry uses a large amount of energy to power a diverse range of manufacturing and resource extraction processes. Many industrial processes require large amounts of heat and mechanical power, most of which is delivered as natural gas, petroleum fuels and as electricity. In addition some industries generate fuel from waste products that can be used to provide additional energy.

Because industrial processes are so diverse it is impossible to describe the multitude of possible opportunities for energy efficiency in industry. Many depend on the specific technologies and processes in use at each industrial facility. However there are a number of processes and energy services that are widely used in many industries.

Various industries generate steam and electricity for subsequent use within their facilities. When electricity is generated, the heat that is produced as a by-product can be captured and used for process steam, heating or other industrial purposes. Conventional electricity generation is about 30 per cent efficient, whereas combined heat and power (also called co-generation) converts up to 90 per cent of the fuel into usable energy.

Advanced boilers and furnaces can operate at higher temperatures while burning less fuel. These technologies are more efficient and produce fewer pollutants.

Over 45 per cent of the fuel used by US manufacturers is burnt to make steam. The typical industrial facility can reduce this energy usage 20 per cent (according to the US Department of Energy) by insulating steam and condensate return lines, stopping steam leakage, and maintaining steam traps.

Electric motors usually run at a constant speed, but a variable speed drive allows the motor's energy output to match the required load. This achieves energy savings ranging from 3 to 60 per cent, depending on how the motor is used. Motor coils made of superconducting materials can also reduce energy losses. Motors may also benefit from voltage optimisation.

Industry uses a large number of pumps and compressors of all shapes and sizes and in a wide variety of applications. The efficiency of pumps and compressors depends on many factors but often improvements can be made by implementing better process control and better maintenance practices. Compressors are commonly used to provide compressed air which is used for sand blasting, painting, and other power tools. According to the US Department of Energy, optimizing compressed air systems by installing variable speed drives, along with preventive maintenance to detect and fix air leaks, can improve energy efficiency 20 to 50 per cent.

Vehicles

The estimated energy efficiency for an automobile is 280 Passenger-Mile/10^6 Btu. There are several ways to enhance a vehicle's energy efficiency. Using improved aerodynamics to minimize drag can increase vehicle fuel efficiency. Reducing vehicle weight can also improve fuel economy, which is why composite materials are widely used in car bodies.

More advanced tyres, with decreased tyre to road friction and rolling resistance, can save gasoline. Fuel economy can be improved by up to 3.3 per cent by keeping tyres inflated to the correct pressure. Replacing a clogged air filter can improve a cars fuel consumption by as much as 10 per cent on older vehicles. On newer vehicles (1980's and up) with fuel-injected, computer-controlled engines, a clogged air filter has no effect on mpg but replacing it may improve acceleration by 6-11 per cent.

Energy-efficient vehicles may reach twice the fuel efficiency of the average automobile. Cutting-edge designs, such as the diesel Mercedes-Benz Bionic concept vehicle have achieved a fuel efficiency as high as 84 miles per US gallon (2.8 L/100 km; 101 mpg_{-imp}), four times the current conventional automotive average.

The mainstream trend in automotive efficiency is the rise of electric vehicles. Hybrids, like the Toyota Prius, use regenerative braking to recapture energy that would dissipate in normal cars; the effect is especially pronounced in city driving. plug-in hybrids also have increased battery capacity, which makes it possible to drive for limited distances without burning any gasoline; in this case, energy efficiency is dictated by whatever process (such as coal-burning, hydroelectric, or renewable source) created the power. Plug-ins can typically drive for around 40 miles (64 km) purely on electricity without recharging; if the battery runs low, a gas engine kicks in allowing for extended range. Finally, all-electric cars are also growing in popularity; the Tesla Roadster sports car is the only high-performance all-electric car currently on the market, and others are in preproduction.

Energy Conservation

Energy conservation is broader than energy efficiency in including active efforts to decrease energy consumption, for example through behavioural change, in addition to using energy more efficiently. Examples of conservation without efficiency improvements are heating a room less in winter, using the car less, or enabling energy saving modes on a computer. As with other definitions, the boundary between efficient energy use and energy conservation can be fuzzy, but both are important in environmental and economic terms. This is especially the case when actions are directed at the saving of fossil fuels. Energy conservation is a challenge requiring policy programmes, technological development and behavioural change to go hand in hand. Many energy intermediary organisations, for example governmental or non-governmental organisations on local, regional, or national level, are working on often publicly funded programmes or projects to meet this challenge.

Sustainable Energy

Energy efficiency and renewable energy are said to be the 'twin pillars' of a sustainable energy policy. Both strategies must be developed concurrently in order to stabilize and reduce carbon dioxide emissions. Efficient energy use is essential to slowing the energy demand growth so that rising clean energy supplies can make deep cuts in fossil fuel use. If energy use grows too rapidly, renewable energy development will chase a receding target. Likewise, unless clean energy supplies come online rapidly, slowing demand growth will only begin to reduce total carbon emissions; a reduction in the carbon content of energy sources is also needed. A sustainable energy economy thus requires major commitments to both efficiency and renewables.

Rebound Effect

If the demand for energy services remains constant, improving energy efficiency will reduce energy consumption and carbon emissions. However, many efficiency improvements do not reduce energy consumption by the amount predicted by simple engineering models. This is because they make energy services cheaper, and so consumption of those services increases. For example, since fuel efficient vehicles make travel cheaper, consumers may choose to drive farther and/or faster, thereby offsetting some of the potential energy savings. This is an example of the direct rebound effect.

Estimates of the size of the rebound effect range from roughly 5 per cent to 40 per cent. The rebound effect is likely to be less than 30 per cent at the household level and may be closer to 10 per cent for transport. A rebound effect of 30 per cent implies that improvements in energy efficiency should achieve 70 per cent of the reduction in energy consumption projected using engineering models.

Since more efficient (and hence cheaper) energy will also lead to faster economic growth, there are suspicions that improvements in energy efficiency may eventually lead to even faster resource use. This was postulated by economists in the 1980s and remains a controversial hypothesis. Ecological economists have suggested that any cost savings from efficiency gains be taxed away by the government in order to avoid this outcome.

19

Conservation Movement

The conservation movement, also known as nature conservation, is a political, environmental and a social movement that seeks to protect natural resources including plant and animal species as well as their habitat for the future.

The early conservation movement included fisheries and wildlife management, water, soil conservation and sustainable forestry. The contemporary conservation movement has broadened from the early movement's emphasis on use of sustainable yield of natural resources and preservation of wilderness areas to include preservation of biodiversity. Some say the conservation movement is part of the broader and more far-reaching environmental movement, while others argue that they differ both in ideology and practice. Chiefly in the United States, conservation is seen as differing from environmentalism in that it aims to preserve natural resources expressly for their continued sustainable use by humans. In other parts of the world conservation is used more broadly to include the setting aside of natural areas and thc active protection of wildlife for their inherent value, as much as for any value they may have for humans.

Jones (1991) argues that from an economic perspective the Western nations have been no more destructive of natural resources than any other civilization. He rejects the suggestion that Christianity, by destroying animism, facilitated the ruination of nature in the West, stating he finds no empirical evidence that any culture was or is less exploitive of the natural world than Christianity. He notes that Eastern agricultural history has numerous examples of massive deforestations, erosion, silting of rivers, and infestation with waterborne parasites. He points to large-scale animal extinction and wasteful agricultural practices by North American Indians before 1492. Jones allows that economic growth in the West did result in a higher level of resource use, but finds no evidence to support the view that such resource exploitation was a product of religion, culture, or geography.

History of Conservation Ideas

The nascent conservation movement slowly developed in the 19th century, starting first in the scientific forestry methods pioneered by Prussia and France in the 17th and 18th centuries. While continental Europe created the scientific methods later used in conservationist efforts, British India and the United States are credited with starting the conservation movement.

Foresters in India, often German, managed forests using early climate change theories (in America, see also, George Perkins Marsh) that Alexander von Humboldt developed in the mid 19th century, applied fire protection, and tried to keep the 'house-hold' of nature. This was an early ecological idea, in order to preserve the growth of delicate teak trees. The same German foresters who headed the Forest Service of India, such as Dietrich Brandis and Berthold Ribbentrop, travelled back to Europe and taught at forestry schools in England (Cooper's Hill, later moved to Oxford). These men brought with them the legislative and scientific knowledge of conservationism in British India back to Europe, where they distributed it to men such as Gifford Pinchot, which in turn helped bring European and British Indian methods to the United States.

ASIA

India

Sivaramakrishnan (2009) explores the boundaries between wildness and civility in Indian society, as well as connection of ideas of nature to different aspects of social life, especially labour, aesthetics, politics, commerce, and agriculture. These interconnected historical processes inform environmental history in India. Everyone knows kinnari is great. At present forest history is the area of environmental history in which the most important scholarly debate is underway in India, with special interest in questions of water, air, industry, and climate change.

WESTERN EUROPE

Pyrenees

Vaccaro and Beltran, (2009) examine the Pyrenees mountains as an environmental reservoir, where most of the population has emigrated and the state has taken over much of the mountainous territory to implement conservation policies. One result is the return of fauna, via reintroduction or natural regeneration, especially bears, wolves, beavers, river otters, marmots, mouflon, feral goats, and deer. The work and living space of the mountain communities has fallen under the jurisdiction of external institutions and constituencies that value conservation and ecotourism above local subsistence. This has led to controversy among scientists and residents. Local herders see wild animals as unregulated public property subsidized by the work of the local people. Farmers complain that their fields are invaded on a daily basis by animals they cannot kill because of their protected status. Ranchers, under extremely strict sanitation regulations, see their cattle and sheep coming into biological contact with these unchecked wild populations.

EASTERN EUROPE

Russia

In Russia the regime of Joseph Stalin (1924-53) concentrated on large-scale industrialization, and has earned a historical reputation for paying little heed to the human and environmental costs of such rapid transformations. One exception was the logging industry, in which conflicting needs and ideologies enabled the preservation of significant tracts of forest.

Latvia

Galbreath and Auers (2009) examines history of environmental politics in Latvia, especially the formation of the Latvian Green Party, known as Zala Partija as part of the Green/Farmers' Union or Zalo un Zemnieku Savieniba (ZZP). The depoliticization of environmentalism emerged from the nationalist, corporate, and environmental elements of the ZZP. The three aspects of the environmentalism here are represented by the colours green, brown, and black. Green represents: ecological preservation and reversal of industrial side effects. Brown stands for civic and ethnic nationalism. Black represents the oil and gas pipeline industry and its influence on the 'Green' agenda in Latvia.

UNITED STATES

Progressive Era

Both Conservationism and Environmentalism appeared in political debates during the Progressive Era in the early 20th century. There were three main positions. The laissez-faire position held that owners of private property—including lumber and mining companies, should be allowed to do anything they wished for their property.

The Conservationists, led by President Theodore Roosevelt and his close ally Gifford Pinchot, said that the laissez-faire approach was too wasteful and inefficient. In any case, they noted, most of the natural resources in the western states were already owned by the federal government. The best course of action, they argued, was a long-term plan devised by national experts to maximize the long-term economic benefits of natural resources.

Environmentalism was the third position, led by John Muir (1838-1914). Muir's passion for nature made him the most influential American environmentalist. Muir preached that nature was sacred and humans are intruders who should look but not develop. He founded the Sierra Club and remains an icon of the environmentalist movement. He was primarily responsible for defining the environmentalist position, in the debate between Conservation and environmentalism.

Environmentalism preached that nature was almost sacred, and that man was an intruder. It allowed for limited tourism (such as hiking), but opposed automobiles in national parks. It strenuously opposed timber cutting on most public lands, and vehemently denounced the dams that Roosevelt supported for water supplies, electricity and flood control. Especially controversial was the Hetch Hetchy dam in Yosemite National park, which Roosevelt approved, and which supplies the water supply of San Francisco.

Roosevelt put conservationist issue high on the national agenda. He worked with all the major figures of the movement, especially his chief advisor on the matter, Gifford Pinchot. Roosevelt was deeply committed to conserving natural resources, and is considered to be the nation's first conservation President. He encouraged the Newlands Reclamation Act of 1902 to promote federal construction of dams to irrigate small farms and placed 230 million acres (360,000 mi^2 or 930,000 km^2) under federal protection. Roosevelt set aside more Federal land for national parks and nature preserves than all of his predecessors combined.

Roosevelt established the United States Forest Service, signed into law the creation of five National Parks, and signed the 1906 Antiquities Act, under which he proclaimed 18 new U.S. National Monuments. He also established the first 51 Bird Reserves, four Game Preserves, and 150 National Forests, including Shoshone National Forest, the nation's first. The area of the United States that he placed under public protection totals approximately 230,000,000 acres (930,000 km^2).

Gifford Pinchot had been appointed by McKinley as chief of Division of Forestry in the Department of Agriculture. In 1905, his department gained control of the national forest reserves. Pinchot promoted private use (for a fee) under federal supervision. In 1907, Roosevelt designated 16 million acres (65,000 km^2) of new national forests just minutes before a deadline.

In May 1908, Roosevelt sponsored the Conference of Governors held in the White House, with a focus on natural resources and their most efficient use. Roosevelt delivered the opening address: 'Conservation as a National Duty'.

In 1903 Roosevelt toured the Yosemite Valley with John Muir, who had a very different view of conservation, and tried to minimize commercial use of water resources and forests. Working through the Sierra Club he founded, Muir succeeded in 1905 in having Congress transfer the Mariposa Grove and Yosemite Valley to the National Park Service. While Muir wanted nature preserved for the sake of pure beauty, Roosevelt subscribed to Pinchot's formulation, "to make the forest produce the largest amount of whatever crop or service will be most useful, and keep on producing it for generation after generation of men and trees".

1930s

In the 1930s, the dominant view was the conservationism of Theodore Roosevelt, endorsed by Democrat Franklin D. Roosevelt, that led to the building of many large-scale dams and water projects, as well as the expansion of the National Forest System to buy out sub-marginal farms.

Since 1970

Environmental issues reemerged on the national agenda in 1970, with Republican Richard Nixon playing a major role, especially with his creation of the Environmental Protection Agency. The debates over the public lands and environmental politics played a supporting role in the decline of liberalism and the rise of modern conservatism. Although Americans consistently rank environmental issues as 'important', polling data indicates that in the voting booth voters rank the environmental issues low relative to other political concerns.

The growth of the Republican party's political power in the inland West (apart from the Pacific coast) was facilitated by the rise of popular opposition to public lands reform. Successful Democrats in the inland West and Alaska typically take more conservative positions on environmental issues than Democrats from the Coastal states. Taking the conservationist position, conservatives drew on new organizational networks of think tanks, industry groups, and citizen-oriented organizations, and they began to deploy new strategies that affirmed the rights of individuals to their property, to hunt and recreate, and to pursue happiness unencumbered by the federal government.

Areas of Concern

Deforestation and overpopulation are issues affecting all regions of the world. The consequent destruction of wildlife habitat has prompted the creation of conservation groups in other countries, some founded by local hunters who have witnessed declining wildlife populations first hand. Also, it was highly important for the conservation movement to solve problems of living conditions in the cities and the overpopulation of such places.

Boreal Forest and the Arctic

The idea of incentive conservation is a modern one but its practice has clearly defended some of the sub Arctic wildernesses and the wildlife in those regions for thousands of years, especially by indigenous peoples such as the Evenk, Yakut, Sami, Inuit and Cree. The fur trade and hunting by these peoples have preserved these regions for thousands of years. Ironically, the pressure now upon them comes from non-renewable resources such as oil, sometimes to make synthetic clothing which is advocated as a humane substitute for fur. Similarly, in the case of the beaver, hunting and fur trade were thought to bring about the animal's demise, when in fact they were an integral part of its conservation. For many years children's books stated and still do, that the decline in the beaver population was due to the fur trade. In reality however, the decline in beaver numbers was because of habitat destruction and deforestation, as well as its continued persecution as a pest (it causes flooding). In Cree lands however, where the population valued the animal for meat and fur, it continued to thrive. The Inuit defend their relationship with the seal in response to outside critics.

Latin America (Bolivia)

The Izoceño-Guaraní of Santa Cruz, Bolivia is a tribe of hunters who were influential in establishing the Capitania del Alto y Bajo Isoso (CABI). CABI promotes economic growth and survival of the Izoceno people while discouraging the rapid destruction of habitat within Bolivia's Gran Chaco. They are responsible for the creation of the 34,000 square kilometre Kaa-Iya del Gran Chaco National Park and Integrated Management Area (KINP). The KINP protects the most biodiverse portion of the Gran Chaco, an ecoregion shared with Argentina, Paraguay and Brazil. In 1996, the Wildlife Conservation Society joined forces with CABI to institute wildlife and hunting monitoring programmes in 23 Izoceño communities. The partnership combines traditional beliefs and local knowledge with the political and administrative tools needed to effectively manage habitats. The programmes rely solely on voluntary participation by local hunters who perform self-monitoring techniques and keep records of their hunts. The information obtained by the hunters participating in the programme has provided CABI with important data required to make educated decisions about the use of the land. Hunters have been willing participants in this programme because of pride in their traditional activities, encouragement by their communities and expectations of benefits to the area.

Africa (Botswana)

In order to discourage illegal South African hunting parties and ensure future local use and sustainability, indigenous hunters in Botswana began lobbying for and implementing conservation practices in the 1960s. The Fauna Preservation Society of Ngamiland (FPS) was formed in 1962 by the husband and wife team: Robert Kay and June Kay, environmentalists working in conjunction with the Batawana tribes to preserve wildlife habitat.

The FPS promotes habitat conservation and provides local education for preservation of wildlife. Conservation initiatives were met with strong opposition from the Botswana government because of the monies tied to big-game hunting. In 1963, BaTawanga Chiefs and tribal hunter/adventurers in conjunction with the FPS founded Moremi National Park and Wildlife Refuge, the first area to be set aside by tribal people rather than governmental forces. Moremi National Park is home to a variety of wildlife, including lions, giraffes, elephants, buffalo, zebra, cheetahs and antelope, and covers an area of 3,000 square kilometers. Most of the groups involved with establishing this protected land were involved with hunting and were motivated by their personal observations of declining wildlife and habitat.

Forest Conservation, Afforestation and Reforestation in India

India is a large developing country known for its diverse forest ecosystems and is also a mega-biodiversity country. Forest ecosystems in India are critical for biodiversity, watershed protection, and livelihoods of indigenous and rural communities. The National Communication of the Government of India to the UNFCCC has reported that the forest sector is a marginal source of CO_2 emissions.

India has formulated and implemented a number of policies and programmes aimed at forest and biodiversity conservation, afforestation and reforestation. Further, India has a goal to bring one-third of the geographic area under forest and tree cover by 2012. All forest policies and programmes have implications for carbon sink and forest management. This chapter presents an assessment of the implications of past and current forest conservation and regeneration policies and programmes for forest carbon sink in India. It also estimates the carbon stocks under current trend scenario for the existing forests as well as new area brought under afforestation and reforestation for the period 2006-30.

The forest sector could be a source or a sink of carbon. Forest carbon stock includes biomass and soil carbon pools. Biomass carbon can be further disaggregated into aboveground and belowground biomass and dead organic matter. Change in forest carbon stock between two time periods is an indicator of the net emissions of CO_2 from the sector. Carbon stocks are estimated and projected for the period 2005-30.

Methodology

The COMAP model13 is a set of versatile models with the ability to analyse the mitigation potential as well as costeffectiveness of diverse activities such as forest conservation (e.g. Protected Areas and halting forest conversion), natural regeneration (with no logging) and afforestation/ reforestation through plantation forestry, including short- as well as long-rotation forestry (with logging or harvesting).

Assessment of mitigation activities using the COMAP model would involve consideration of the following:

- Land availability for different mitigation activities during different years.
- Wood product demand and supply to ensure that socio-economic demands are met with and real additional mitigation is feasible.
- Developing a baseline or current trend scenario to enable estimation of incremental carbon mitigation.
- Developing a mitigation scenario incorporating the extent of area to be covered for meeting different goals.

Data required for assessing different activities: The data required for assessing the mitigation potential of afforestation and reforestation include land area-related information, baseline carbon density (tC/ha) in above-ground vegetation and soil, rotation period, above-ground woody biomass accumulation rate (tC/ha/yr), soil carbon enhancement rate (tC/ha/yr), and cost and benefit flows.

Outputs of the COMAP model: These include mitigation potential estimates per ha and aggregate tonnes of carbon benefit, annual carbon stocks, carbon stocks for a given year such as 2008 and 2012 and cumulative over a period, and cost-effectiveness parameters.Carbon stock projections for the existing forests as well s new area brought under afforestation and reforestation for the current trend scenario are made for the period 2006-30. The carbon stock projections are made using the COMAP model. The forest cover data were obtained from the projections made using the FSI area trends and afforestation rates were obtained from the past trends (average annual rate of 1.32 mha). The biomass and soil carbon stock and growth rates were obtained from published literature. The afforestation rate of 1.32 mha/annum was allocated to short- and long-rotation and natural regeneration at 63.7, 32.2 and 4.1 per cent respectively, based on the previous years' trend. The carbon stock in the existing forests is projected to be nearly stable over the 25-year period at 8.79 GtC). When afforestation and reforestation is included, the carbon stock is projected to increase from 8.79 GtC in 2006 to 9.75 GtC by 2030, about 11 per cent increase. It is important to note that COMAP model accounts for harvests and the resulting emissions. Thus, Indian forests will be a net sink over the next 25 years.

Factors Contributing to Stabilization of Carbon Stocks in Indian Forests

India is one of the few countries where deforestation rate has been reduced and regulated and forest cover nearly stabilized, unlike most other tropical countries. Further, the projections of carbon stocks for the period 2006-30 showed that the carbon stock will increase. Thus, it is important to understand the likely factors contributing to the observed and projected stabilization of forest cover as well as forest carbon stocks in India. The factors include legislations, forest conservation and afforestation programmes, and community awareness and participation.

Forest Conservation Act, 1980

This Act is one of the most effective legislations contributing to reduction in deforestation. This was enacted to reduce indiscriminate diversion of forest land for nonforestry purposes, and to help regulate and control the recorded forest land-use changes.

Compensatory Afforestation

According to Forest Conservation Act, 1980, when after careful consideration forest land is released for any infrastructure projects, it is mandatory for compensatory plantations to be raised on an equivalent non-forested land or equal to double the area on degraded forestland.

Wildlife Parks and Protected Area

In India, 15.6 mha is Protected Area, where all human intervention or extraction is banned.

Afforestation

India has been implementing large-scale afforestation/ reforestation since 1980 under social forestry, Joint ForestManagement, silvi-pasture, farm forestry and agro-forestry programmes, covering over 30 mha. This may have reduced pressure on the forests.

National Forest Policy, 1988

It envisages people's participation in the development and protection of forests. The basic objective of this policy is to maintain environmental stability through preservation of forests as a natural heritage.

Joint Forest Management (JFM), 1990

The Forest Policy 1988 set the stage for participatory forest management in India. The JFM programme recognized the rights of the protecting communities over forest lands.

The local communities and the Forest Department jointly plan and implement forest regeneration programmes and the communities are rewarded for their efforts in protection and management. The total area covered under the JFM programme is over 15 mha. This has enabled protection of existing forests, regeneration of degraded forests and raising of forest plantations, potentially contributing to conservation of existing forests and carbon stocks.

Significance of Stabilization of Forest Carbon Stocks in India

India is one of the few countries in the world, particularly among the tropical countries, where carbon stock in forests has stabilized or is projected to increase. This has implications for reducing the carbon emissions from forest sector, potentially contributing to stabilization of CO_2 concentration in the atmosphere. This Indian achievement is significant due to the following:

High Population Density and Low Per Capita Forest Area

India is a large developing country with a population density of 363 persons/km^2. Even more significantly, the forest area per capita is only 0.06 ha, compared to the world average of 0.62 ha/capita and Asian average of 0.15 ha/ capita. A comparison of key developing countries and Western European countries is provided in Forests and wooded land area per 1000 population in Germany and France is nearly two and five times that of India.

Similarly, forest and wooded land in other major developing countries such as Brazil, China and Indonesia are also higher by 3 to 40 times, as compared to India.

Low Deforestation Rate Compared to Other Developing Countries

According to the Global Forest Resources Assessment, countries such as India and China are experiencing an increase in forest area since 1990. However, majority of the other tropical countries with large area under forests are experiencing deforestation on a significant scale since 1990. Majority of the countries (42-65%) are experiencing reduction in forest area or net deforestation.

High Dependence of Human Population on Forests

In India, nearly 196,000 villages are in the forests or on the forest fringes. Fuelwood is a dominant source of cooking energy for the rural population with forests contributing significantly to this. Apart from fuelwood, village communities depend on forests for small timber, bamboo and non-timber forest products.

High Livestock Density

India accounts for 2.3 per cent of the world's geographic area, but accounts for 15 per cent of the global livestock population. The cattle (cows, bullocks and buffaloes) population density is nearly one per hectare. When sheep and goats are included along with cattle, the livestock population density further increases to 1.5 per hectare. However, if only forest land is considered, the livestock density is 7 per hectare, which is among the highest in the world. Dominance of agrarian economy rural areas in India are characterized by large dependence of the population on land resources, particularly cropland and forest land, leading to more human pressure on land.

Implications of Indian Forest Conservation and Development Programmes and Policies for Global Change

India is a large developing country with a high population density and low forest area per capita. The livestock population density is among the highest in the world. Further, nearly 70 per cent of the population residing in rural areas depends on forest and other biomass resources for fuelwood, timber and non-timber forest products for its energy needs and livelihood. In such a socio-economic scenario, one would have expected the forest area to decline, leading to large emissions of CO_2 from the forest sector.

The analysis of forest cover, afforestation and reforestation has shown that the forest cover has stabilized in the past 15 years (64-67 mha). Projections under the current trend scenario indicate that the forest cover is likely to increase in the period 2006-30. Further, model-based projections of carbon stocks in the Indian forest sector show a likely increase (from 8.79 GtC in 2005 to 9.75 GtC in 2030). This is a significant achievement for a developing ountry such as India, despite high human and livestock population density, high dependence of rural communities on forests for biomass resources and low per capita forest area. The factors contributing to the current and projected trends of stable or increasing carbon stocks in the forests are progressive and effective forest conservation legislations, afforestation and reforestation programmes and community participation in forest protection, regeneration and management.

The progressive conservation-oriented forest policies and afforestation programmes are contributing to reduction in CO_2 emissions to the atmosphere, stabilization of carbon stocks in forests and conservation of biodiversity. Thus, the Indian forest sector is projected to keep making positive contributions to global change and sustainable development. This projected estimate and conclusion excludes any potential decline in forest carbon stocks due to forest conversion, forest degradation, biomass extraction, fire, etc.

Index

D

E